Publication Sponsored by the W. K. Kellogg Foundation

The W. K. Kellogg Foundation was founded in 1930 with a clear mission: "To help people help themselves through the practical application of knowledge and resources to improve their quality of life and that of future generations." The private foundation that began funding programs to meet the health and educational needs of Michigan children has grown to a position of national and international prominence for its assistance to communities in the United States, Latin America, the Caribbean, and southern Africa. Today, the W. K. Kellogg Foundation is one of the largest philanthropic organizations in the world.

As a private grantmaking institution, the W. K. Kellogg Foundation provides seed money to nonprofit organizations and institutions that have identified problems and designed constructive action programs aimed at solutions. Most grants are awarded in the areas of health; food systems and rural development; youth and education; and philanthropy and volunteerism. Grants are also awarded under the cross-cutting themes of leadership; information systems and technology; capitalizing on diversity; and social and economic community development.

The Insider's Guide
to Grantmaking

The Insider's Guide to Grantmaking

How Foundations Find, Fund, and Manage Effective Programs

Joel J. Orosz

A publication of the W. K. Kellogg Foundation

JOSSEY-BASS
A Wiley Company
San Francisco

Jossey-Bass books and products are available through most bookstores. To contact Jossey-Bass directly, call (888) 378-2537, fax to (800) 605-2665, or visit our website at www.josseybass.com.

Substantial discounts on bulk quantities of Jossey-Bass books are available to corporations, professional associations, and other organizations. For details and discount information, contact the special sales department at Jossey-Bass.

Manufactured in the United States of America on Lyons Falls Turin Book. This paper is acid-free and 100 percent totally chlorine-free.

A publication of the W. K. Kellogg Foundation

Credits appear on page 304.

Library of Congress Cataloging-in-Publication Data

Orosz, Joel J.
  The insider's guide to grantmaking: how foundations find, fund, and manage effective programs / Joel J. Orosz.—1st ed.
      p. cm.—(The Jossey-Bass nonprofit and public management series)
  Includes bibliographical references and index.
    ISBN 0-7879-5238-9 (hardcover: alk. paper)
    1. Charities.   2 Charities—Finance.   3. Endowments.   4. Subsidies.
  5. Research grants.   I. Title.   II. Series.
  HV41.O76   2000
  658.15'224—dc21   00-008263

FIRST EDITION
HB Printing   10 9 8 7 6 5 4 3 2 1

The Jossey-Bass
Nonprofit and Public Management Series

This book is dedicated to the memory of Dr. Peter R. Ellis. During his seventeen years as a program director with the W. K. Kellogg Foundation, he exemplified Aristotle's dictum that excellence in giving away money is "rare, praiseworthy, and noble." The lessons he taught as a mentor, coach, and compassionate critic can be found, quite literally, on every page of this book.

Contents

Preface   xi

Acknowledgments   xiii

The Author   xv

Prologue: Foundations—Their History, Structure,
  and Societal Role   1

1   Making Sense of the Grantmaking Universe   25

2   Grantmaking: The Human Factor   38

3   Building Relationships with Applicants   53

4   Reviewing Proposals   66

5   Declining Proposals   96

6   Responding to Proposals   110

7   Site Visits   130

8   Writing the Funding Document   143

9   Presenting the Funding Document   153

10   Managing the Project   167

11   Closing the Project   183

12   Leveraging Impact   196

13   Influencing Policy   210

14   Initiative-Based Grantmaking   232

15   The Ethics of Grantmaking   252

Epilogue: The Future of Formal Philanthropy   262

References   281

Bibliography   285

Index   293

Preface

Foundation work is a calling with no preemployment training courses, no qualifying entrance exam, and few formal postemployment training programs. There is a literature that describes sound practices for certain aspects of grantmaking, but it is scattered and fugitive, appearing mostly in periodicals, a few specialized monographs, and ephemeral pieces such as annual reports. Only by a determined and persistent bibliographical search can foundation employees pull it all together, and even then, gaps would appear in areas where precious little has been written on the responsibilities and roles of the program officer.

An Inside View of Professional Practice

This book represents a first attempt to examine, from a base of experience, the full range of the duties of a program officer. It is not a comprehensive manual, nor is it a checklist. It offers, instead, an introductory discussion about the essential skills needed to be an effective and ethical program officer. Although it was written specifically for newcomers to the field to help them understand the basic principles of good practice, it will also be useful to veteran grantmakers as a means of reflecting on their performance. It should also be of interest to grantseekers for the "inside view" of foundations that it provides.

Although the text was written by a single author, the manuscript was critiqued and improved by a panel of more than twenty program officers and CEOs from foundations, large and small, located all over the United States. The focus of the book is entirely on U.S. institutions, and it is written primarily from the perspective of a grantmaking private foundation (although many, if not most, of the practices described are also applicable to community and corporate foundations). It is important to note that this is a first effort and as such is bound to contain errors and gaps. I hope, however, that the book will begin a dialogue on sound practices in the field, one that will, over time, lead to generally accepted standards of best practice.

Overview of the Contents

The book opens with a prologue introducing you to foundations: their history, structure, and function in society, and the role of the foundation program officer. There follow chapters on setting grantmaking priorities and on grantmaking considered as a human enterprise. These chapters address such questions as these: Is grantmaking a calling or a profession? What kind of person should become a grantmaker? How can you avoid the "seven temptations" of philanthropy?

Chapters Three through Fourteen focus on your essential work as a program officer: meeting with applicants, reviewing proposals, declining proposals, conducting site visits, recommending proposals for funding, making oral presentations to the board or funding committee, managing and evaluating funded projects, increasing the impact of funded projects, and managing program initiatives. The final chapter discusses the ethics of grantmaking, and the book concludes with an epilogue considering the possible future of foundation philanthropy.

As a grantmaker, you are a steward of funds that are precious— funds that often provide the margin between progress and stagnation, between development and decay. It is incumbent upon you, and all grantmakers, to maximize the good these funds can do by enhancing your ability to effectively and ethically invest them for the common good. It is to that end that I conceived and wrote this book and now offer it to you.

Kalamazoo, Michigan   JOEL J. OROSZ
January 2000

Acknowledgments

I have more than the usual number of acknowledgments to make, for in an effort to reflect the varieties of practice in the field, I submitted drafts of the manuscript to a panel of colleagues at the W. K. Kellogg Foundation and to a panel of selected grantmakers from foundations around the nation. These panelists have given freely of their time and expertise, detecting a number of errors and suggesting many valuable additions. To them, endless thanks are in order.

The following people served with distinction on the Kellogg Foundation panel: Leah Austin, Caroline Carpenter, Robert DeVries, Cynthia Koch, Christine Kwak, Robert Long, Ricardo Millett, Dan Moore, Betty Overton, Tom Reis, Frank Taylor, and Kathy Whitesell.

Two members of the Kellogg panel must also be cited for going "above and beyond" in their review of the work. Ricardo Millett lavished attention on the evaluation sections of the chapters and improved them immensely. Frank Taylor, in addition to his insightful critiques, shuttled research materials and manuscripts back and forth between Battle Creek and Kalamazoo.

The panelists from other foundations or related organizations who were so helpful in critiquing this book are Willis Bright, Hugh Burroughs, Stephanie Clohesy, Ernie Gutierrez, Dorothy Johnson, Lisa Wyatt Knowlton, Janice Kreamer, Linda D. May, Michael Seltzer, and Benjamin Shute.

I gratefully acknowledge the W. K. Kellogg Foundation for providing a six-month professional study leave, which allowed me to research and write the first draft. Special thanks in this connection go to Dan Moore, vice president for programs at the foundation, who championed the leave, and to Sonia Barnes, program associate at the foundation, who shouldered the lion's share of my daily responsibilities while I was away.

I owe an unpayable debt to Ruth Ann Hoiles, program assistant at the Kellogg Foundation, for covering numerous responsibilities for me while I was on leave, and especially for her herculean effort in transcribing every word and every revision of the manuscript. Her trenchant editing also materially improved the quality of the final product.

Deep appreciation is owed as well to the communications staff of the Kellogg Foundation, particularly to Karen Lake and Mike VanBuren, who guided me through the technical and contractual mazes of book production.

Kellogg Foundation librarians Antonio Gomez, Angela Graham, and Wendy Carter are to be commended for their prompt and resourceful research assistance. No fact proved too arcane or obscure for them to unearth. Thanks go as well to Kellogg Foundation colleagues Pat Babcock, who helpfully reviewed the chapter dealing with public policy issues, and Ann McKinstry, who assisted with the legal aspects of foundation work.

I am grateful as well to my wife, Florence, for living with the annoying clutter of a work in progress, and to my children for their understanding when their father was too busy writing to play soccer.

Finally, I wish to express my gratitude to a fine team of professionals at Jossey-Bass: to CEO Lynn Luckow, who believed in this project from the beginning; to senior editor Alan Shrader, whose suggestions created a much stronger manuscript; to Dorothy Hearst, the senior editor who saw the manuscript through to publication; to assistant editor Johanna Vondeling, who proved a deft guide through the maze of book writing and publishing. I am also indebted to Michele Jones, who copyedited the manuscript with both rigor and sensitivity, and to Carolyn Uno of Tigris Productions, who ordered the manuscript into a printed work.

To all of these people, my debts are profound, but to none of them is attached any of the responsibility for errors or omissions; this is reserved for me alone. Finally, it should be noted that although I am an employee of the W. K. Kellogg Foundation, this book is neither a description of Kellogg Foundation operational methods nor a "how-to" manual for securing grant support from the foundation. The text is, instead, a description of sound approaches and techniques more generally practiced among private foundations.

J.J.O.

The Author

Joel J. Orosz is a program director in the Philanthropy and Volunteerism programming area of the W. K. Kellogg Foundation, of Battle Creek, Michigan. He earned his B.A. degree in American history (1979, cum laude) from Kalamazoo College, and both his M.A. degree in history and museum studies (1981, magna cum laude) and his Ph.D. degree in nineteenth-century American social history (1986) from Case Western Reserve University.

Before joining the Kellogg Foundation, Orosz was employed by the Howard Dittrick Museum of Historical Medicine in Cleveland, Ohio, as a curatorial assistant and by the Kalamazoo Public Museum in Kalamazoo, Michigan, as curator of interpretation. His main research activities have focused on museology and philanthropy. In 1990, the University of Alabama Press published his doctoral dissertation, *Curators and Culture: The Museum Movement in America, 1740–1870*. He served as the editor of *For the Benefit of All: A History of Philanthropy in Michigan* (Council of Michigan Foundations, 1997), which won the first-ever special award for merit in communications from the Council on Foundations in 1999. He has also authored a number of articles in both fields. In addition, he has written two books and numerous articles about his avocation of numismatics, three of which have won awards from the American Numismatic Association and the Numismatic Literary Guild.

Orosz has served on a number of professional committees, including chairing the Council on Foundations' Committee on Legislation and Regulations, and he holds memberships on the Program Committee of the Points of Light Foundation, the Government Relations Committee of the Council of Michigan Foundations, and the Michigan Nonprofit Research Program Advisory Council of the Aspen Institute Nonprofit Sector Research Fund. He is also a charter commissioner on the Michigan Community Service Commission.

Orosz is married to Florence Upjohn Orosz, and they have four children: Carly, Anita, Marianna, and Andrew. The Orosz family makes their home in Kalamazoo, Michigan.

Foundations—Their History, Structure, and Societal Role

Program officers work in foundations, so before we discuss the work that program officers do, it is important to begin by discussing how foundations have developed in the United States. The idea of a foundation—an endowment established, whether for a fixed term or in perpetuity, the income from which is dedicated to charitable or philanthropic purposes—is a very old one, indeed. As Warren Weaver notes in *U.S. Philanthropic Foundations: Their History, Structure, Management, and Record* (1967), the notion can be traced, in Western cultures at least, as far back as Plato's academy, founded in Athens about 387 B.C. Plato left the academy, along with its supporting farmland (in effect, an endowment), to his nephew, stipulating that it be administered for the benefit of Plato's followers. His nephew proved a better manager than most nephews tend to be, and the academy endured for more than five centuries.

It was a pupil of Plato, Aristotle, who was one of the first to conceive of the difficulties inherent in administering such endowments for the good of others. In Book Two of *Nicomachean Ethics*, Aristotle stated: "Anyone . . . can give away money or spend it; but to do all this to the right person, to the right extent, at the right time, for the right reason, and in the right way, is no longer something easy that anyone can do. It is for this reason that good conduct [in such matters] is rare, praiseworthy, and noble" (Aristotle, 1962).

Greeks of Aristotle's time developed a tradition of making benefactions for the good of the populace as a whole. The Athenian Herodes Atticus, for example, made gifts of a theater to Corinth and a stadium to Delphi. These charitable acts were performed during his lifetime, however, and even bequests like Plato's academy were generation-to-generation transmissions that lacked the permanency essential to truly develop the foundation concept.

In 150 B.C., Roman law took an important step toward laying the basis for foundations by declaring charitable corporations to be both "sentient reasonable beings" and "immutable undying persons." These principles opened the way for the establishment of long-term endowments that could endure for generations after the death of the donor or, if desired, in perpetuity. For the remainder of the Roman republic and throughout the era of the Roman Empire, foundationlike societies, such as guilds and collegia, gained endowments and carried out programs of good works. The Julian emperors gradually extended the right to accept and administer bequests of funds to cities, towns, and villages.

The Roman emperors pioneered in foundation scandals as well, looting municipal endowments for their own uses between A.D. 192 and 324. Partly as a corrective to this problem, Constantine I issued an edict allowing the Christian Church to receive legacies and administer them as ecclesiastical foundations in accordance with the will of the donor. Roman law also made another critically important contribution to the foundation concept: the doctrine of cy pres. This principle recognizes that the terms of a perpetual trust can, over time, become outdated or impossible to fulfill, and allows for modifications to render the trust able to meet new needs and changing conditions. The Emperor Justinian used these doctrines to dissolve Plato's academy, by then nearly six hundred years old, on the grounds that it taught heretical ideas. (Actually, the academy was teaching the ideas that it had taught for almost six centuries; it was the beliefs of the Roman Empire that had changed.)

Ecclesiastical foundations grew in size and importance during the Middle Ages. In England, churches and monasteries were becoming so well endowed that the sovereigns feared their growing power. Henry VIII and Edward VI both met the perceived threat by expropriating ecclesiastical wealth for the Crown and its favorites. These confiscations met with general approval, but there was considerable resentment about how the proceeds were distributed. In 1601, partly as a result of this discontent, Parliament passed the Statute of Charitable Uses, the bedrock law by which both British and U.S. charitable and philanthropic organizations, including foundations, are essentially governed, even today. Perhaps the most important principle laid down by the statute was that of *fundatio incipiens,* which required charitable foundations to secure legal incorporation from the state. In practice, this principle meant that all foundations were destined to have a dual character: endowed privately but chartered publicly. Although it seems not to have been the original intent, *fundatio incipiens* created the concept of a foundation as an instrument for transforming private funds into a public benefit.

Foundation History in the United States

The foundation idea came to America with the English diaspora. Puritans preached benevolence (John Winthrop's sermon "A Modell [sic] of Christian Charity" is an example) and practiced it, particularly in the construction and support of their churches. It was that emphatically unpuritanical Benjamin Franklin, however, who undertook the first substantial American experiment with the foundation concept. As Weaver (1967) has chronicled, Franklin's will left bequests to Boston and Philadelphia of £1,000 for two hundred years. For the first hundred years, the funds (each worth $4,444.49 at the time of Franklin's death in 1790) were to be loaned out at 5 percent to "young married artificers of good character." The principal and interest were to accumulate, and in 1890 each fund was to be divided into two portions, with three-quarters to be expended on public works "of the most general utility" and the remaining one-quarter to be invested and allowed to accumulate for a second one hundred years. In 1990, the full amount of the remainder of the fund was to be distributed, earmarked once again for generally useful purposes.

Over the years, Bostonians proved far better money mangers than Philadelphians. In 1890, Philadelphia had but $90,000 for distribution, whereas Boston had $298,602. Both cities used their windfalls to build Franklin Institutes. The Boston fund was augmented by a matching grant from industrialist Andrew Carnegie, and the two funds seeded an endowment for Boston's Franklin Institute.

During the second hundred years, both cities used the cy pres doctrine to modify the terms of Franklin's bequest in order to expand the pool of those to whom loans could be made. When the trusts were finally terminated in 1990, Boston again outmanaged Philadelphia, $5 million to $2 million.

The Franklin bequest, although not a modern foundation (it did not, for example, make grants from the interest earned by its endowment), nonetheless illustrates several of the themes that would later characterize foundations in the United States. Franklin endowed it with his private funds but dedicated its income to public purposes. He left specific instructions as to how the principal was to be employed, but he also allowed for distributions for general purposes and gave trustees discretion to decide how these distributions might best be made. And, although he made his trust a long-term benefit, he did limit its life span. Finally, his trustees, recognizing the requirements of changing conditions and customs, exercised the cy pres doctrine to make needed changes in the bequest. All these themes recurred, to a greater or lesser degree, during the following two centuries of foundation development in the United States.

What is generally regarded as the first true U.S. foundation was the Magdalen Society, established in Philadelphia in 1800 as a perpetual trust "to ameliorate the distressed condition of those unhappy females who have been seduced from the paths of virtue, and are desirous of returning to a life of rectitude." Weaver (1967) notes that the Magdalen Society also became the first foundation in the United States to experience difficulty in fulfilling its philanthropic mission. Distressingly, the society had difficulty in finding many prostitutes who were interested in "returning to a life of rectitude," and the minutes of the society complained that most who were recruited were "insubordinate." It even discovered that one volunteer was an "impostor." (Whether the imposture was a matter of gender or of professionalism, the minutes unfortunately did not explain.) After struggling to pursue their original mission for many years, the trustees finally threw in the proverbial towel and reorganized as the White-Williams Foundation, with an interest in youth development.

The Magdalen Society learned a lesson that every foundation must absorb sooner or later: those whom the foundation wishes to help do not appreciate having that help thrust upon them without their knowledge or consent. As laudable as a foundation's intentions and objectives might be, its efforts will come to naught unless it consults and respects the wishes and needs of those to whom its aid is directed.

Throughout the nineteenth century, a number of endowments were established, often for the relief of the poor and frequently entrusted to churches or units of local government for administration. The first foundation established in the United States whose organization and aims would seem "modern" to us was the Peabody Education Fund, endowed by George Peabody in 1867. His gift, of about $2 million, was directed to aid the Southern states that had been devastated by the recently concluded Civil War. Peabody stipulated that his fund could be dissolved after thirty years, and indeed, in 1914, the remaining assets were transferred to the John F. Slater Fund, which had been established in 1882.

The Prototypical Private Foundations: Carnegie and Rockefeller

The general-purpose charitable foundation—which supports projects in fields as diverse as health care, social services, religion, education, arts and culture, and the environment—is the general standard of organization at the dawn of the twenty-first century. This style of organization, however, was not invented until the early part of the twentieth century, and the prototypical foundation exemplars were established, ironically enough, by two of the nineteenth century's robber barons.

Andrew Carnegie: The Steward

Andrew Carnegie was the avatar of the self-made man: starting in 1848 as a bobbin boy in a textile mill at a salary of $1.20 per week, fifty-three years later he sold the Carnegie Company to J. P. Morgan's newly organized United States Steel Company for $492 million. Carnegie's philanthropy began long before, however, for in 1868, at the age of thirty-three, he resolved to devote all of his surplus wealth to charity. He kept this resolution according to a carefully thought out philosophy. In 1889, Carnegie published an essay, simply titled "Wealth," in the *North American Review* (Carnegie, [1889] 1992b). When it was reprinted in Britain in the *Pall Mall Gazette,* the editors styled it "The Gospel of Wealth," by which title it is remembered today. This essay, along with a second installment (Carnegie, [1889] 1992a) subtitled "The Best Fields for Philanthropy" and also published in the *North American Review,* laid out a coherent theory of philanthropic giving.

"The problem of our age is the proper administration of wealth," wrote Carnegie ([1889] 1992b), and he called on his fellow millionaires to regard their fortunes as being held in trust for the public good. In bestowing gifts, he proclaimed, "the main consideration should be to help those who will help themselves." Carnegie made a forceful case for the wealthy to establish foundations and to use them, not for charity (the relief of immediate needs or wants), but for philanthropy, "to provide ladders upon which the aspiring can rise." Moreover, the wealthy should dedicate all of their fortunes to this work, as opposed to enriching their heirs with unearned wealth. Carnegie was adamant on this point: "The man who dies thus rich dies disgraced." In his second essay, Carnegie ([1889] 1992a) outlined the seven best uses for philanthropy:

1. Founding a university
2. Establishing free libraries
3. Founding or extending hospitals, medical colleges, laboratories, and other institutions connected with the alleviation of human suffering, and especially with the prevention rather than the cure of human suffering
4. Establishing public parks
5. Providing halls suitable for meetings of all kinds and for concerts of elevating music
6. Establishing public swimming baths
7. Assisting one's own church and churches in poor neighborhoods

Carnegie was that rarest of pundits: one who followed his own advice. He gave, for example, $10 million to the Scottish University's trust. In the years between 1901, when he sold the Carnegie Company to J. P. Morgan, and 1919, when he died, he made challenge grants for public library construction (conditioned upon the local communities providing the site and pledging to pay operating costs) totaling 2,509 buildings across the United States. But this was only the beginning; he went on an unprecedented (and still unmatched) spree of philanthropic institution building: he endowed the Carnegie Institution of Washington, the Carnegie Hero Fund, the Carnegie Foundation for the Advancement of Teaching, and the Carnegie Endowment for International Peace. After all of this he was still worth $150 million. Determined to avoid dying rich and "disgraced," he established the Carnegie Corporation of New York and made gifts of $125 million to endow it. At the first meeting of the corporation's trustees, Carnegie read a document in which he revealed his hopes for the corporation's future (Hendrick, 1932):

> My desire is that the work which I have been carrying on, or similar beneficial work, shall continue during this and future generations. Conditions upon the earth inevitably change; hence no wise man will bind Trustees forever to certain paths, causes or institutions. I disclaim any intention of doing so. On the contrary, I give my Trustees full authority to change policy or causes hitherto aided, from time to time, when this, in their opinion has become necessary or desirable. They shall best conform to my wishes by using their own judgment. . . . My chief happiness as I write these lines lies in the thought that, even after I pass away, the wealth that came to me to administer as a sacred trust for the good of my fellow men is to continue to benefit humanity for generations untold.

Carnegie's shadow looms large over the foundation world. His insistence on giving his foundation wide scope was a bold and ultimately influential stroke. His international gifts ensured that U.S. foundations would look beyond the boundaries of their own nation. His focus on prevention rather than on the cure of suffering—striking at causes rather than treating symptoms—was revolutionary. And his refusal to lay "the dead hand of the donor" on his trustees—his faith that they would wisely adapt the foundation to changing conditions and needs—preserved the flexibility that he had originally conferred upon his corporation. Today, virtually all the larger foundations in the United States owe their basic approach and underlying philosophies to the Scottish immigrant who came to America poor and died comfortably situated but who, in between these events, epitomized stewardship by enriching humankind immensely.

John D. Rockefeller Sr.: The Patriarch

Like Carnegie, John D. Rockefeller Sr. had humble beginnings, was a shrewdly successful businessman, and proved a faithful steward of his wealth. The two men were also very different in many respects. Rockefeller's charity started earlier. His ledgers show that he was a tither even while eking out a meager living as a junior clerk in Cleveland. Rockefeller Sr. did not see any disgrace in dying a rich man nor in enriching his heirs. Perhaps the most significant difference between the two lay in their business practices: Rockefeller was the most ruthless player in a rough-and-tumble trade. But when all the dust had settled, the first John D. Rockefeller left an imprint on U.S. philanthropy nearly as profound as that of Andrew Carnegie.

Rockefeller read and was impressed by Carnegie's essays. In 1892, he had a fateful meeting with the Reverend Frederick Gates, a Baptist minister who became his philanthropic adviser. Rev. Gates heeded the advice of his contemporary, the architect Daniel Hudson Burnham, and made no little plans. He found that he could stir the blood of one of the world's richest men by using a combination of bold visions and blunt assessments. It was Rev. Gates who convinced Rockefeller that the Baptist denomination needed a flagship university, and forty million of Rockefeller's dollars were dispatched to establish the University of Chicago. In 1902, Rev. Gates led the formation of the General Education Board, which spent the next sixty years bringing improvement to primary and secondary education in the U.S. South. Rockefeller himself insisted that African Americans benefit from the board's work as fully as did whites, and improvement in educational opportunities for black southerners was dramatic. After 1912, the board turned its sights on medical education in the United States. A committee chaired by Abraham Flexner, and funded by the Carnegie Foundation for the Advancement of Teaching, had documented the woeful inadequacy of U.S. medical schools, and the board followed up with grants of nearly $100 million to upgrade the entire system. The Flexner committee found medical education in the United States mired in the dogmas of the eighteenth century and, with General Education Board funding, led it into the health sciences of the twentieth. In the meantime, the Rockefeller Sanitary Commission, established in 1909, took aim at the scourge of hookworm. By 1915, the commission reported that hookworm had been effectively eradicated across the U.S. South.

It was also in 1909 that Rockefeller launched an enterprise that significantly influenced the future development of U.S. philanthropy. He conveyed $50 million to a trust in order to establish the Rockefeller Foundation and sought to have it chartered by the federal government (as opposed to having it chartered by a state, the more familiar method used by pioneering foundations). His plan was loosely modeled on that of the Smithsonian Institution and would have given Congress the right to appoint the foundation's trustees. Rockefeller floated this plan, however, at the height of the Progressive Era, when muckraking journalists, such as Ida Tarbell, had made his name synonymous with monopolistic greed. When a bill to incorporate the Rockefeller Foundation was introduced in Congress in 1910, critics, echoing Washington Gladden's phrase "tainted money" (1895), charged that Rockefeller was trying to paper over his business atrocities with stacks of greenbacks. Some speculated that the proposed Rockefeller Foundation was in fact a Trojan horse that the biggest robber baron of them all could use to get inside the government, and even Attorney General George Wickersham objected that the foundation was "an indefinite scheme for perpetuating vast wealth" (Bremner, [1960] 1987). The bill was defeated, and after making a few more fruitless attempts, Rockefeller retreated from Washington to Albany, incorporating his foundation under the laws of New York State.

One can only speculate how different the course of U.S. philanthropy might have been if one of its exemplar foundations had been chartered by—and had its trustees chosen by—the U.S. Congress. The rejection of the federal charter request guaranteed for the Rockefeller Foundation—and for the many foundations that followed its pattern—an independence from political control that has been essential to its success. Thus, in losing his battle, Rockefeller inadvertently won a far more important war.

The new foundation immediately set out on an ambitious course of national and international grantmaking. It sought to eradicate hookworm on a global basis, and challenged malaria and yellow fever as well. The Rockefeller Foundation also led an enormous effort to establish schools of public health and public health nursing in the United States and abroad.

Just as Andrew Carnegie had reposed great faith in his trustees, so too did John D. Rockefeller Sr. In 1935, shortly before Raymond B. Fosdick became president of the foundation, Fosdick called on the elderly founder to brief him on changes in the program. Rockefeller waved Fosdick off, saying that he had complete confidence in the organization and its board. And well he might, for to say that men like Frederick Gates took their responsibility seriously is to understate the matter considerably. At his last meeting of the board, Rev. Gates admonished his fellow trustees: "When you die and come to approach the judgment of Almighty God, what do you think He will demand of you? Do you for an instant presume to believe that He will inquire into your petty failures or trivial virtues? No! He will ask just one question: *What did you do as a trustee of the Rockefeller Foundation?*" (Fosdick, 1952).

John D. Rockefeller Sr. was a founding father of U.S. foundations, but he also spawned a remarkable family tradition of philanthropy. His son John D. Rockefeller Jr. was a philanthropist perhaps best remembered for all but single-handedly restoring Colonial Williamsburg; his grandson John D. Rockefeller III, among many other philanthropic achievements, played a key role in the establishment of INDEPENDENT SECTOR, the national advocacy organization for foundations and national charities. And literally dozens of Rockefeller descendants of both genders have distinguished themselves in acts of public and private philanthropy throughout the twentieth century and into the twenty-first. Truly, Rockefeller can claim the greatest personal legacy of any U.S. philanthropist.

The Flowering of Foundations

Once Carnegie and Rockefeller had shown the way, many others followed in their footsteps. One of the more outstanding of the smaller followers was the Russell Sage Foundation, established in 1907 as a widow's revenge on the deceased "donor." By all accounts, Russell Sage was America's answer to Ebenezer Scrooge, except that he never was visited by three spirits. His biographer, Paul

Sarnoff, wrote, "to the world at large . . . he was the meanest, most miserly skinflint that ever lived" (1965). Upon his death, Mrs. Sage used a goodly portion of the $64 million that he had left behind to establish the Russell Sage Foundation. The naming of the foundation fairly dripped with irony, as did its first major grant, which funded an exposé of the usurious practices by which Sage had gathered his fortune. Despite its miserable antecedents, however, the Russell Sage Foundation quickly distinguished itself in the fields of social work and social reform. Another foundation deserving of mention is the Julius Rosenwald Fund, which contributed to the construction of 5,357 public schools and teachers' homes across the U.S. South, focusing its efforts so as to bring maximum benefit to the African American population. Rosenwald chose to spend his fund out of existence, which goal was achieved in 1946.

In 1914, a banker named Frederick Goff, an employee of the Cleveland Trust Company, conceived the notion of a foundation that would be made up of a collection of trusts large and small, which would enable individuals from all walks of life to become philanthropists. The Cleveland Foundation thus became the world's first community foundation and the prototype for hundreds more to follow, first in the United States and, more recently, worldwide.

Corporate foundations also made their appearance during the twentieth century, although most are not endowed but rather what are called pass-through operations—that is, a portion of the corporation's profits are channeled through the corporate foundation to be given as charitable grants. Naturally, pass-through operations work well in good years, but when profits drop, so do contributions. The relatively few endowed corporate foundations are able to keep their programs on a steady keel, in both good years and bad. The typical corporate foundation usually confines its giving to those communities in which the corporation has operations, although there are some that carry on national and even international giving programs. Some corporate foundations also make matching grants to augment contributions made by employees.

As the twentieth century rolled on, the process of foundation formation accelerated rapidly. There were but eighteen foundations in the United States in 1900. That number doubled in the decade from 1900 to 1909, more than doubled during 1910 to 1919, and almost doubled again during the Roaring Twenties. Not even the Depression decade of the 1930s slowed the "foundation express," as the number formed doubled yet again. The rate more than tripled during the 1940s. (More were formed during that decade than in all the previous history of the nation.) In the 1950s, the feat of the 1940s was nearly repeated. As the 1960s dawned, there were over five thousand foundations in operation across the United States. Foundations, it seemed, were multiplying faster than mushrooms after a rain, and apparently nothing could slow the growth.

The Tax Reform Act of 1969

In the early 1960s, the seemingly irresistible force met the truly immovable object. As Thomas A. Troyer recounts in "The Cataclysm of Sixty-Nine" (1999), Rep. Wright Patman (D-Tex.), a populist down to his socks, was hearing disturbing reports about underhanded doings at foundations, some of which were located in a region of the country he found highly suspect (the Eastern seaboard). In 1961, Patman requested a broad range of data from more than five hundred foundations. He was furious about the abuses his survey uncovered—a tiny percentage of his sample, to be sure, but probably, he suspected, only the tip of the iceberg. Among the findings were foundations that paid out little or nothing for charitable purposes, foundations used to enrich the donor and the donor's family and friends, and foundations formed not for philanthropic purposes but to avoid payment of taxes. Only a handful of foundations were involved, some of which had multiple problems. The vast majority operated efficiently and honestly, but Patman focused on the feckless few.

In 1962, Patman launched what was to become an ongoing campaign against foundations. In that year, he called on the Internal Revenue Service to suspend issuance of tax exemption rulings to all foundations. Every few months thereafter for the next six years, Patman convened hearings, fired off press releases, and issued reports on his latest concerns about foundations. Patman was soon joined by Senator Albert Gore Sr. (D-Tenn.), whose son Albert Jr. would later become vice president of the United States.

They jointly proposed that a twenty-five-year limit be placed on the life of all foundations.

By 1964, Patman and Gore's steady drumbeat threatened to derail the Tax Reform Act of 1964, then pending in the Senate Finance Committee. To prevent that, Secretary of the Treasury Douglas Dillon promised to conduct a comprehensive survey on foundations and report to the Finance Committee. Dillon, a former investment banker with a good understanding of the foundation field, appointed an advisory committee, which helped the Treasury Department survey a sample of thirteen hundred foundations, including all of those with assets of $10 million or more, and which gathered information from other sources as well. A young treasury staffer named Thomas A. Troyer drafted most of the report, which offered high praise for the work of most private foundations. The report did, however, document many of the abuses alleged by Patman, but found that these transgressions had been committed by a small minority of the foundations studied. The report recommended remedies including laws to curtail self-dealing, establish minimum payout requirements, and place limits on how much of a for-profit enterprise a foundation could own (U.S. Treasury, 1965).

The treasury report stopped the Patman-Gore juggernaut in its tracks. Their proposed twenty-five-year limit on the life span of foundations went down to defeat, and the Tax Reform Act of 1964 proceeded on schedule. The two lawmakers were down but not out, however. They attacked the "soft on foundations" stance of the report and redoubled their efforts to shackle foundations with legal irons. Patman and Gore found their opportunity in the issue of tax loopholes. It was unfortunately true that a small number of foundations had been formed strictly as a means of evading income and other taxes. In January 1969, the secretary of the treasury reported on some examples of loopholes. The House Ways and Means Committee promptly launched hearings on tax reform, and foundation leaders were called as witnesses. For the most part, these CEOs were largely unsophisticated in the ways of congressional testimony, and their artlessness only made matters worse. Ironically, the foundation leader who *was* intimately familiar with the ways of Congress, former Kennedy administration aide and then Ford Foundation president McGeorge Bundy, adopted a combative tone for his full day of testimony and alienated key members of the committee. After a long week in the witness chair, foundations were depressed, on the defensive, and lacking a plan to recover the ground they had lost.

The mood of doom, defeat, and despair intensified in late May, when the Ways and Means Committee introduced punitive legislation that would restrict the types of grants that foundations could make, deny tax advantages for contributions to them, and slap them with a 5 percent excise tax on investment income. This news caused the larger foundations to finally mobilize behind their "trade association," the Council on Foundations (established in 1949), to launch a counterattack. As the legislation moved from the House to the Senate, foundation leaders concentrated their fire on the upper house of Congress. They called supportive witnesses from nonprofits, including Dr. Jonas Salk, to testify about their good works. They found champions in the Senate, including Walter Mondale (D-Minn.), who led the fight for them on the floor. The counterattack worked; the Senate version of the bill greatly reduced the programmatic restrictions imposed by the House bill, liberalized the treatment of donations to foundations, and slashed the proposed excise tax rate.

Unfortunately for foundations, a key member of the House-Senate Conference Committee convened to reconcile the two bills was Rep. Wilbur Mills (D-Ark.), the House member second only to Patman in his distaste for foundations. Mills exerted his considerable clout to make sure the Tax Reform Act of 1969 that emerged from the Conference Committee looked much more like the House version than the Senate version of the bill. The act placed restrictions on fellowship programs and voter registration drives. It made charitable deductions for gifts to private foundations less attractive than those to public charities. It placed restrictions on self-dealing and on the percentage of a business a foundation could own. Most disturbing, it set the excise tax for foundations at 4 percent, and the payout rate at 6 percent of asset value or all of net income, whichever was greater. In addition, the legislation allowed the treasury to use its discretion to raise or lower the payout rate as desired.

The Tax Reform Act of 1969 fell like a bomb among foundations. The rate of new foundation formation dropped precipitously. Several existing private foundations terminated their existence, passing their assets to community foundations or public charities. Most foundations that remained realized that the one-two punch of a 4 percent excise tax and a 6 percent payout rate, combined with legitimate administrative expenses, would create a yearly demand that their endowment could not meet. Hence it was clear that over time their corpus would inevitably erode, and eventually the foundation itself would cease to exist.

The Council on Foundations, however, took a different view. As the council's leaders examined the 1969 act, they decided that some of its provisions, especially the prohibitions against self-dealing and excessive business holdings, were actually needed reforms. The programmatic restrictions were more annoying than alarming. The only truly dangerous provisions were the excise tax and the payout rate, both of which had been set too high. If these could be rolled back, foundations could live quite comfortably with the changes wrought in 1969. The council, under the leadership of David Freeman, set about building a capacity in foundations to do public policy work. This took some time, but the council and its members quite effectively enhanced their capabilities in this vital arena.

In 1976, when the treasury adjusted the payout rate upward to 6.75 percent, the council and its member foundations flexed their new policy muscles and were able to convince Congress to reduce the rate to a flat 5 percent of net asset value. Heartened by this victory, the council redoubled its efforts, and in 1978, it succeeded in getting Congress to cut the 4 percent excise tax in half. In 1981, Congress repealed the bothersome rule that required foundations to pay out all of their income if it exceeded 5 percent of net asset value. Finally, in 1984, Congress passed a law containing a formula allowing foundations that could meet certain requirements to cut their excise tax from 2 percent to 1 percent.

The immediate effect of these victories, of course, was to stop the erosion of foundation endowments. The repeal of the more punitive aspects of the Tax Reform Act of 1969, combined with the big bull stock market that began in 1982, resulted in the foundation birthrate taking a sharp turn upward. The 1980s surpassed the 1950s as the best decade ever for foundation formation.

On balance, then, the Tax Reform Act of 1969 proved beneficial to foundations. As Troyer (1999) has written, "Profoundly traumatic as it appeared at the time, the act rid the field of abuses that undercut philanthropic goals, that were, sooner or later, bound to precipitate Congressional action." To be sure, the act contained some burdensome and unwise provisions, but nearly all of these have been corrected by subsequent legislation or regulation. The Tax Reform Act of 1969 set the stage for the foundation field as we know it today, and for these reasons, surprisingly enough, there should be a framed picture of Wright Patman hanging in every foundation boardroom in the country.

Foundations: Their Types and Structure

In his book *Philanthropic Foundations*, F. Emerson Andrews (1956), a former director of the Foundation Center, the premier information source on U.S. philanthropy, defined a U.S. philanthropic foundation as a "nongovernmental, nonprofit organization, having a principal fund of its own, managed by its own trustees or directors, and established to maintain or aid social, educational, charitable, religious, or other activities serving the common welfare." U.S. foundations are the legal descendants of the *fundatio incipiens* principle in that they are endowed with private funds but established to serve a public purpose. In practice, this principle allows people who have been successful in creating wealth in the private sector to dedicate that wealth to supporting public benefits in the nonprofit sector. And, not unimportant, it allows successful entrepreneurs to keep part of that wealth out of the hands of tax collectors.

The Tax Reform Act of 1969 made an important distinction between community foundations and private foundations. Under the act, community foundations are public charities, exactly like other nonprofit organizations. They are designated under section 501(c)(3) of the Internal Revenue Code; gifts to them are fully tax deductible; and they must meet the public support test—that is, they must be able to prove that in any given four-year period, at least one-third of their income is derived from public sources. Private foundations, in contrast, are 501(c)(3) entities under section 509(a) of the Internal Revenue Code. This classifies them as non-profit charitable foundations, not public charities, and they are exempt from the public support test. Gifts to private foundations are tax deductible, but at a less attractive rate than gifts to public charities. Thus, although community foundations and private foundations have many things in common (they both have a corpus and make grants from that corpus), they also have two fundamental divergences: community foundations must raise money to meet the public support test, and private foundations, for the most part, do not raise money due to the unfavorable tax treatment of gifts made to them.

Other kinds of foundations include corporate foundations, either endowed or pass-through, as previously discussed; family foundations, which are usually private foundations, the boards of which are usually composed of members of a single family; and operating foundations, which exist not to make grants but to manage projects or institutions of their own creation. Operating foundations are complex creatures, and they cause no end of misunderstanding among the general public. Occasionally a crusading reporter will "expose" an operating foundation for making no grants—not understanding that such foundations run programs rather than make grants. To add to the confusion, several foundations are a hybrid of grantmaking and operating, which can make their grantmaking totals appear low in comparison with those of their strictly grantmaking cousins. It should also be noted that the term *foundation* is not strictly defined, so that organizations that neither make charitable grants nor operate philanthropic programs can use it with impunity. Hence many public charities that are in fact fundraising institutions call themselves foundations. People who work in grantmaking foundations must resign themselves to explaining repeatedly what their organization is, what it does, and why it differs from other organizations that are similarly named but very different in their missions. Foundations as a field should make it a priority to do a better job of educating the public on their roles and the benefits they offer to society. If the public misunderstands foundations, it is because foundations have not clearly explained themselves.

Foundations: Their Societal Role

The role of foundations in society is, of necessity, many roles. Considering that there were more than fifty-eight thousand foundations in existence as of 1999, sheer numbers dictate that there will be many varieties of form and function. Many foundations, especially smaller ones, limit their funding to their own local areas. Some, especially the larger foundations, support national or global projects (or both). Many foundations fund a wide range of organizations, but a few, especially operating foundations, drastically limit the number of entities they support. Making any sort of meaningful generalized statement about the roles that foundations play in society is all but impossible.

Despite this wide diversity, the great majority of U.S. foundations would probably agree with the following four statements:

1. Foundations should primarily concentrate on philanthropy (root causes) as opposed to charity (meeting immediate needs).
2. Foundations should primarily concentrate on supporting innovation as opposed to supporting ongoing programs.
3. Foundations should primarily concentrate on leveraging funds as opposed to being the sole funder.
4. Foundations should primarily concentrate on helping good ideas get a trial and a start as opposed to funding tested and proved approaches.

These statements require some explanation, for they lie at the heart of the mission of most U.S. foundations.

1. *Focus on philanthropy.* Most foundations would agree that their mission is *not* to meet immediate needs—to provide food, shelter, and clothing. As laudable and as necessary as these charitable acts are, foundations should not attend to them. According to figures compiled by the American Association of Fund-Raising Counsel Trust for Philanthropy, as listed in their annual publication, *Giving USA* (Kaplan, 1999), foundations provide only about 7 percent of the charitable dollar in any given year. (Corporations provide about 4 percent; the balance comes from individuals.)

Obviously, if foundations tried to meet basic needs, their funds would quickly be swallowed up, and nothing would fundamentally change. Foundations instead should aim at *causes* of problems. For example, instead of providing food, clothing, and shelter to homeless people, foundations should strive to strike at the *causes* of homelessness: poor education, structural unemployment, deteriorating housing stock, and inadequate social service programs. This is an approach analogous to focusing on the prevention of disease rather than on treating illnesses. Of course, there are some foundations, especially smaller family foundations, that give for direct charitable relief, but these are more the exception than the rule.

2. *Focus on innovation.* Most foundations focus on encouraging innovation rather than on supporting the ongoing programs of nonprofit organizations. This is widely resented among nonprofits, who complain that such policies force them to continually start new activities, while existing solid programs wither for lack of support. Foundation leaders reply that the dollars that foundations provide are so few that they would quickly be swallowed up by support of ongoing programs. In so saying, they have research results on their side. According to data compiled by Lester M. Salamon (1992), philanthropy of all kinds provides about 18 percent of the income of nonprofit organizations, and the *Giving USA* data indicate that foundations provide only about 7 percent of this 18 percent. Thus, philanthropy provides only about 1.2 percent of nonprofit income, and the only way that this small amount can have an impact is if it backs new ideas and promising approaches.

3. *Focus on leveraging funds.* Most foundations do not see themselves as sole funders of projects. For one thing, relatively few are big enough to go it alone. Even large foundations, however, generally prefer to stimulate other funders to join them in support of good ideas. Some foundations do this quite explicitly by issuing challenge grants, which are essentially promises to give a certain amount if the grantee organization can raise funds from other sources to match it. Most foundations do this implicitly by making their outright gifts in such a way as to stimulate other support (such as by giving early in the process or by supporting parts of a project that are hard to "sell" to other givers). By leveraging funds in this way, foundations can multiply their impact without increasing their expenditures. In fact, the ability to leverage funds is one of the main strengths of any philanthropic organization. It gives foundations the ability to put up seed money, which in turn allows the

grantee to demonstrate the value of its project and thus attract other sources of support, whether that support comes from other foundations, public charities, for-profit corporations, units of government, or individuals. Leveraging allows a foundation's reach to exceed its grasp, in effect to put a down payment on progress that it could not afford to pay for in full.

4. *Focus on start-up.* Most foundations see themselves as the research and development arm of society; that is, their mission is to support the experimental and the untried. They find good ideas, back them, nurture them, leverage other dollars for them, and then reduce and eventually cease to support them altogether. This approach causes friction with some applicants, who understandably would like to see foundations support their tried-and-true efforts indefinitely. Although such support might be possible for one or two "special grantees," it is not possible to pursue it as a general policy. Foundations must continuously stop supporting "old" grantees so that they will have funds available to meet new opportunities. Grantees do have a point, however, in that foundations often end their support prematurely, before an organization has secured a sufficient base of earned income and grants from other sources that will allow them to continue their operations. In order to avoid fostering dependence and to wean organizations from support, many foundations give by the "descending stair step" method: for multiyear commitments, the biggest year comes first, with the amount pledged for each subsequent year declining. This model is somewhat counterintuitive; after all, it costs more year after year to run a growing program, not less. However, if the goal is to make the organization gradually less dependent on foundation funds, it does make sense to steadily reduce the amount given over time.

Foundations: The Role of the Program Officer

The character of work in foundations is anomalous, truly a vocation like no other. When you become a foundation program officer, you discover that you have entered a truly distinctive trade. What other calling, for example, cannot agree on a name by which to refer to itself? A kiss is just a kiss, but you may be called a philanthropist, a funder, a grantmaker, a changemaker, a philanthroper (even a philanthropoid!), and, more recently, a social investor or social venture capitalist. Weighty objections can be arrayed against each term: *philanthropist* properly describes the foundation's donor, not its employee; *funder* is too generic, for it could describe any entity, human or corporate, that donates money; *grantmaker* is rather reductionist regarding your responsibilities, which involve more than just making grants; *changemaker* is at once pompous and misleading, implying delusions of grandeur on the one hand, or the post of cashier on the other; *philanthroper* and *philanthropoid* share the disadvantage of evoking visions of aliens with which Captains Kirk or Picard might do battle in the starship *Enterprise; social investor* and *social venture capitalist* are more common terms among corporations than among foundations. For purposes of this book, its shortcomings notwithstanding, *grantmaker* is the term of choice. Although the word does not explain the full range of your responsibilities as a program officer, it does at least convey a sense of your core work. Moreover, it has the advantage of not sounding too jargonish or grandiose. Perfect it is not, but it will do until a better term is invented.

Another anomaly that distinguishes grantmaking is the fact that there is really no good way to prepare for a career as a program officer. Every doctor, it is safe to say, has graduated from a medical school; every program officer, it is equally safe to say, did *not* take pre-philanthropy courses as an undergraduate. If one were to conduct a survey of educational backgrounds at any sizable conclave of grantmakers, one would discover a range spanning astronomy to zoology. Nor is there any uniformity of prior career experience; whereas many program officers come from posts in the nonprofit sector, others come from backgrounds in the world of business or government service. Just about the only safe generalization to make about the education and experiential background of any program officer is that it prepared him or her to do something else entirely.

Whether this fact is good or bad depends largely on one's point of view. Every lawyer must pass the bar exam to demonstrate a minimal level of proficiency prior to entering practice. There being no comparable philanthropy exam, it is true that some unqualified people become program officers. A strong counterargument can be made, however, that the riotous diversity of backgrounds in philanthropy brings a strength—a sort of hybrid vigor—to grantmaking that monolithic training leeches out of the formal professions. The sheer variety of education and life experience encourages a greater breadth of ideas and approaches, and it is no doubt useful for program officers to have real-world experience in the fields in which they will be making grants. Nonetheless, in a world dominated by the credentialed professions, grantmaking stands out as one of the last bastions of the (one hopes) enlightened generalist.

Perhaps the greatest peculiarity of grantmaking lies in its distinctive relationship to the bottom line. In virtually every other type of organization, operating funds must be either earned or raised before anything else can be achieved. This is true even of community foundations, which must raise sufficient funds every year to maintain their tax status as public charities. Not so for private foundations, however, which need only cash the checks generated by their endowments to satisfy their own financial requirements.

Actually, private foundations do have a bottom line of their own, albeit an inverted one: they must *spend* money to make their numbers come out right. Thanks to the regulations instituted by the Tax Reform Act of 1969, foundations must spend a minimum of 5 percent of their net asset value in any given year, or suffer a 100 percent penalty tax on the shortfall. As in most law and regulation, there is some wiggle room (foundations are allowed to carry forward a certain percentage of the requirements from year to year), but the fact remains that there is a yearly minimum that foundations must pay out. As the rest of the world industriously goes about the business of amassing money, private foundations must with equal industry spend it. Small wonder, indeed, that newcomers to the field sometimes secretly wonder if they have wandered through the looking glass.

The savor of Wonderland can also be interpreted in a positive light. Foundations, without the limiting factors of the need to attend to a bottom line, raise a budget, or face an electorate, have a greater degree of freedom to act than do any other institutions in society. This freedom is hardly absolute—it is limited by regulatory bodies, the performance of financial markets, and concern about public opinion—but it is still considerable. For anyone interested in making social change to serve the common good, there can be no better platform.

Grantmaking is clearly a singular enterprise, but what is it: a calling or a profession? A calling might be defined as a job that one is inspired to do, whether by intellectual curiosity or by spiritual enthusiasm. It can be done in many different ways by many different people. Its hallmarks are openness and experimentation. A profession, in contrast, has an esoteric body of knowledge that can be practiced only by a highly trained and rigorously selected group of people. It has a defined set of accepted practices, and experimentation around these practices must be within limited boundaries. Its hallmarks are exclusivity and set standards.

Those who see grantmaking as a calling cite the virtues of flexibility to make their case. The variety of educational preparations and life experiences grantmakers bring to their calling matches the complexity of the problems with which they grapple. A rigid set of standards would never be able to cope with the variegated and ever-changing problems permeating modern society. Professions tend to rely primarily on the cognitive in their approach, leaving little room for the spirit in dealing with the problems of people. Finally, advocates of the "calling" interpretation say that grantmakers should never spend an entire career making grants. They should begin in other fields, get real-world experience, become grantmakers for a few years, then leave so as to avoid falling into complacency or, worse, arrogance and unresponsiveness.

Those who feel grantmaking should be a profession argue that grantmaking has been, in too many institutions, the "original amateur hour." People unprepared by either education or life experience to make grants are thrown into the fray without a universally accepted set of standards by which to navigate. The result is performance that is all over the map—from exemplary to abysmal. How can grantmakers demonstrate success and be accountable unless they first develop adequate preparation, self-regulation, and agreed-on methods?

This book will take a middle view, holding that grantmaking should have more standards than a calling but more fluidity than a profession. Grantmakers must be open and experimental, to avoid rigidity, but they also need recognized standards, to avoid arbitrary and capricious behavior. Perhaps the best way to put it is that grant-making must be a hybrid—a "calling with a canon"—in order to be most effective and socially useful.

What are we to make, then, of this distinctive field, which has no name, no single means of preparation, no entrance exam, no direct bottom line, and no mortal fear of risk? The cynic might say it is amateurish, unaccountable, and arbitrary. The booster might say it is flexible, responsible, and gutsy. Perhaps a balanced view might apply to the philanthropic realm Winston Churchill's judgment of free enterprise in the economic sphere: "It is the worst system ever devised—except for all of the others."

Chapter One

Making Sense of the Grantmaking Universe

All grantmaking is done in a context—in fact, in many contexts simultaneously. There is the financial context (How large is the asset base?), the social context (Is society kindly disposed toward foundations and the types of social change they promote?), and the historical context (What has the foundation accomplished in the past?). The most influential of them all, however, is the institutional context of the foundation itself. All foundations have a dominant ideology, and given the large number of foundations in the United States, these ideologies span the spectrum from the loony left to the rabid right. The ideology, in turn, does much to shape the foundation's "theory of change": its beliefs about what type and intensity of intervention will best facilitate social movement toward the common good. The wide scope given to people to create private foundations in the United States virtually mandates that there will be nearly as many theories of change as there are foundations themselves.

Within this ideological welter, we can nonetheless discern that theories of change cluster around four main types. These types can be plotted as points along a single continuum. Because all the types begin with the letter *P*, this will hereafter be referred to as the 4-P continuum. As illustrated in Figure 1.1, the types are the passive, proactive, prescriptive, and peremptory. A brief description of each type will highlight the very real differences among them.

1. *Passive.* The passive foundation essentially responds to unsolicited requests—in foundationese, requests that come in "over the

Figure 1.1. The 4-P Continuum.

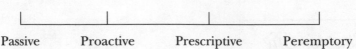

transom." The passive foundation may (but more often does not) publish an annual report listing some general guidelines for giving, but it does little or nothing more than that to generate proposals. It simply chooses for funding the best proposals in hand when the funding cycle comes to an end, and it usually does very little to share with others the lessons it is learning from programs it supports. Among those who could benefit from the lessons are applicants, other foundations, and policymakers. Among the lessons are what sorts of interventions are effective and ineffective, what are key leverage points for social change, and whether there are better ways to provide needed services. The motto of the passive foundation might be "We fund the best of those who find us."

2. *Proactive.* The proactive foundation is more energetic in making its interests known, through annual reports, brochures, Web pages, and other means. It tends to have well-defined priorities, and sends its program officers out actively searching for good grantees. Still, it is quite open to considering unsolicited good ideas. Generally, proactive foundations make grants clustered around related subjects, and they sometimes actively network their grantees, thus maximizing the number of lessons that they can learn from them and also maximizing the benefits that those grantees can provide to society. Most proactive foundations also have an interest in sharing those lessons learned with others, such as fellow funders or members of Congress. The motto of the proactive foundation might be "We fund the best we can find."

3. *Prescriptive.* The prescriptive foundation clearly defines its interests. It expects its program officers to identify relatively narrow fields of activity and to concentrate their efforts in those fields. The prescriptive foundation tends to do its grantmaking in an initiative-based format—that is, through a strategically structured grants program based on applicants responding to a formal and well-defined request for proposals (RFP). The prescriptive foundation usually

retains the capacity to respond to a few unsolicited requests, and it sometimes operates its own programs (that is, it manages charitable programs directly, with its own employees, rather than makes grants). No matter what its precise structure, however, the prescriptive foundation keeps its sights clearly focused on its defined interests. Its motto might be "We fund the best we can define."

4. *Peremptory.* The peremptory foundation is totally agenda-driven. It chooses its grantees, sometimes by means of an RFP but often simply by selecting them without public notice or competition. Peremptory foundations often operate their own programs and rarely if ever accept unsolicited proposals. Some peremptory foundations create reports on their grantmaking, but others do minimal reporting or none at all so as to avoid creating a demand they have no intention of fulfilling. The motto of the peremptory foundation might be "We fund the best we can imagine, and no others need apply."

Choosing a Grantmaking Style

A foundation's theory of change has a direct effect on its style of grantmaking. The passive foundation is highly likely to make a series of isolated, unconnected grants based solely on the proposals it receives during a given time period. The proactive foundation is likely to make clusters of individual grants tied together by a subject or a theme, while remaining very receptive to requests from outside. The prescriptive foundation is apt to carve out well-defined and strategically conceived initiatives, leaving relatively little receptivity to requests from outside. The peremptory foundation chooses grantees according to its own specific and strongly held visions, and it is not at all receptive to unsolicited requests.

The great majority of all U.S. foundations fall somewhere in the middle section of the 4-P continuum. They are either proactive or prescriptive, thus tending to make grants by cluster or by initiative. The lines frequently cannot be drawn with such sharp precision, however, and many foundations practice a mixture of two—or even more—styles. For example, a foundation may be for the most part proactive, but it may operate a program or conduct one or more initiatives that would typically be more characteristic of a prescriptive foundation. This book will consider both the proactive and prescriptive styles, but will make less effort to cover the much rarer passive and peremptory styles.

Just where on the 4-P continuum a foundation locates itself is affected by ideology, but not completely determined by it. In general, the more ideologically charged the foundation, the more it tends to favor highly directed theories of change. Despite their vast political differences, highly ideological liberal and highly ideological conservative foundations both would be likely to favor a peremptory style of operation. When views are strongly held in a foundation, the organization tends to be less receptive to over-the-transom grantmaking.

The 4-P continuum provides a basis for understanding the trade-offs inherent in embracing different theories of change. The passive foundation is open to good ideas and can react quickly to unexpected opportunities, but it pays a cost in its lack of systematic programming, which in turn causes, in most cases, weak or indifferent outcomes. It has great breadth but little depth. The peremptory foundation can be extremely strategic in identifying highly specific projects and following through on them to achieve measurable results, but it pays a cost in lack of flexibility and inability to respond to unexpected opportunities. It has great depth but little breadth. Proactive and prescriptive foundations seek to find their own versions of the happy medium between these two extremes. All, however, must cope with the essential trade-offs of opportunity versus strategy and breadth versus depth. Figure 1.2 illustrates these trade-offs in relation to the 4-P continuum.

Choosing a Mode of Operation

In addition to embracing a theory of change and a grantmaking style, the foundation must choose a mode of operation. There are essentially two ways that a foundation may conduct its business: as a grantmaking or an operating organization. The vast majority of U.S. foundations are grantmaking; that is, they make awards to mainly nonprofit organizations for charitable purposes. In order to do this, the foundation (if it is of a significant size) usually needs employees of its own, but because the foundation does not itself manage the projects that it supports financially, it need not employ a large staff. An operating foundation, in contrast, makes few or no awards to other organizations. Instead, it manages institutions,

Figure 1.2. Trade-Offs on the 4-P Continuum.

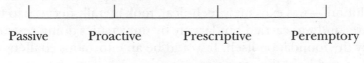

⇐ More open and greater breadth

| Passive | Proactive | Prescriptive | Peremptory |

More strategic and greater depth ⇒

such as museums; or oversees activities, such as fellowship programs; or conducts research. Two of the largest operating foundations are the Howard Hughes Medical Research Institute and the J. Paul Getty Foundation. Because they actually manage programs, operating foundations tend to have a relatively larger number of employees than their grantmaking counterparts.

Although there is a distinct difference between the two modes of operation, one is not intrinsically better or worse than the other. Grantmaking foundations are able to support a wider range of good causes, but operating foundations are able to support work in greater depth and for longer duration. The distinction between the two is sometimes muddied by the fact that certain foundations combine both modes, having both a grantmaking side and an operating side. The most common example of this "mixed" approach is the grantmaking foundation that also operates a significant fellowship program, but there are other models as well. Proponents of this approach see benefits deriving from cross-fertilization, for the lessons learned from grantmaking should sharpen the foundation's management of its operated programs; the lessons learned from running programs should inform and improve the foundation's grantmaking. The great majority of U.S. foundations are nonetheless exclusively grantmaking entities, so this book will focus on the grantmaking mode of operation.

Choosing a Public Profile

It is essential that each foundation decide on the type of public profile that it wishes to present. This profile ranges from the spotlight-seeking to the camera-shy. Historically, for the most part foundations have been very little in the news. The work they do is complex and takes a long time to show results, and, in any case, much of their work is done through others. For example, the research supported by the Rockefeller Foundation to increase global crop yields—the "Green Revolution"—was extremely technical, took literally decades to fully mature, and was carried out largely by universities doing research, not by the foundation itself. It would be an enormous challenge to capture and hold the attention of the media on such arcane subjects for such a long span.

Many foundations have deliberately sought to avoid publicity. Reasons for their doing so can range from the laudable (a desire to do good works quietly without receiving credit) to the questionable (it's no one's business how we choose to do good works). Operating without press scrutiny can lead to quietly effective outcomes. It can also lead to insular, narrow-minded, and anachronistic outcomes. And even when the work thus done is effective, it is done so quietly that few people learn about it.

Another reason for the relative invisibility of foundations in the press can be deduced from the types of stories that have appeared about foundations. Largely due to the penchant for anonymity that many foundations display, most of the attention given to them by the fourth estate has been during times of trouble. Typically, it has come during congressional investigations (such as that of the Patman committee, which led to the Tax Reform Act of 1969) or when an individual foundation becomes embroiled in a scandal. Many foundations, as a result, have come to equate publicity with regulatory assaults or lurid exposés and have become reflexively leery of any kind of limelight.

As with most other questions facing the field, there is no ideal stance regarding which public profile a foundation should choose. Those who argue for the low-profile approach say that the media cares only about negative stories, so any news about foundations will be, by definition, bad news. The complexity of the projects supported by foundations makes it challenging for reporters to understand them, thus causing inaccuracies to appear in print. Once made, these errors are difficult to correct and could excite the suspicion of those who regulate foundations. Besides, at least in the case of grantmaking foundations, it is the grantee that does the work, and therefore it is the grantee that should take the bow.

Finally, worrying about what the media might say is likely to skew the performance and decision making of foundations. Just as politicians hesitate to take necessary but unpopular steps for fear of igniting a firestorm in the press, so too will foundations obsessed with their media image shy away from controversy and venturesome decisions.

Those who argue for a higher profile say that, contrary to popular belief, the media are not obsessed with negativity; the media will, however, be more likely to go negative if they are not provided with examples of the good work that foundations do. The danger of a low profile is that when the foundation finds itself in the midst of a controversy, it will have no on-staff expertise in dealing with the press and no contacts within the press who are knowledgeable about philanthropy, and it will suffer for its past isolation. Although the projects supported by foundations are complex, and although grantees do most of the work, foundations do have a vital role to play in society, and it is important that people understand that role. Without cultivating such an informed constituency, foundations will find themselves in trouble whenever regulators become interested in them. A working relationship with the press can help foundations help their grantees disseminate innovations and ideas. Finally, good relations with the media will make foundations more venturesome, not less, for foundations will be able to tell their side of the story in any controversial situation and thereby become less fearful of controversies.

On balance, it appears that those who favor a more open stance have the stronger case. Foundations should be supporting work of real public utility, and if they are, the public has a right to know about it. Although there are risks involved in opening one's program to public scrutiny, there are greater risks inherent in pursuing a policy of secrecy. Any organization operates better in the long run when it is accountable to others outside its own narrow ambit. Foundations therefore should pursue a policy of openness and accountability to the many publics they serve.

Whatever a foundation's theory of change, style of grantmaking, mode of operation, and level of public profile, as a program officer you must thoroughly understand them and be able to operate comfortably within them. On the one hand, if you are working at a foundation that is proactive and low profile and that engages in cluster grantmaking, it will not do to be a highly prescriptive, micromanaging, and personally flamboyant program officer. On the other hand, these qualities might be highly valued in an operating foundation that is peremptory and high profile.

Setting Grantmaking Priorities

"No people," observed Mandell Creighton, "do so much harm as those who go about doing good." While Mr. Creighton was undoubtedly exaggerating in order to make a point (Joe Stalin, for example, probably did more harm than even the most avid do-gooder), there is more than a little truth to this remark. Foundations that have not bothered to set goals for their funding—or those that have, but have decided not to share them with the grant-seeking public—comprise an excellent example of Mr. Creighton's point. Foundations can waste buckets of their own money—and hours of grantseeker time—if they have not firmly set their priorities for social change and clearly communicated these priorities to the public.

It is obvious that grantmaking institutions with different styles will set their priorities very differently. A passive foundation will allow its priorities to be set pretty much by the postman (that is, by whatever proposals it receives). A peremptory foundation will set its priorities exclusively to advance its predetermined agenda without reference to what the other six billion people in the world might think. For the great mass of foundations that fall into the proactive and prescriptive categories, however, there is an ongoing attempt to strike a balance in setting programming priorities between listening to the needs, dreams, and aspirations of those outside the foundation, and heeding the ideas, insights, and plans of those inside the foundation.

Grantseekers complain, often with justification, that foundations do not regularly consult them before setting their priorities. Those people whom foundations aim to help—such as the impoverished, or victims of inequities—complain with even more justification that they are not usually asked their opinions before programs are crafted to help them. Scholars point out, with considerable justification, that priorities and programs devised by foundations without outside input invariably disappoint and nearly always fail. Effective grantmaking depends on foundations constructing their agenda in consultation with others. Fortunately, there are many ways to do so.

The easiest of these potential partners to consult is the grantseeker. As a program officer, you are in frequent contact with grantseekers, and there is even a national professional organization—the National Society of Fund Raising Executives—for those who raise money for a living. Getting the input of informed grantseeking professionals, therefore, is not particularly difficult; it is merely a matter of deciding to do so and following through. Securing the input of people on the margins of society, however, presents a greater challenge. First of all, in your position as a program officer, you encounter impoverished people much less often than you encounter professional grantseekers. Nor is there a single association by and for the disenfranchised to whom you can turn for counsel. This advice is absolutely essential, but you must be sure that those whom you choose to give the advice are knowledgeable about the needs, assets, and aspirations of their own community and have the respect of their peers. Just because they live there does not mean that they automatically have attained such knowledge and esteem. Foundations, which reside at a great remove (often physically, but almost always attitudinally) from stressed communities, have a lot of legwork to do in this process.

Precisely because it is so difficult to do that legwork, program officers often fall into the trap of claiming to have consulted those on the margins because they met with their intermediary representatives. For example, if the foundation wishes to work in an impoverished neighborhood, the foundation's representatives may consult with the local community development corporation or tenant's association and then proclaim that they have secured input from the people living in the neighborhood. It is important, of course, to consult such intermediary grantseeking organizations; however, although they might plausibly claim to represent some of the people living in that area, they still may not represent a true cross section of the residents. If as a program officer you truly want to get advice from the people, you will need to talk to a representative group of the people themselves. Doing so involves much work on the ground to get the right set of people at the table. There are no shortcuts when it comes to heeding the voices of those whom foundations wish to help.

The Five Steps in Setting Priorities

Step one: Identify a niche. In some cases, a foundation's area or areas of interest are determined by the will of the donor, and there is no need to consider any other area of work. In the case of the donor giving the foundation wide leeway (as did Carnegie and Rockefeller), the first step the foundation must take is to identify areas that need work or possible niches where the foundation could make a difference. Are there places where a little extra effort might achieve a breakthrough? Areas of promise that have been ignored by others? Preliminary work that could lead to greater things later on?

Step two: Review the literature. Once a possible niche has been identified, the foundation will need to learn what is already known about that subject, and the best place to start is with a literature review. If the foundation wishes to support research on a cure for a certain disease, for example, what research has already been done? There can be no point in demonstrating yet again something that has already repeatedly been demonstrated and verified.

Step three: Scan the field. If the literature search suggests that valuable lessons could be learned by grantmaking within a certain niche, the next step is to discover what other foundations and corporate giving programs have been doing on this subject. Other funders are probably working on this subject, or related subjects, already. They may be willing to share the lessons they have learned. The best way to learn about what other funders are doing is to consult the Foundation Center library, which is the premier source of information about grantmaking. The data supplied by the Foundation Center will give a baseline of information about the state of opportunity within the contemplated niche.

Step four: Consult those most affected. To continue with the example of research on a disease, the foundation would wish to consult university-based researchers, practicing physicians, researchers seeking cures in pharmaceutical companies, and those working on the problem from other perspectives (that is, other medicocultural traditions, alternative medicine). Besides these professional viewpoints, the foundation should also solicit the opinions of those having the disease and their primary caregivers, families, and support groups.

These opinions can be sought rather formally, through carefully designed stakeholder studies, which seek to compare responses made to a common survey instrument. It can be done less formally, through the use of polling techniques. And it can be done in a more face-to-face mode, with focus groups, advisory panels, or community-based meetings. Each of the methods presents trade-offs. Generally speaking, the more formal the approach, the more objective the data; the more informal the approach, the more subjective the data. The more formal the setting, however, the greater the chance that respondents will not answer with complete candor; they may even become downright intimidated. Formally gleaned data, therefore, may be consistent and replicable yet still be unsound.

This phenomenon deserves a little more explanation. Any time a foundation reaches out to others for advice on priority setting, one thing is certain: distribution of a lot of money is riding on the outcome. To ensure that the cash starts to flow, many—perhaps most—respondents are likely to feel pressure to say what he or she thinks the foundation wants to hear.

The rationalization goes something like this: "I'd like to tell the foundation the whole truth, but if they hear how bad things are, they probably will not start this work at all. So I will tell them just enough to get them interested. After all, it is better to get half a loaf than no loaf at all." Therefore it is incumbent on any foundation engaged in consulting others to constantly reassure the people whom they are asking for advice that they want a "warts and all" picture, not just happy talk. The difference in the power dynamic will always be there. Foundations will always have the money, and people outside will always need it, but foundations can, and must, do everything in their power to reduce the gaps that impede honest communication when they are consulting with others.

At no time does this power differential loom larger than when the foundation is getting input from disenfranchised people. A phalanx of Ph.D.'s in suits is not likely to put anyone at ease, particularly not in the austerely formal settings that characterize many foundation headquarters. It thus makes sense to go to the community when asking its residents their views. Informal meetings, held on familiar turf, go a long way toward reducing the intimidation factor.

Another key ingredient is simple respect. If community residents are treated with any less dignity and credibility than university experts, the foundation can forget any hope of receiving honest input. These are not occasions to quibble with advisers or, worse yet, to lecture them on conditions in their own backyards. This is not to say that you cannot disagree with residents on legitimate issues. There must be an open dialogue for the process to work. But the dialogue should be kept strictly within the bounds of respectful and actively attentive discussion. The minute a community delegation realizes that it is being disrespected, all is lost.

Given the obvious importance of getting input from those most affected, you might wonder why this is the fourth step rather than the first. The reason is simply that any such indication of interest on the part of a foundation will raise hopes and expectations of assistance within a community. It is preferable, therefore, to wait until later in the priority-setting process, when a foundation is more certain of its interest in a prospective niche, to seek a community's input. No good can come from raising expectations frivolously.

Step five: Make some learning grants. Once the prospective niche is identified, the literature is reviewed, the field is scanned, and those most affected are consulted, the foundation may begin to finalize its priorities. Each foundation will have a different process for doing so, with varying degrees of involvement—and autonomy—for the program officer. A fully formed set of priorities can emerge from the process at this point; there is, however, one other tool in priority setting that is often overlooked: the act of grantmaking itself. It is possible, indeed desirable, to have the fifth and final step in setting priorities consist of making exploratory or learning grants. Such grants are usually modest in size, short-term, and carefully evaluated. The lessons that emerge from them provide a real-world test of the priority-setting process and allow the foundation to make needed adjustments before launching full-blown programs of grantmaking.

Conclusion

Foundations are notoriously difficult to pigeonhole by means of generalizations. They are liberal and conservative, sluggish and hyperkinetic, grantmaking and operating, reclusive and brash. In this variegated diversity, they very much resemble the American people whence they sprang.

In priority setting, though, these wildly different organizations begin to find common ground: a shared sense of good practice.

Grantmaking, of course, can be done in a vacuum without going to the trouble of setting priorities. No matter how ill conceived the grantmaking program, no matter how arbitrarily it may have been devised, cash-starved organizations can always be found to become the foundation's grantees. One is reminded, however, of the wisdom found on a dental poster that admonishes, "You do not have to brush all of your teeth. Just the ones that you want to keep." Foundations do not need to identify prospective niches, search the literature, do funding scans, consult those affected, and conduct exploratory grants for all of their projects—just for the ones they want to improve society.

Chapter Two

Grantmaking:
The Human Factor

*Above all other aspects of foundation work, I would
put the human factor. I mean by this the attitudes and
behavior of foundation staff members. If they are arrogant,
self-important, dogmatic, conscious of power and status,
or filled with a sense of their own omniscience—traits
which the stewardship of money tends to bring out in some
people—the foundation they serve cannot be a good one.
If, on the other hand, they have genuine humility, are
conscious of their own limitations, are aware that money
does not confer wisdom, are humane, intellectually alive
and curious people—men and women who above all else
are eager to learn from others—the foundation they serve
will probably be a good one. In short, the human qualities
of its staff may in the end be far more important to what a
foundation accomplishes than any other considerations.*

PIFER, 1973

The passage of more than a quarter-century has not eroded an
iota of truth from Alan Pifer's insight that grantmaking is ineluc-
tably a human enterprise. It follows from this truth that the quality of any foundation's work, and the amount of positive change
that it can effect in the world, is directly dependent on the capabilities of its employees. And of all these employees, no position
matters more than that of the program officer. Everything that the

foundation knows of its grantees—and everything that the grantees know of the foundation—ultimately filters through this individual. Program officers are truly at the vital center of the entire enterprise.

Because all roads in philanthropy lead to (and through) program officers, it matters greatly what kind of people they are, how well they can resist the peculiar temptations of philanthropy, how they treat applicants and grantees, and what kind of qualities they need to excel at their position. Surprisingly little attention has been paid to these matters, and philanthropy has suffered from this oversight. It is time—in fact, past time—that such issues receive the consideration they deserve.

It must be acknowledged at the outset that the sheer number of foundations and the bewildering variety of their interests render it all but impossible to come up with a universal set of best practices that will fit all program officers, in all settings, at all times. There are, nonetheless, a certain number of generic challenges and a certain level of general skills and aptitudes that characterize efficient, ethical, and humane ways to conduct grantmaking. Perhaps by laying out some tentative definitions of these challenges, skills, and aptitudes, we can work toward generally accepted guidelines for good practice for program officers.

The Temptations of Philanthropy

In his study of the Ford Foundation, author Dwight Macdonald puckishly defined a foundation as "a large body of money completely surrounded by people who want some" (1956). To change the metaphor, a foundation, to most people, is the pot of gold at the rainbow's end, and program officers are its guardian leprechauns. This means, of course, that everyone wants to catch—or at least, catch the attention of—grantmakers. The competition to capture the interest of program officers is intense, which ensures that their paths will always be strewn with numerous snares and temptations. If you are taking on the role of program officer, your first test is to avoid the blandishments of seven temptations: philanthropy's version of the Seven Deadly Sins. Surrendering to any one of these can utterly destroy your effectiveness as a grantmaker.

Believing the Flattery

Clearly some grantseekers feel that flattery will get them every-where—or, at any rate, somewhere. Grantmakers actually receive letters with opening lines that read like this one: "What a delightful, sincere, knowledgeable individual you are!" A little flattery does wonders for anyone's self-esteem, but a steady diet of it distorts the perspective and raises the danger that the recipient may actually begin to believe it uncritically. To be a successful program officer, you must learn to discount a large proportion of the praise that you will receive from those outside the foundation. You need to equip yourself with an internal gyroscope to allow for self-assessment of performance. After all, those who want a grant or who have gotten a grant have a vested interest in praising the grantmaker. Even those whose grant requests have been declined have a vested interest (the hope of securing a grant in the future) in avoiding overt criticism of the program officer. As a result, all feedback you receive is highly likely to be skewed unrealistically to the favorable side, thus making the internal gyroscope an indispensable tool.

Surrendering to the Whims of Arrogance

The unending flattery leads directly to this second temptation. Few grantseekers are so bold—or so foolhardy—as to disagree with you to your face. A prolonged drought of constructive criticism, coupled with the ongoing cloudburst of flattery, leads almost inevitably (unless you strenuously resist) to a growing sense of entitlement and infallibility—in short, arrogance. Pifer (1984) framed the problem perfectly: "These are the individuals—and we all know some—who go around exuding an air of self-importance and apparent infallibility, who have fallen into the habit of pontificating rather than listening, who have become name droppers, who surround themselves with an aura of wealth, power, and prestige, and who are patronizing toward grantseekers and are largely insensitive to their feelings and inconsiderate of their needs. These people would be shocked if they were charged with such faults because they quite genuinely believe that simply being part of a profession as worthy as philanthropy automatically makes them worthy people too."

It is difficult, indeed, to resist this overblown sense of self-worth when so many people, day after day, line up to proclaim your worthiness. People toiling in more feedback-rich environments (an umpire perhaps, or a public school teacher) experience no shortage of those willing to be critical, whether constructively or otherwise. In contrast, you will only rarely find anyone so bold. One solution to this problem comes from the David and Lucile Packard Foundation, which in 1996 and again in 1998 mailed anonymous surveys to their grantees and those whose grant requests they had turned down. The cloak of anonymity served to protect the respondent while providing the foundation with valuable unfiltered feedback on its performance. As a result of this approach, the foundation received constructive criticism—including specific ideas for improvement—that they could have received in no other way. Such anonymous responses are a powerful corrective to the flattery and fear that prevents honest feedback from occurring naturally.

It is worth noting, however, that there is another, cheaper method of receiving candid criticism. It is also a somewhat older approach, having been in operation as long ago as A.D. 43. In that year, the Roman emperor Claudius returned from his successful campaign in what is now Great Britain. The Roman Senate voted him the exceptional right to make a triumphal entry into Rome at the head of his legions. Mindful of the dangers of arrogance, however, the Senate prescribed that the slave who stood behind the emperor, holding the laurel wreath above his head, repeatedly whisper the words "Remember, you are not a god." You should have at least one friend who is empowered specifically to provide you with such timely and unminced words.

Before leaving this topic, it is worthwhile to note that, in larger foundations in particular, there is a different twist on the problem of arrogance. Grantmakers in such settings are often tormented by the disjunction between how they are treated outside the foundation and inside. Externally, they are lionized. Internally, they are just another employee in the hierarchy. One program officer advises that there is a mathematical formula that balances it all out: "I find that I'm only half as good as they think I am out there, but I'm twice as good as my supervisors think I am in here." Here, again, the internal gyroscope is an essential tool.

Surrendering to Cynicism

The third temptation of grantmaking is really an overreaction to the first two. It is entirely possible for you to overdiscount the flattery and to overestimate the amount of criticism you might receive if only people dared to offer it. A program officer can become tempted to consider every compliment, no matter how sincerely meant or well intended, as immediately suspect. "They only love me for the money I might get for them" becomes the mantra of this poor soul. After a while, it may occur to the suspicious grantmaker that the *only* reason that she or he is treated with respect is because of employment with the foundation. The program officer therefore slides into a cynical Catch-22. To stay at the foundation is to be inundated with praise that is insincere and unmerited, but to leave the foundation would mean risking being treated as a nonentity.

To avoid this situation, again you must be able to assess your self-worth. If you are able to walk the line between arrogance on the one hand and cynicism on the other, you must have a self-generated sense of just how many of the compliments are truly earned.

Regarding the Foundation's Money as Your Own

Grantseekers report this as a widely indulged peccadillo among program officers, complaining that their requests for grants are sometimes treated as if they were pleas for personal loans. This attitude toward grantseekers is fundamentally unkind, but more than that, it is dead wrong. The corpus of the foundation, of course, is not your property. Nor is it any longer the property of the donor or donors of the corpus. It is not, strictly speaking, even the property of the foundation that employs you. U.S. foundations exist as a result of a social contract: the U.S. government has agreed to forego taxes on the donor's capital in exchange for the donor's irrevocably dedicating that capital to projects that will advance the common good. Thus the corpus ultimately belongs not to any single entity but to the public. Ironically, the money belongs just as much to those who are seeking it as to those who are dispensing it.

The fifth and sixth temptations of grantmaking are mirror images of each other, and were identified in a jocular vein some years ago by a California community foundation executive named Jack Shakely (1988).

Doubting the Worthiness of All Applicants

The fifth temptation, says Mr. Shakely, is to believe that no applicant is worthy of funding. As a program officer, you are essentially in the business of making decisions about who gets money and who does not, and for every applicant who gets money there is a long line of those who do not. Your critical faculties must be sharp, you must make hard decisions, and people (unfortunately, many very good people) must be disappointed. Every program officer must have a strongly analytical streak and must be decisive in making the call as to which proposals are funded and which are rejected. If taken to excess, however, a purely analytical approach will miss many of the most creative and daring ideas. Compassion, imagination, and a generous spirit must also come into play. As Shakely notes, you can reach a point at which you find fault with everything. Overanalyzing proposals, if taken to its logical conclusion, results in the foundation being unable to fund anything. Grantmaking requires you to have a good head, but that is not enough; you also need to have a good heart.

Finding Value in All Applicants

If all head and no heart is a problem, so too is its mirror image, all heart and no head. Bighearted grantmakers see worthiness in every proposal and try to nurture them all to funding. Such an approach cannot work, for foundations get more proposals than they can possibly fund, and some are much more worthy of funding than others. As a program officer, you simply must make hard decisions and disappoint good people. Bighearted grantmakers frequently respond to this hard truth by dithering—that is, they defer making decisions and neither decline nor fund proposals. Typically, the proposal does not fit the foundation's guidelines, but the submitting organization is so admirable or the people leading it are so likable that the program officer cannot bear to say no, so the proposal goes into limbo. The grantmaker might hope that a change in foundation priorities or a need to pay out more funds due to endowment growth (to take but two rationalizations) will allow him or her eventually to slip the proposal through. What almost always happens instead is an endless, inconclusive wait for the grantseeker, and frustration for all involved. It seems safe to say that neither the pure head approach nor the pure heart approach works in philanthropy; these are two temptations that must be strenuously resisted.

Taking the Easy Way Out

The life of the average program officer is nothing if not hectic. Grantseekers continually clamor for meetings, both face-to-face and by telephone. Projects must be visited, both prior to and after funding. Colleagues within the organization require attention, as do colleagues working for other foundations or potential funding partners. And there is always a mountain of material to read: proposals, annual report narratives, reports from evaluators, and background material needed to keep current in fields of the foundation's interests. Add to this imposing workload the knowledge that most grantmakers are driven by a desire to serve good causes, and it all totals overload. "None of what I do is rocket science," commented one program officer, "but the sheer volume of it all is overwhelming." The typical program officer works very hard. It is commonplace for grantmakers to take home work at night, put in hours on weekends, even to toil on holidays and while on vacation. Against this background of sheer busyness, there is sometimes an overwhelming temptation to cut corners. Phone messages are easy to ignore, general correspondence can be tossed in the circular file, long proposals can be skimmed or not read at all. Grantseekers are unanimous in complaining that too many program officers are unresponsive, not even giving the simple courtesy of a civil reply to a polite inquiry.

Such behavior on the part of grantmakers, no matter how busy they might be, is simply inexcusable. It is, for starters, unprofessional. It is also a train wreck in the making. Sooner or later one of these ignored applicants will turn out to be a key player in a critical field, or a friend or relative of a foundation trustee, or, worse, a prominent constituent of a member of the House Ways and

Means Committee. Any ephemeral savings in time or spurious increase in efficiency realized by ignoring grantseekers will be more than counterbalanced by the damage that discourtesy and unprofessional behavior inevitably cause.

This discourtesy, it should be noted, too often crosses the line into rudeness. Grantseekers have horror stories to tell of repeated phone calls that are never returned, urgent letters that are pointedly ignored, contemptuous and dismissive behavior during meetings, and broken promises of follow-through. Regrettably, this boorish behavior is probably the most common failing among grantmakers. Again, there can be no possible justification for such performance on the part of program officers, for though grantmakers must deliver bad news regularly, there is no reason why they must deliver it badly.

There is, moreover, a subtler form of the seventh temptation. Every program officer knows the dilemma of reading a proposal that describes a potentially great idea but that has significant problems. It might be poorly written, or the applicant may be an unknown quantity, or possibly the organization doing the asking is new and fragile. All of these things are fixable, but all of them take lots of time to fix. Concurrently, there are requests on the table to support ideas of middling potential, but the proposals are well written, or the applicants are old reliables, or the organizations are seasoned in the arts of grantseeking. The temptation is to reject the highly promising but enormously time-consuming proposal and to embrace the humdrum but easy-to-process idea.

As easy as it is to settle for supporting mediocre requests that are easy to fund, you should never tolerate such a lazy approach. Excellence in grantmaking is no accident, and it is achieved by a lot of hard work. This is the value that effective program officers add to the grantmaking process. Anyone can process a blah proposal; if that is all grantmakers do, they could (and should) be replaced by a cash machine.

There is no effective way for a foundation to keep watch over you to ensure that you return all phone calls, answer all letters, or take on the promising but complex requests. You must ultimately be self-accountable in ensuring that you see to these tasks. Much depends on this. The image of the foundation—as open or arrogant—and the impact of the foundation's work—whether its outcomes lead the wave or founder in the backwash—will largely be determined by the integrity (or lack of same) of its program officers.

It is worth noting that a promising effort to improve the behavior of program officers emanates not from inside but rather from outside the foundation field. *Foundation News and Commentary*, the journal of the Council on Foundations, reported that Michael H. Shuman, former executive director of the Institute for Policy Studies, has designed a survey titled "A Report Card on Progressive Funders," which he mailed during summer 1998 to thousands of progressive activists (White, 1998). Shuman intends to disseminate the results in a publication to be titled "The Insider's Guide to Progressive Foundations." Interestingly, Shuman noted in the article that the initial response rate was disappointing, a fact that he attributed to grantees' concerns about disclosing their full level of dissatisfaction—even anonymously. However, he has vowed to make this report card an annual event, and if he succeeds, it will bring—at least to the progressive spectrum of funders—a measure of much-needed accountability.

A Grantseeker's Bill of Rights

A straightforward way to systematize this kind of "right behavior" for program officers is to draw up a bill of rights for grantseekers. A number of attempts have been made over the years to do just that, with the number of grantseekers' rights ranging from less than ten to more than twenty. The list that follows takes into consideration its predecessors (most of which, over the years, have been published in *Foundation News and Commentary*) and adds a few new twists. My choice of offering ten rights is a deliberate one. Not only is this pleasing historically, but my aim is to present a concise statement of the most important things that all program officers should honor in their dealings with applicants:

1. The right to receive a clear statement of the foundation's funding interests
2. The right to have all communications answered
3. The right to an explanation of, and timeline for, the foundation's proposal review process

4. The right to a prompt acknowledgment of receipt of a proposal
5. The right to have all proposals read in full and seriously considered
6. The right to a timely and unambiguous funding decision
7. The right to receive an explanation of the reasoning behind funding decisions
8. The right to have all requirements for the grant relationship clearly spelled out, in writing (including the right to have any components of the grant *required* by the foundation *paid for* by the foundation)
9. The right to have all reports completely read and carefully considered
10. The right to be informed if continued funding is a possibility

For the most part, with apologies to Mr. Jefferson, these truths certainly are self-evident, but this does not mean that they are universally honored. In fact, many foundations fall short of completely respecting this bill of rights. For example, there are still a number (a minority to be sure, but a significant minority) of foundations that publish neither an annual report nor a brochure explaining their programming interests. Grantseekers are thus forced to do considerable detective work before they can even determine whether the foundation might be interested in receiving a proposal. This is a waste of their time and resources, and it could easily be prevented by the issuance of a simple brochure.

The third right is often violated by review processes that are shrouded in as much mystery as the fate of Amelia Earhart. Such foundations seem determined to appear as a black box, in which proposals are inserted at one end, and grants—or more likely, rejection letters—emerge at the other end in a totally inexplicable fashion. A foundation need not share every detail of the grantmaking process, but an explanation of its broad outlines and an estimate of its likely duration would be of significant help to the grantseeker. Unfortunately, even something as simple and painless as acknowledging receipt of proposals by return mail is not universally practiced.

Perhaps the most inexcusable lapse occurs when foundations require a certain component as a condition for receiving a grant but refuse to cover its cost. This is the moral equivalent of the un-funded mandate in government. Some foundations are notorious for requiring, for example, that projects they fund be evaluated by a third party—but they are unwilling to pay for evaluation. Foundations should require nothing unless they are willing to pay (at a minimum) the lion's share of the costs for the requirement.

Living up to the bill of rights outlined here is an essential element of professional practice for any foundation, and not an onerous task. All that is needed is a commitment to open and honest communications with the public. Any foundation that aspires to a professional level of operations—or that simply values its integrity—should not find it difficult to comply with these ten rules.

What Qualities Should Grantmakers Possess?

Given the temptations of philanthropy, and given the imperatives for right treatment of grantseekers, what are the necessary qualities for fitness as a grantmaker? This question has been considered many times over the years, most often in the pages of *Foundation News and Commentary*. Large numbers of lists have been compiled, each containing many traits in common and a few that are distinctive. Of these dozens of potentially valuable qualities, there seem to be six that are irreducible requirements.

Integrity

Some wag once remarked that "the most important thing in life is integrity. Once you have learned to fake that, you've got it made." Facetiousness aside, as a program officer you must possess and model trustworthiness. All transactions between grantmakers and grantseekers ultimately depend on trust. Any program officer who cannot be trusted cannot ultimately be effective. Not only is it wrong to lie, but it is also bad policy. Grantseekers form a surprisingly small and well-connected society, and their grapevine functions well. Lies are soon discovered. The consequences of these lies hurt more than just the program officer; they affect the reputation of the foundation itself. And, because program officers *are* the foundation to grantseekers, a mendacious program officer is tantamount to a mendacious foundation.

People Skills

The story is told of a Civil War surgeon who was amputating, without benefit of anesthetic, limbs of wounded soldiers. A concerned observer asked, "Isn't that terribly painful?" The surgeon quickly replied, "Only if I carelessly cut my thumb." More than a few grantmakers are the spiritual descendants of that surgeon: brilliant but insensitive. Philanthropy being an eminently human enterprise, it is absolutely essential that you be an empathic and respectful listener, articulate speaker, clear writer, and intuitive and sensitive observer. A program officer who cannot listen is quite simply useless; one who cannot communicate is quite simply dangerous. As a program officer, you must listen without unduly raising expectations, communicate interest without making unfounded implications or empty promises, and, above all, say no without crushing spirits or making enemies.

Many program officers were hired for their penetrating intellect, their impressive scholarship, or their valuable experience, all without regard to their ability to communicate or their respect for others. In a foundation context, brilliance without humanity is not just unfortunate: it crushes good ideas and makes lasting enemies. An anecdote related by a program officer underlines the importance of empathy: "I brought along a half-dozen proposals to a conference I was attending," she said. "One evening I skipped the host event and read them all. None were competitive, so I dictated letters declining each request. As I finished the last one, I felt great because I had gotten so much accomplished that evening. Then it suddenly hit me. That pile of rejected proposals represented the hopes, the aspirations, and the dreams of hundreds of people who wanted to help thousands of other people. I had just crushed those dreams—and here I was feeling great about it. I suddenly felt ashamed of myself." There should be no shame in turning down uncompetitive requests, but there should be no pride in inflicting pain—even unavoidable pain—on applicants. And always there is a danger of what might be called "creeping numbness": a loss of sensitivity for the impact on others of the decisions made by the foundation. The responsibility of deciding who gets money and who does not is one that should never be taken lightly and one that requires a healthy respect for the dreams and feelings of others.

Analytical Ability *and* Creativity

A cynic, as defined by Oscar Wilde, is one "who knows the price of everything and the value of nothing." The post of program officer requires a healthy balance between "knowing the price" (having the ability to analyze ideas, test their internal logic, and rate their external value) and "knowing the value" (having the ability to grasp the possibilities of ideas, to envision how they might develop and change society). As mentioned before, you must possess a balance of "head" and "heart"—must at once be logical and passionate. Too much "head," and you will analyze promising ideas to death. Too much "heart," and you will fund ludicrous or embarrassing ideas. In short, the ideal program officer is a mixture of equal parts accountant and entrepreneur, with a dash of coach and a pinch of cleric added to the mix.

Spirituality

Genius, Thomas Edison once explained, "is 1 percent inspiration, and 99 percent perspiration." In philanthropy, these proportions should not exactly be transposed, but inspiration should play a greater role in your work as a program officer than a mere 1 percent. People who wish to make money tend to be drawn to the commercial sector. People who wish to wield power tend to be drawn to the government sector. People who wish to make positive change in the world tend to be drawn to foundation work. Making money and wielding power are essentially rational ambitions, proceeding from the cognitive side of people's lives. The desire to transform society, however, issues from a different part of people's lives, one that is less logical and more affective. In fact, for many, foundation work becomes a secular expression of spirituality. It demonstrates love for fellow humans, provides an avenue to transform faith into action, and satisfies a craving to connect to others in a profound way. Rob Lehman (1998), president of the Fetzer Institute, has eloquently defined this phenomenon as "the heart of philanthropy": bringing into balance and into a conscious relationship the inner life of the spirit and the outer life of action and service.

Ironically, foundations as organizations are usually uncomfortable with these impulses, often in the mistaken belief that spirituality equates with conventional religion. Indeed, sometimes it does, but more often it transcends any particular organized system of faith. "Spirit," as Robert Greenleaf (1977) noted, "represents the divine behind the urge to serve." Spirituality should be seen as a source of strength to the foundation and to philanthropy as a whole, for when the spirit is exorcized from foundation work, such work becomes indistinguishable from any other calling: making grants becomes pretty much the same as making widgets.

Sense of Balance and Proportion

Few things in life are more potentially dangerous than an overzealous person, particularly one with lots of money and an urge to do good works. New program officers are highly likely to experience the "kid in the candy store" problem, being unable to resist each new opportunity, making too many commitments, overextending their calendar, and ultimately sapping their physical and mental energy. It would be simpler, of course, if there were a dearth of good opportunities, which would make it easier to choose only the best. As it is, there are more opportunities to do good than any one person can possibly pursue. You must have the self-discipline to bring balance to your life. If you are to do things well, you will have to sacrifice many good opportunities (or at the very least, hand them over to others). The program officer who is overcommitted, overstressed, and overwhelmed does nothing well. In foundations, almost universally, program officers report that the responsibility for keeping that sane balance between work and family, between internal and external responsibilities, and among professional, volunteer, and personal commitments falls squarely on their own shoulders. The officers of the foundation do not take on such tasks, nor should they be expected to do so. Effective grantmakers pace themselves, working steadily and working hard, but also controlling the amount and the intensity of that work. And always, the hardest part is passing up exciting and promising chances to do good.

Compassion

Grantmaking is more than the making of grants. It is also the breaking of hearts. Declining proposals is a weekly, if not daily, part of the routine. Moreover, many of the proposals that must be declined represent good ideas from good people and are a good fit with the foundation's priorities—and yet must be declined because the grantmaking budget is not large enough to support everything. The last thing an applicant needs is for the program officer to heap insult on injury by being disrespectful or insensitive while delivering disappointing news. As a grantmaker you need to keep this in mind always and to practice compassion constantly. This is not to say that you can avoid hard decisions; rather it is to say that you should not be unnecessarily hard on applicants when you deliver and explain the foundation's decisions to decline requests. Without compassion and empathy, you become part of the problem that your foundation is trying to overcome.

Conclusion

Alan Pifer was right: in foundation work, the human element is all-important. No one type of personality, no one sort of profession, produces the kind of people who become good program officers. The best grantmakers have the strength of character to resist philanthropy's manifold temptations; they have a strong respect for the rights of their opposite numbers among grantseekers; they possess innate integrity and the ability to listen carefully and communicate well; they are able to be at the same time creative and critical; they are imbued with a spirituality that informs and renews them; and they have an internal gyroscope that keeps all these elements in an effective balance. If a foundation hires people like these and treats them well, it will succeed. As Russell G. Mawby, the retired CEO of the W. K. Kellogg Foundation, is wont to say: "Only people are important, because only people make things happen."

| Chapter Three |

Building Relationships
with Applicants

It is a commonplace of foundation wisdom that grantseekers need money, and therefore they need grantmakers. Program officers are reminded of this fact every day in ways both subtle and blatant. It seems to occur to foundation types much less often that grantmakers also need grantseekers. Money is a necessary condition for social change, but it is hardly sufficient. Without grantseekers and their assorted partners, foundations would be in the bizarre position of having a lot of money but possessing no way to put it to work.

Grantmaking: A Relational Enterprise

Grantmaking is inescapably a relational enterprise, which means that what passes between grantmaker and grantseeker is more than mere socializing; their relationship is the strategic bridge over which money, lessons learned, and ultimately social change must pass. It works only if it is a mutually respectful relationship of peers, not a patron-supplicant system. Given the inequalities of the power dynamic, however, this relationship of peers is easier to conceptualize than to accomplish.

The relational nature of grantmaking offers many opportunities for abuse. "It's not what you know, but who you know" goes the cynical old saw, and nowhere is it potentially more true than in foundations. It is unfortunately not unknown for a program officer to take this principle to the extreme by maintaining a largely closed circle of favorites and distributing largess to them on a regular schedule. The rationalization is that in making any grant, one is betting on the integrity of the grantee, so it is sensible to back people whom one knows to be honest and capable. There is some merit in this argument, but it does not begin to justify setting up a small and exclusive clique of recipients.

The degree of openness you can display will, of course, depend largely on where your foundation falls on the 4-P continuum. Grantmakers in passive foundations will be far more open than their counterparts in peremptory foundations. Grantmakers in proactive foundations should be quite open, for they will need new partners to add to their grant clusters, whereas program officers in prescriptive foundations will probably be much less so, because their agendas are largely set. No matter where your foundation falls on the continuum, however, it behooves you to retain at least a certain level of openness, for no institution has ever cornered the market on innovation or worthwhile ideas. To be completely closed is to turn off the agitator in the foundation washing machine: the rest of the apparatus may still work, but the outcomes will not be as satisfying.

Although openness is a virtue, it is not without its costs. The responsibilities on the shoulders of the typical grantmaker on any given day are daunting and time-consuming. The last thing an overloaded calendar needs is an unexpected meeting. Cold telephone calls are even worse, for they arrive without warning, interrupt workflow, and often come in unwanted clusters. It becomes very tempting to decline meeting requests and refuse to take phone calls, simply to keep control over one's day. Yet as time-consuming and unproductive as these can sometimes be, they are frequently a prime source for great new ideas. (There are many other sources, such as reading widely, working networks, surfing the Web, and the like, but these are more easily scheduled.)

The grantmaker who does not return calls or accept invitations to meet may gain in efficiency over the short term, but he or she loses touch with the flow of promising ideas, not to mention giving the foundation field a reputation for unresponsiveness. The temptation to do so, however, is great. When you are overbooked, many things are difficult to cut from the "to do" list, such as projects ordered by the boss, or standing internal meetings. You can cut meetings with applicants, however, with no immediate negative consequences. Such temptations must be strenuously resisted. It is obviously very important for you to manage your relations with applicants so as to maximize the value of the time for both you and them.

Communicating Requirements with Clarity

The essential first step in managing relations with applicants is to make proper use of paper and pixels. Communicating with clarity is essential to establishing and maintaining good relations with the outside world, so the foundation should print brochures and annual reports, and if possible create videos or websites, all clearly spelling out programming priorities and detailing the application procedure. If these communication tools are not in place, you will spend endless hours imparting such essential but basic information to grantseekers. There are better uses for your time, and all those asking for such information should be politely but firmly referred to such resources.

Writing the copy for the communications tools is no easy matter. Defining the foundation's interests too vaguely (as in, "The foundation funds proposals that improve society") tells the grantseeker nothing. Setting out the criteria in too much detail imparts the wrong message. Many program officers tell stories of receiving phone calls from grantseekers in which the excited applicant says, in effect, "My idea meets every one of the seventeen criteria listed on your website. I sent my proposal to you this morning. How soon will you send me the money?"

To be effective, the communications vehicle must explain the main grantmaking priorities of the foundation and share the most important criteria by which proposals will be judged. It must also convey the fact that the foundation will receive many more proposals that fit the criteria than it can possibly fund. Meeting the criteria in itself, therefore, will not guarantee funding.

The communications vehicle should tell the would-be grantee how to make the initial approach to the foundation (phone call, letter, e-mail, written proposal?). Is there a specific person or office to whom the proposal should be directed? How long can the proposal be? What are the deadlines for submission? What attachments are required? How many copies should be sent? Are specific types of funding, such as support for operating expenses or endowment, proscribed? Is there a specific geographic focus or monetary ceiling on the foundation's grantmaking? How can the applicant get more information? This list is not necessarily exhaustive, but the communications vehicle should contain, at the very least, all the elements named.

The communications instrument should also coach applicants to avoid a couple of classic grantseeker errors. First, it should strongly advise them to avoid sending in "laundry list" proposals. In essence, this type of proposal lists a number of proposals (sometimes more than ten) that the applicant *could* submit, and asks you to pick the one most congenial to the foundation. Although the laundry list is useful as an item of information (it does reveal the range of interests of the grantseeking organization, and often the interlocking strategies it is pursuing), it poses any number of problems as a means of putting forward a proposal. First, it puts you in an awkward position, for now having chosen the proposal, you will have to sit in judgment on it. There is also a fundamental problem in that your choice will be the top priority on the list for the foundation, but it may well be a much lower priority for the applicant. In any case, it is the applicant, not you, who should be making that prioritizing decision. Should an applicant ask you to do it anyway, the best response is simply to suggest that the applicant choose its top priority and send that in as a proposal. If that proposal is not congenial to the foundation, the applicant can always submit its second priority after the first has been declined.

The second major error occurs when the grantseeker, whether overtly or covertly, asks you to write the proposal. Once again, this puts you into a very awkward position of having to sit in judgment on a proposal that you had a strong hand in creating. As program officer, you should function as a coach, making suggestions to improve a proposal's chances for funding. However, just as coaches stay on the sidelines in a game, so too should you stay on the sidelines while the proposal is being written.

Telephone Calls and Meetings with Applicants

No matter how well worded the foundation's external communications may be, there will still be a never-ending parade of requests from grantseekers to talk with and to meet with you. Grantmakers often feel besieged by this insatiable demand. Some spend too much of their time trying, without success, to meet it. Some throw up their hands and refuse to be disturbed. Both approaches are counterproductive in the long run. There is a happy medium between becoming enthralled by nonstop outside demands and turning into the second coming of Greta Garbo. Achieving this happy balance requires a disciplined approach to grantmaking.

Many new program officers have vowed to pursue an open-door policy: being accessible on demand to anyone who phones or who asks for a face-to-face meeting. If they religiously follow this policy for any length of time, they soon discover that they have lost control of their schedule and that they no longer have sufficient time to devote to other important parts of their job, such as managing funded projects. There are ways, however, to preserve accessibility while protecting your calendar.

Telephone calls are the bane of many grantmakers because of their utter unpredictability. They interrupt meetings, derail trains of thought, and imperil deadlines. However, there are ways to handle even this bugaboo. A simple policy is to take an unsolicited telephone call *only* if you are not doing something more important, such as trying to meet a deadline imposed by the CEO. One variation on this policy is to demur on taking the phone call now but to ask the caller to try again during specified office hours. Another and more precise variation is to make a firm telephone appointment time. Either approach has the virtue of placing telephone calls under your control and, by bunching, minimizing the constant interruption that the telephone brings in its train.

Controlling meetings presents a somewhat different set of challenges. Most foundations require grantseekers to make an appointment in order to visit a program officer but leave the details of the arrangements up to him or her. It is always in the interest of the grantseeker to have a face-to-face meeting with you; sometimes it is in your interest as well. There are two tests you can apply to decide if a meeting (or for that matter, a phone call) is warranted. The first test is whether the person seeking the meeting has a substantive agenda. It is always in the interest of the grantseeker to have "get acquainted" meetings with you before proposing anything specific. In fact, such meetings sometimes turn into fishing expeditions, with the grantseeker-angler trolling for information from you, the fish. Sometimes, for political reasons, you cannot avoid such meetings. If possible, however, you should insist that there be something substantive on the table to discuss, such as a concept paper or a proposal. This imposes some discipline on the grantseeker and gives the meeting a definite purpose.

The second test is whether the applicant will agree to a reasonable time limit. From the standpoint of the grantseeker, the longer the meeting, the better: it gives him or her a greater chance to get to know you and the foundation you represent. From your point of view, as the length of a meeting increases, you experience diminishing returns, and valuable time is lost. Set a time limit and stick to it. An hour is usually sufficient; anything longer than two hours should be reserved for those who have traveled great distances or have a complex, expensive proposal to present. Courtesy meetings should be limited to a half hour, if at all possible, as it is highly unlikely that a grant relationship will develop from them.

The meetings themselves must be conducted with enormous sensitivity. The late Dr. Peter Ellis, a long-time program director with the W. K. Kellogg Foundation, was a master of foundation meeting etiquette. More than fifteen years of experience as a grantmaker led him to propound Ellis's Iron Law of Meetings and to derive eight rules for conducting meetings based on it. Ellis's Iron Law of Meetings states, "All grantseekers are optimists searching for affirmation; therefore they are prone to misinterpret any communication from a grantmaker, whether verbal or nonverbal." Dr. Ellis was adamant that grantmakers must be direct and clear in their oral and written communications with applicants. They must be especially conscious of the signals they are sending, whether overt or subtle, whether intentional or unintentional. If program officers are careless or imprecise in their communications, grantseekers will leave the meeting with precisely the opposite message than the one intended, leading to needless misunderstandings and potentially dangerous consequences. The eight rules that Dr. Ellis formulated for meetings are aimed to minimize this threat of miscommunication and to remove ambiguity from the grantmaker-grantseeker relationship. They apply equally to telephone conference calls.

Ellis's First Rule: Define the purpose and predict the probable outcome of the meeting very clearly at the time of setting it up.

In his experience, Ellis noted that because the process of foundations is largely a mystery to most grantseekers, some of them actually believe that getting a meeting is tantamount to getting a grant. In order to demystify the process, therefore, you should inject clear expectations at the beginning. For example, if the purpose of a meeting is merely a courtesy call, then you should convey to the applicant, as tactfully as possible, that it is highly unlikely that the meeting will lead to a grant. It is far better to deliver disappointment early, before expectations are built up.

ELLIS'S SECOND RULE: Begin the meeting with a disclaimer.

Ellis used to tell of a frustrated grantseeker who, when Ellis declined his request, blurted "Why not? You are *the* program officer, aren't you?" The title of program officer may suggest to some people that its bearer has the authority to make unilateral decisions about funding requests. It is wise, therefore, to begin by saying (as is true of most foundations) that you propose but others dispose. No decisions can be made at this meeting, so the most the applicant can expect is to educate the foundation about the applicant's idea. Nor can you make any guarantees that the final decision about the request, once made, will be favorable.

ELLIS'S THIRD RULE: Remember that it is vitally important to qualify statements, especially positive statements.

Such words as *if, should, in case,* and *possible* are your best friends. Unless you qualify a statement, the grantseeker will interpret it to be true. For example, Ellis told of a young grantmaker who was asked by an applicant to explain the foundation's proposal review process. "Well," responded the program officer, "first we read your proposal, then we recommend it for funding, then the officers of the foundation sign off on it, and finally the board approves it." The program officer thought he was delivering a hypothetical scenario, but the applicant interpreted the affirmative statements to mean that the request was already approved. Later, after the proposal had been declined, the applicant called in great anguish to say that he had already informed *his* board that the proposal would be approved by the foundation. According to Ellis, here is what the grantmaker should have said: "Well, first we will read your proposal. *If* it meets our criteria and *if* it is competitive, then it is *possible* that we *might* recommend it for funding. *Should* the officers of the foundation sign off on it, then it would go to the board. The board does not approve every proposal we send for funding, but *in case* they should approve this one, then it would be officially a grant." This statement contains no fewer than six qualifications. That may sound like overkill, but you must remember that an applicant will likely seize on *any* unqualified statements, so it is necessary to qualify *every time* when discussing the probable fate of a proposal. Another of Ellis's aphorisms should be mentioned here: "There is a word for program officers who unilaterally promise people grants. That word is *unemployed*."

ELLIS'S FOURTH RULE: In grantmaking, the possibility of failure *does* exist (in contradiction to the apocryphal doctrine once attributed to Queen Victoria).

You must explicitly state this possibility to the applicant during the course of the meeting. "Every time I failed to mention during the meeting that the proposal could be declined," said Ellis, "after I declined it later, I would get a phone call from the disappointed grantseeker, who would say 'But you never said that it might be turned down.'" Of course, any proposal can be turned down, but it is better not to leave unstated that simple fact of foundation life. If worse comes to worst, it is extremely helpful to be able to remind the applicant that you had uttered those very words of warning during the meeting.

ELLIS'S FIFTH RULE: We send important messages not only through words but also through nonverbal cues, tone of voice, and general demeanor.

Ellis often told of a meeting he attended when he was new to the foundation, at which an applicant was asking for $6 million for a project that was clearly outside the scope of the Kellogg Foundation's programming interests. The senior officer conducting the meeting gave the applicant this message, but he did it with such warmth and in such an encouraging tone of voice that the applicant came away believing that her proposal had only to be submitted to be funded. It later fell to Ellis to disabuse the grantseeker of this notion. Clearly, she had not heard the words: what came through were the smiles, the empathy, the warm tone of voice. Unfortunately, this story has been repeated many times in many different foundations. Grantmakers tend to be positive people who wish to be affirming even when they cannot give someone money. So if it becomes necessary to deliver bad news, or even a tough disclaimer, they try to soften the blow. What comes across to the grantseeker, unfortunately, is not the negative message but rather the warm and fuzzy nonverbal cues. A similar problem arises when you become enthusiastic about the concept under discussion. Your verbal disclaimers duly offered are drowned out by the sense of enthusiasm in your voice. You need first to be aware of this phenomenon, then to alter your behavior accordingly. It is important to be attentive but not overenthusiastic, cordial but not overwarm, affirming but not overencouraging. Finally, you should issue a specific disclaimer about behavior, such as, "If I appeared enthusiastic about your idea, I would suggest that you do not attach any significance to it. Decisions about your request will be made by a committee, so one person's opinion will not be decisive."

Ellis's Sixth Rule: Be sure before the meeting ends to clearly summarize what happened during its course and to review the next steps that were agreed on.

As Ellis used to remark, "It is quite possible for two people to attend two entirely different meetings together." In the course of an hour or more of intense conversation, it is easy indeed for the parties to misunderstand such points as whether a formal or informal proposal should be submitted, the amount that should be requested, or the timetable for next steps. Discussing these outcomes explicitly near the end of the meeting ensures that both parties have a chance to iron out any misconceptions, achieve a common understanding of what transpired, and agree on what comes next.

Ellis's Seventh Rule: Close the meeting by reiterating every disclaimer uttered during its course.

Again, it may appear to be overkill, but as Ellis was fond of saying, "I'd rather have them consider me redundant now than have them consider me repugnant later." It simply saves infinite trouble in the long run if every applicant understands that you cannot unilaterally say yes; that the foundation can, and may very well, unilaterally say no; and that your nonverbal reactions are not a reliable forecast of the outcome of the request.

ELLIS'S EIGHTH RULE: Document the results of every meeting.

"I have never regretted writing meeting notes," said Ellis, "but I have always regretted it on every occasion when I thought I was too busy to do it." Take notes during the meeting and translate these notes into a document as soon as possible afterwards. This is sensible for at least two reasons. First, if the meeting leads to a proposal that is eventually funded, then the meeting notes become the first entry in the file that must be kept on the project. Second, if the proposal is eventually declined, you will have a record of the meeting in case the grantseeker complains about the decision to a higher authority within the foundation.

It is worth repeating that all of Ellis's rules for meetings, including the eighth rule, apply to telephone conferences as well as to face-to-face encounters. It is all too easy to make a promise over the telephone, then to completely forget about it after hanging up. Documenting phone calls is not always convenient (or even safe, if the conversation is taking place over a car phone), but it is professionally sound practice to document it as soon as possible afterwards.

A final note on meetings: the vast majority of all grantseekers are honest and ethical professionals, but a tiny percentage are not. In the best of all possible worlds, grantmakers would never attend meetings without a colleague present. Every program officer with a few years of experience in the field has a horror story in which one of the few unscrupulous grantseekers deliberately lied about something he or she supposedly said or did during a meeting. Of course, it will not be possible, especially in smaller foundations, to avoid solo meetings. If, however, you have any reason to be concerned—or a "gut" instinct is aroused—it is always a good idea to have a witness, or at least to document the meeting all the more carefully.

Project File Documentation

The project file is the most overlooked aspect of relationships with both applicants and grantees. No program officer can possibly remember all of the important details of every project, especially when he or she is responsible for multiple projects, so recording them on paper or on disk is essential. Grants are legal contracts between the foundation and the grantee, so there are also good legal and fiduciary reasons to keep an up-to-date file on each project. The file serves as a key source of the data that enable the project to be properly evaluated, disseminated, or brought to scale. The file also is essential as a record of the project should the foundation be audited by the Internal Revenue Service, which can and occasionally does happen.

Finally, there is the issue of self-protection. As a program officer, you are, like it or not, quite often in the business of disappointing people. For the most part, it is applicants that you must turn down, but occasionally you must also disappoint the leaders of previously funded projects. One program officer tells of a time when he inherited, from a colleague who had passed away, a three-year project just beginning its final year. After that year was up and the program officer had declined the grantee's request for a second grant, the foundation's president received an angry letter from the CEO of the grantee. The letter claimed that the program officer had totally ignored the project over its last year and had never once contacted the grantee. The letter closed with an angry demand for a meeting with the president of the foundation. The program officer was able to document, from the file, nine separate occasions over the twelve-month period in question when either the program officer or his secretary had been in touch with the grantee, and even once when another colleague from the foundation had made a brief site visit to the grantee. Unsurprisingly, when confronted with this evidence, the chastened CEO withdrew the request for a meeting with the foundation's president.

The project file is in many ways the program officer's best friend; thus it needs to be created and tended with care. You will need to exercise discretion, however, in choosing which documents to include in the file and which not to. Among the documents that belong in the file are meeting notes, field notes from site visits, all drafts of a proposal, all foundation responses to proposal drafts, funding documents (which recommend to an internal committee or board of trustees that a proposal be supported), commitment letters, commitment revision letters, annual progress reports, and evaluation reports. Other items might be included in the main file or placed in a supplemental file, such as newsletters, press clippings, videos, and the like.

Among the documents that *do not* belong in the file are any that contain libelous material of any sort about individuals, or unsubstantiated charges about institutions. For example, if a document quotes someone who says that an employee of the grantee is a notorious adulterer, that document should not go into the file. A good rule is never to include in the file any document that would embarrass you, the foundation, or the grantee if it were to be reproduced verbatim on the front page of a national newspaper.

Relations with Colleagues

In any foundation large enough to employ more than a single program officer, it is important to consider the relationships between and among staff members. Perhaps the most obvious of these considerations is a concern for how the daily flow of work is handled. For example, if a proposal is sent to you by the applicant, do you automatically handle it, or is there a mechanism for transferring it to a different program officer who may have more expertise in the area covered by the proposal? If you are planning on meeting with an applicant, by what criteria will it be decided whether or not colleagues are invited to attend the meeting?

You can avoid much friction with your colleagues by reaching an agreement as to how the duties of reading and deciding on the merits of proposals will be handled. Will every proposal be read by a team? Will decisions about recommending proposals for funding be made in group meetings? Will unanimity be required for recommendation, or will a majority suffice? How will the presentations to the board of trustees or internal committee of officers to get funding approval be handled?

Because program officers frequently are confronted with making judgments about matters that are beyond their areas of personal expertise, it is essential for all grantmakers on a foundation staff to work collegially, cooperatively, and, whenever possible, collaboratively. There is a place in philanthropy for the solitary genius, but the gregarious generalist is usually the most effective program officer.

Conclusion

Grantmaking is a relational enterprise, and like any relationship it has its moments of sublime connection and its moments of frustrating miscommunication. It is an enterprise in which inequalities of wealth and power must be overcome, in which opposite numbers must find ways to communicate, and in which every phone call offers new opportunities for misunderstandings. Unlike Richard Nixon's press secretary Ron Ziegler, you do not have the luxury of saying "I misspoke myself" and soldiering on. You must choose words carefully, employ them with the proper tone, and work to banish ambiguity from all communications, whether with those outside the foundation or with colleagues. In short, excellence in grantmaking requires the specialized knowledge of the technocrat, the communication savvy of the diplomat, and, some would say, the breathtaking agility of an acrobat.

| **Reviewing Proposals**

The job descriptions of program officers in the more than fifty-eight thousand foundations across the United States vary widely, but if there is a single task that all share, it is that of reading, declining, and recommending proposals for funding. Doing this consistently well is at the heart of any program officer's job, but defining what is meant by "well" is notoriously difficult. Proposals are received in a truly infinite array. They can focus on virtually any subject, whether the foundation is interested in that subject or not; they can be terse or verbose, elegant or clumsy, brilliant or vapid, typeset or scrawled in pencil. No two are ever exactly alike, and no one can formulate a one-size-fits-all set of rules for assessing them.

Reviewing proposals is, inescapably, a subjective business. Although it is possible to compare one proposal with another, these comparisons are rarely, if ever, exact. When the foundation's board or the internal committee ultimately chooses one proposal over another, the basis for that choice is apt to be less a mass of data and more a matter of judgment or hunches based on experience, and sometimes it is even a leap of faith. There is no science of proposal review, but fortunately there are some reliable guideposts along the way.

The policies of the foundation employing you serve as your first guidepost. Some foundations, especially those in the peremptory range of the 4-P continuum, do not accept unsolicited proposals. They either choose their grantees without any proposal process at all or send requests for proposals to selected potential grantees, but in either case, they accept no unsolicited submissions. Most of the foundations that are open to receiving unsolicited proposals have deadlines for receiving them and deadlines for completing the review process so that the proposals may be recommended for funding to the board or to an internal committee. The discipline of the deadline is useful, for it promotes timely decision making. Nothing could be more frustrating for a grantseeker than to wait a year or so for a foundation to finally make a decision, only to have the proposal declined.

The preferred form of the initial submission serves as another key organizational guidepost. Many foundations insist that this first written proposal be truncated in some fashion. Short initial submissions spare the grantseeker the trouble of preparing a full-blown proposal "on spec" only to learn that the foundation has no interest in it. They also spare you the burden of reading long proposals that have no hope of being supported. Typically, a foundation will request that the initial submission be in the form of a three- to five-page letter that sketches out the opportunity to be seized, the work plan for seizing it, a strategy for continuation of the project after the foundation's funding would cease (if this is applicable), an evaluation plan, and a simplified line-item budget. Some foundations even require that all of this information be condensed into a single-page outline.

In justice to the grantseeker, it should be noted that requiring such abbreviated preliminary proposals is more of a time saver for the grantmaker than for anyone else. "I have made this letter longer than usual," wrote Blaise Pascal, "because I lack the time to make it short." This is more than a witticism. In many ways, it is easier to write a rambling proposal than it is to distill its essence into a few pages. Foreshortening does, however, force the grantseeker to concentrate on the essentials of the proposal and thereby saves you a world of time and effort.

There are some foundations that prefer a longer first submission, and even a few that wish to see a full-length proposal before they see anything else. Still others prefer the less formal option of the concept paper. With more narrative than an outline but less verbiage than a full proposal, a concept paper is a compromise between a long proposal and a short letter. Grantseekers tend to like concept papers because this format gives them extra pages in which to tell their stories. And because some foundations do not, as a matter of policy, decline informal concept papers, grantseekers also prize the flexibility the concept paper allows them to adjust and revise their presentation before submitting a formal request.

As always, there are trade-offs involved in whatever "first submissions" policy the foundation chooses to adopt. One-pagers are quick to read, but much of the richness of the idea is necessarily omitted along with the extraneous detail. The richness is amply found in full proposals, but these novellas take many times longer to read and consider than do one-pagers. Concept papers allow for a greater level of detail than one-pagers (although less than full proposals), but also take longer to consider (although not as long as full proposals). As one grantmaker puts it, a concept paper is "too short to contain meaningful detail, but still long enough to contain a filibuster." No method is ideal, but unless a foundation has a very low proposal volume, it makes sense to require some type of foreshortened first submission. Reading full proposals as a preliminary step is simply too time-consuming for you—which means, in turn, that the decision process is slowed, thus hurting grantseekers.

The leeway to make decisions on proposals that is extended to program officers serves as another important guidepost. Some private foundations, especially smaller ones, make all decisions by committee. Nothing can get funded without that committee's approval, nor can any proposal be declined without the committee's say-so. In larger foundations with bigger proposal volumes, however, it simply is not practical to make all decisions regarding proposals in a corporate fashion.

For better or for worse, then, many foundations follow a policy that allows program officers to unilaterally decline proposals but not to unilaterally approve them. Approval usually requires a favorable decision first by the review team, then by an internal committee of officers, and often by the foundation's board of trustees. The theory is that bad ideas can thus be expeditiously declined, and good ideas can benefit from the "two heads are better than one" principle. This is an effective system for the most part, guarding well against arbitrary approvals. It does, however, place program officers in the rather peculiar position of being able, in theory at least, to say no to any request while being unable to say yes to any request. One grantmaker summed up the situation succinctly: "It's a weird job. I can decline a request from a prince, but I can't approve a request from a pauper."

In practice, however, most foundations attempt to limit unilateral declines to only those proposals that are out of scope or clearly inferior in quality. The tougher calls are usually made by consensus of a committee. The word *consensus* is chosen advisedly; sometimes the decision is unanimous, and other times it is not. This means that there is always the potential for conflict between you and the internal committee. Inevitably, there will be times when the committee disagrees with your recommendation to fund a particular request. These disagreements are to be expected; as long as everyone handles them openly and professionally, they should not outweigh the benefits of bringing a team of talent to bear on the opportunities presented by proposals.

Typology of Proposals

Once the initial submission has arrived, you can use a typology of proposals as another guidepost for review. Some foundations have strictly defined areas of interest, which limits the types of proposals they receive. At foundations with broader interests, proposals come in a bewildering array of varieties. Even in the latter case, however, we can discern some patterns.

All proposals can be divided into at least two broad categories: those that are calculated to provide a personal benefit to individuals and those that would provide a public benefit. An example of a proposal for personal benefit would be a request to a foundation from an incarcerated person asking assistance to appeal his or her sentence. This level of personal benefit is disallowed by law. When the individual in question is the grantmaker or a close relative, the issue becomes one of self-dealing. If the grantmaker chairs the board of the local symphony, a large grant to the orchestra, especially one that would pay the grantmaker's honorarium, would constitute self-dealing and likewise be illegal. Nor can a foundation make grants to that class of individuals known as for-profit corporations (unless it is willing to undertake what the Internal Revenue Service calls expenditure responsibility). You can therefore decline personal benefit requests quickly and unambiguously.

Proposals that would provide a public benefit make up the vast majority of those you receive. Traditionally, this category is divided into three types of grant requests: capital, operating, and programmatic.

Capital Proposals

Capital proposals seek support for what might be called, in the language of accounting, durable goods and services. One of the most common of capital proposals is for assistance in constructing or renovating buildings (in foundationese, bricks-and-mortar requests). Another is for the purchase of durable equipment, such as heating, ventilating, and cooling apparatus, furniture, or vehicles. Still a third is for funds to augment or begin an organizational endowment.

For various reasons, most foundations have traditionally been cool toward capital requests. (A conspicuous exception to this general disdain is the Kresge Foundation, which has created a distinguished record of support for bricks-and-mortar campaigns.) Building construction and renovation is an ongoing—in fact, never-ending—need for most organizations and is likely to appeal to other types of funders, such as individuals. The same "bottomless pit" argument is employed to disallow requests to buy equipment and is also often used regarding endowment requests. There is a strongly held belief among many foundation leaders that foundation funds, which are generated by an endowment, should be reserved for supporting programmatic activities and not merely transferred to another organization's endowment. There are several exceptions to this widespread tendency, the most notable being those foundations that make program-related investments instead of grants in response to capital requests; but as any seasoned grantseeker will affirm, securing capital grants from most foundations is an uphill struggle.

Operating Proposals

Operating proposals seek support for what might be called, again in the parlance of accounting, recurring charges. An organization must pay its bills every month, and certain classes of expenses recur: heating, lighting, cooling, and maintenance of the building; rent and insurance; supplies; and costs of ongoing programs. Many grantseekers argue that operating costs are the biggest expenses they face, and criticize foundations for being, virtually across the board, reluctant to support them. Foundation leaders counter that, according to research done by the American Association of Fund-Raising Counsel Trust for Philanthropy (Kaplan, 1999), only about 7 percent of the charitable dollar in any given year comes from foundations; clearly the big money in philanthropy comes from other sources. In addition, according to research done by Salamon (1992), charity provides only about 18 percent of the nonprofit sector's total income. Combining these two pieces of data yields the fact that foundations provide only about 1.2 percent of the total income of the nonprofit sector. If it were used to support ongoing operations, this modest amount would quickly disappear without a trace. When this money is used judiciously, however, to support innovation—the novel, the untried, the promising—it can make a considerable impact. Moreover, foundations are the only reliable source of dollars for innovation. Very few individuals are wealthy enough to provide such funds; corporations tend to support projects that are more certain of results; and units of government have been, since the 1980s, reducing their role in funding innovation in the nonprofit sector. The 1.2 percent of the sector's income that foundations provide is thus very precious and must be earmarked for programmatic innovation. With this rationale in mind, it comes as no surprise that foundation support for operating expenses is even rarer than grants for capital support.

Programmatic Proposals

Programmatic proposals seek support for innovative ideas. Accountants would liken such grants to investing venture capital in the for-profit realm. Getting new programs up and running, and testing their practicality, requires support for such activities as attending meetings (including travel and lodging), and for such costs as salaries, space, and materials. It quickly becomes obvious that many of the items that fit under the rubric of operating requests also fit under the heading of programmatic needs: salaries, space, supplies, meetings, and so forth. Indeed, what distinguishes the two is not so much the type of activity as the *tenure* of that activity. If the activity is of long standing, then it is "more of the same" and classed as operating. If it represents a novel approach, then it is "innovative" and classed as programmatic. Foundations often make grants specifically to build the capacity of an organization; these developmental grants are generally considered to be programmatic as well. Like it or not, most foundations are in the business of supporting innovation, and it is under the heading of programmatic grantmaking that they focus nearly all of their intellectual and financial capital.

A special type of programmatic proposal is the request for what is known as a planning grant. Typically, this would be an effort to research the practicality or feasibility of launching a major project. In some cases, a planning grant explicitly lays the groundwork for undertaking a major effort, including such activities as hiring the first staff or setting up an office in the field. On the one hand, there are sound reasons to make planning grants, not least among them being the opportunity they provide to identify unworkable ideas *before* a major grant is made. They also can jump-start projects by taking care of some of the organizational work before the project is launched. On the other hand, planning grants can introduce complications, particularly in the case of those grants that lay the groundwork for a larger project. These planning grants amount to a virtual promise to fund a larger grant; even if the planning process reveals serious problems, it is often very difficult to decline interest in a larger project. Planning grants are thus a valuable tool for studying feasibility but are dangerous when used to jump-start a project.

Relationship of the Idea to the Proposal

Another guidepost for proposal review is the seeming paradox that it is sometimes better to fund a bad proposal than a good one. Actually this is not a paradox at all. Although grantmakers often informally say that they fund good *proposals,* in fact what they are funding is good *ideas.* The proposal is merely a delivery system for the idea. This can perhaps best be explained by employing a birthday present analogy: it is possible for a terrible gift to be poorly wrapped and for a wonderful gift to be beautifully wrapped; but it is also quite possible for a terrible gift to be beautifully wrapped and for a wonderful gift to be poorly wrapped. Similarly, it is possible for bad ideas to be conveyed by a bad proposal and good ideas to be conveyed by a good proposal; it is also very possible for bad ideas to be conveyed by a good proposal and good ideas to be conveyed by a bad proposal. In shorthand form, the four options look like this:

Bad idea, bad proposal

Bad idea, good proposal

Good idea, bad proposal

Good idea, good proposal

Your life as a grantmaker would be a dream if most of the proposals you received fit into the first or fourth categories. A workable idea to bring about world peace that came wrapped in a well-written, well-supported proposal would be a joy to read and fund. On the flip side, a harebrained scheme to sadistically torture everyone on earth—described in a proposal shot through with logical errors and bad grammar—would be a no-brainer to decline. You will soon discover, however, that you see very few of the bad idea–bad proposal type and, surprisingly, not many more of the good idea–good proposal type. Few dreadful people submit proposals to foundations, which probably accounts for the scarcity of the bad-bad. Although foundations receive many good ideas, relatively few are couched in elegantly written proposals. Most proposals fall into the two mixed-bag categories; you earn your money by guarding against funding the bad ideas couched in good proposals and by finding ways to support the good ideas disguised by bad proposals.

The bad idea–good proposal is an insidious creature. So well written is the narrative, especially in relation to other submissions, that you can be seduced by the sprightly prose and support a real dog of an idea. This happens most often with proposals emanating from large institutions that can afford to hire the best and the brightest of proposal writers. If these institutions do not give the writer a decent idea to pitch, but the writer does a splendid job of pitching it, the project, if funded, will become a gold-plated disaster. One of your prime duties as program officer is to dig beneath the prose to seek the mother lode of great ideas. If, as Gertrude Stein said, "there is no there there," then the proposal, lovely though it may be, must be declined.

The good idea–bad proposal is the ugly duckling of the foundation world. It looks awkward and ungainly on the surface, but it contains the essence of the swan within. Unfortunately, truly lousy proposals often prevent you from perceiving the swan. Since grade school days, we have been taught to equate second-rate writing with second-rate minds. Sometimes, of course, this is absolutely true. At other times, however, the typos, misspellings, awkward constructions, and grammatical goofs conceal a truly innovative idea, and in this case, declining the proposal kills an incipient benefit to society. This happens most often with proposals emanating from smaller and newer organizations, often those led by visionaries who are capable of making social change in the real world but whose prose makes strong people weep. Here is where you must step in as a coach, not to write the proposal but rather to guide the applicant in improving it so that the great idea trapped inside can be liberated.

Whether you step in to do so is a test of your character. It is much easier to recommend for funding an elegantly written proposal than it is to recommend a poorly written one, the quality of their respective ideas notwithstanding. It takes time, skill, and patience to help the ugly duckling become a swan. In making this extra effort, you add value to the idea. And this extra value that you bring is, ultimately, why foundations employ program officers—and not cash machines—to dispense grants.

Unfortunately, proposals do not come through the door clearly marked as good idea–bad proposal or bad idea–good proposal. Making the necessary distinctions is a matter of experience, analytical ability, and, not least important, intuition. Because no one is infallible, some bad ideas will be funded, and some very good ideas will be declined. The essence of being an effective program officer is to sort the wheat from the chaff *most* of the time.

Contract Grantwriters

A small but not insignificant percentage of proposals are apt to be authored not by the applicant but by contract grantwriters. These are the pens-for-hire of the philanthropic world, who will for a fee write a proposal to describe the applicant's ideas. Program officers tend to harbor ambivalent feelings about contract grantwriters. On the one hand, grantmakers like them because they are pros; a proposal authored by a contract grantwriter is generally a pretty good one: clear, well written, and fluent in foundationese. Contract grantwriters can be particularly good at translating the good ideas of community-based organizations into good proposals. By preventing the good idea–bad proposal problem, they can make life much easier for both grantmaker and grantseeker.

On the other hand, program officers do tend to look askance at contract grantwriters when they use their writing skills to wrap a good proposal around a fundamentally bad idea. As an old Spanish proverb goes, "You may dress a monkey in silk, but it remains a monkey," and grantmakers tend to resent anyone who creates more bad idea–good proposal situations for them to sort out.

Regardless of the quality of the idea about which they write, contract grantwriters act as intermediaries between grantmakers and grantseekers. Some do it deftly, others do it clumsily, but inevitably they create a certain distance between grantmaker and grantseeker. All things considered, most grantmakers would rather read the real words of the applicant, however inelegant they might be, than read the more polished but less authentic words of the contract grantwriter.

Sentry or Steward?

The character of the program officer is perhaps the most underrated attribute of good grantmaking. The quality of that character does much to determine which of the grantmaker's dual roles will predominate, that of the sentry or the steward. When you find and decline a bad idea–good proposal, you are quite appropriately guarding the foundation's resources: being a sentry. When finding and funding a good idea–bad proposal, you are wisely spending the foundation's resources: being a steward. Although these are two very different roles, the conundrum is that you must play both, and often must switch back and forth between the two many times in a single day.

The sentry mentality, when taken to extremes, creates what Spiro Agnew once described as a "nattering nabob of negativity." The overzealous sentry lives to seek, expose, and capitalize on flaws in proposals. To the sentry, grantseekers are all more or less unworthy and doing their best to separate the foundation from its money. The essence of doing a good job is to discover reasons why a proposal—or even an applicant—is undeserving of the foundation's support. If the proposal is well written, the smooth narrative only masks nefarious intent; poor writing is in itself grounds for rejection. Good ideas that require development are not good ideas at all. Sentries borrow the approach of retail liquidators: everything must go!

Stewards, by contrast, live to seek, expose, and capitalize on the potential of the ideas contained in a proposal. To be sure, they must turn down proposals, even many that have good ideas embedded in them, for there are always more worthwhile ideas than there are funds to support them. Stewards, however, see the possibilities inherent in the best of the ideas, even if those ideas come wrapped in poorly written proposals and even if the ideas themselves lack polish. Stewards see it as their job to help add value to both the proposal and the idea so that the project can be funded.

Your task as a program officer is to jump back and forth between the negative and positive poles of your job. On first contact with an applicant, you *must* be a sentry, for it would irresponsible to be encouraging about the prospects for funding before learning about the idea. For the majority of proposals received, you must remain a sentry, for you will have to turn them down. For those proposals that have potential, however, you must become, at some point in the process, a champion of the applicant. At that point, you make the transition to being a steward. When program officers lack character, they experience difficulty in making this transition and become perpetually stuck in the sentry mode. It takes no character to do so, for any idea, no matter how good, can be judged and found wanting if the judge is so inclined. It does require character to add value and to take risks when making grants. Besides, can there be anything more useless than a one-dimensional sentry in an organization that must, in order to comply with the law, spend 5 percent of its net asset value every year?

Twelve Characteristics of a Good Proposal

Proposals come in all shapes, lengths, and sizes; as program officer, you can review them according to any number of criteria.

Nonetheless, it is possible to identify some generic characteristics that are hallmarks of a good proposal that contains a good idea. Although it is unlikely that any proposal will include all twelve of these characteristics, better ones should contain more than half of them. These characteristics are listed here in no particular order of priority.

1. *The applicant's idea is innovative.* Because most foundations aspire to be explicitly in the business of funding innovations, this characteristic should be front and center. Depending on how the foundation defines *innovative,* the idea can range from something that has never been attempted anywhere before, to something that has been tried in only a few other places, to something that has been thoroughly piloted and now needs to be brought to wider scale. But whereas what an innovation *is* admits of many different interpretations, most foundations are agreed on what it is *not:* support for an organization's ongoing programs, or the "franchising" of a tried-and-true system. As mentioned earlier, if the proposal describes an idea that is just more of the same, then it cannot make the cut as innovative. A good proposal describes an idea that will solve problems in new ways and create new hope.

2. *The applicant has expertise, but also an understanding of its weaknesses.* There are two types of applicants a foundation should not fund: know-nothings and know-it-alls. A foundation must rely on the expertise of its grantees—they must have the experience and the smarts to operate a successful project. At the same time, issues that applicants tackle are likely to be so complex that no one organization will have on staff all of the needed expertise. A good proposal describes an idea about which the applicant's staff are experienced and capable, but it also demonstrates that the staff recognize their own shortcomings and know how to get consulting help.

3. *The applicant has done the needed homework.* There are always two kinds of homework that an applicant must do before writing a proposal: homework about the project and homework about the foundation to which the proposal will be submitted. The homework about the project is quite important: Has anyone else tried something similar? If so, what were the results? Are there any potential partners for this work? Are they interested in becoming partners? What other funders might support the project? All this

information is necessary in order to place the request into a context. The homework regarding the foundation is less important, but still not trivial. Is the foundation interested in this topic? Has it funded similar projects in the past? Might the proposed project be improved by lessons from those past efforts? It is discouraging to receive proposals that make empty claims about their "uniqueness" yet were clearly written as generic requests sent on spec to many possible funders. A good proposal describes the context of the idea and directly relates that idea and its context to the foundation's programming interests.

4. *The applicant is doing the project* with, *not* to, *those it is trying to help.* If grantmakers have proved anything conclusively, it is that projects designed by "experts" work if—and only if—those experts have devised the projects with the advice and consent of the people whom the project is meant to help. Another way to state this is to ask whether the idea described in the project is being driven by demand welling up from the community or by plans being pushed down by elites. Over the years, the academy and the professions have grown ever more esoteric; they have become ever more remote from the people in general, and from the people whom foundations are most interested in helping, in particular. Many scholars and professionals have come to regard people largely as data to be studied or as problems to be solved, rather than as stakeholders to be consulted and as experts on their own lives, needs, and aspirations. Projects that work are partnerships among all of those who have a stake in the project's success. That partnership should have begun *before* the proposal was conceived, and all the stakeholders should have a significant role in writing the proposal, responding to the program officer's questions about it, and managing the project once it is funded. A good proposal describes an idea that has been formed in full partnership between the applicant and the people the applicant is trying to help.

5. *The applicant is other-centered, not self-centered.* Many proposals purport to benefit an external population but, curiously, request only those things that would directly benefit the organization doing the asking. For example, the title of the proposal may be something like "A Project to Facilitate the Positive Development of Migrant Youth," but the text of the proposal hardly mentions migrant youth. Instead, it eloquently discusses the applying orga-

nization's need for an upgraded computer system, new office furniture, a reliable van, and repairs to its headquarters building. Presumably the new equipment, furniture, vehicles, and capital investment would allow the staff to serve migrant youth more effectively, but because the proposal does not mention such service, perhaps not. An old but effective maxim states that applicants tend to write in the proposal about those things that matter most to them. In this example, what matters most is probably the computers, not the kids. A good proposal will describe an idea that clearly focuses on the audience that the organization purports to help—and mentions organizational concerns only in the context of serving that audience.

6. *The applicant will invest its own money in the project.* This characteristic seems counterintuitive on first glance; after all, if the grantseeking organization had enough money to do the project, it would not need to ask a foundation for grants. On closer examination, however, the logic is compelling. Money is obviously one of the most precious resources for any applicant organization. An applicant's willingness to invest a significant amount of that precious resource in the requested project bespeaks real commitment to the success of the project. Conversely, an applicant's unwillingness to invest suggests that the organization has no real attachment to the project and may be merely chasing grant dollars.

How much the applicant should invest depends very much on the size of the organization. A large and well-endowed institution, such as a university or a hospital, might be expected to commit to the project cash and in-kind resources of at least 50 percent of the amount requested from the foundation. A small and unendowed community-based organization, in contrast, might be doing well to commit 10 percent of the amount requested. A good proposal will describe an idea that includes a significant commitment of the grantseeking organization's own financial wherewithal to the idea's success.

7. *The applicant is determined to do the project, no matter what.* Perhaps the most chilling words you can hear from a grantseeker are "If your foundation won't fund this, the project will die." This sentiment may be meant to flatter you with a sense of indispensability, but if it is literally true, then declining the request will be a salutary form of euthanasia. Why is it, you might ask, when there are

more than fifty-eight thousand other foundations in the United States, plus thousands of corporate giving programs, that a no answer from this particular foundation will prove fatal? Leaders of successful projects invariably have a never-say-die attitude that will not allow them to consider a rebuff, or even multiple rebuffs, as a death sentence. The founder of a prominent curriculum-support organization endured 156 consecutive refusals by foundations to fund the proposal to establish his organization before he finally succeeded in getting a grant to do so. One foundation program officer notes, perhaps only half-facetiously, "I like to support people who would keep seeking funds if I turned them down; who, if all else failed, would shake down kids for their lunch money." A good proposal describes an idea that the applicant is *completely* committed to seeing through to success.

8. *The applicant has devised a comprehensive approach.* The twentieth century has been characterized by two important social trends moving in precisely opposite directions. The problems of people have been growing ever more complex and interconnected, while the scope of the academic disciplines and the professions has grown ever more narrowly differentiated. People have problems, goes the saying, but institutions have departments. The melancholy result is a number of proposals from very specialized perspectives that purport to solve multifaceted problems.

For example, young people leave school at an early age because of a complex web of issues, which for any individual may include such problems as poor nutrition, inadequate early education, nonexistent after-school options, unsafe neighborhoods, poorly funded schools, economic necessity, insufficient remedial opportunities, and teen parenthood. Obviously, these problems cross disciplinary and professional lines and connect with each other in overlapping and interlocking ways. Yet proposals will arrive that claim to "solve" the problem solely by offering improved remedial opportunities. No matter how well remediated, young people who are hungry or pregnant or who fear for their lives in the schoolyard are still not going to finish school. The problem lies in the way in which specialized training eradicates any sense of the bigger picture. As the old Hungarian proverb has it, "When your only tool is a hammer, all problems will look like nails." A good proposal describes an idea that advances solutions that are at least as comprehensive as the problems they are trying to solve, or at minimum conveys an understanding of its part in a complex and comprehensive social context.

9. *The applicant will work collaboratively with others who can help.* Precisely because social problems are so complex and cross so many disciplinary lines, it is unlikely that any one organization, operating in magnificent isolation, can solve such problems by itself. It will need to turn to consultants, of course, but it will also need to partner with other organizations that can bring needed skills to the table. Ideally, the partners can be true collaborators: sharing the funds, the leadership, and the credit for success. A good proposal will describe an idea that mobilizes many different players to meet the complex challenges posed by modern problems.

10. *The applicant is willing to have an evaluator assess the project.* Both the grantmaker and the grantseeker need to learn from the successes and the failures of a project in order to improve their performance in the future. And both need to be able to demonstrate that their work produces tangible results in the real world. Neither is in a position to do this work itself, due to its obvious self-interest. Both need the services of an observer to study the project's process and assess its outcomes at the end. Many grantseekers are reluctant to request evaluation, for fear that grantmakers will be unwilling to pay for it or that a critical report will doom their chances for future funding. You must reassure the grantseeker that the foundation is indeed willing to pay all reasonable costs for an evaluation and that the foundation will not automatically cease funding on receipt of a critical evaluation report. A good proposal will describe an idea that is openly evaluated by a knowledgeable observer.

11. *The applicant will continue the project after foundation funding ceases.* One ancient piece of grantmaking wisdom holds that foundations should not fund any project or organization forever. After all, if a foundation's budget is encumbered by multiple ongoing commitments to past grantees, it will lack the flexibility to respond to new opportunities. As a practical matter, though, there are exceptions to every rule. On rare occasions, a foundation may wish to take on a "signature" project that it expects to support indefinitely. For instance, the Irving S. Gilmore Foundation of Kalamazoo, Michigan, provides ongoing support for the Irving S. Gilmore International Keyboard Festival. There is also no wisdom in arbitrarily setting deadlines for ceasing to fund a project. A few may

need only a year or two of support to take root; many may require a decade or even more to demonstrate their value to others. It makes sense, therefore, to emphasize continuation from the beginning of a project. Other funders should be on board, or at least interested. (Another piece of received wisdom in the foundation field is to avoid funding anything 100 percent: "to assist, but rarely or never to do all" was one of Andrew Carnegie's rules [Hendrick, 1932].) The proposal should contain a plan for gradually weaning the applying organization from foundation support, and a blueprint for securing funding from other sources. A good proposal will describe an idea that has multiple funders and a realistic plan to secure ongoing support for the project from a variety of sources.

12. *The applicant's project has the potential for broader impact.* A demonstration project, if done right, will have a positive impact on the small part of the world that it touches directly. There is nothing wrong with that, but it is highly desirable to expand the project's influence more broadly. Although successful pilot projects cannot be replicated like so many photocopies, it is possible, with careful execution, for a foundation to bring a project to scale by adapting it to other situations in other places. For instance, the Local Initiatives Support Corporation, originally funded as a pilot program by the Ford Foundation, has now spread its residential and commercial development activities around the nation and has broadly diversified its funding base. It is also possible for the applicant—or the foundation—to use lessons learned in projects to affect the way that laws and regulations bearing on the subject are written or rewritten. The Robert Wood Johnson Foundation and the Kaiser Family Foundation, to take only two examples, have had great success in mobilizing lessons learned from their projects to encourage desirable reforms in national and state health policy. A good proposal describes an idea that, when implemented, could have broader than local impact, whether by bringing projects to scale or by working to effect changes in the policy arena.

Continuation and Evaluation

Two of the foregoing twelve points deserve special emphasis. One of the most common errors committed by program officers reviewing proposals is to recommend funding without adequately considering two important elements: how a project, once initiated, can continue to operate without further foundation support, and how the project can be evaluated so as to yield important lessons to the foundation. While it is possible to defer these considerations, experience teaches that it is not wise. Both continuation efforts and evaluation plans prove more effective if they are part of program planning from the beginning. Hence, the time to seriously plan for these elements is while the proposal is still under consideration, not when the project is half over.

Continuation

Continuation is a subject only rarely addressed in most proposals. The applicant is understandably focused on trying to get the project started and on attempting to secure foundation support for doing so. Moreover, few applicants understand how important it is for foundations to continually stop funding old grantees so that they will have the flexibility to support new ones. It is the applicants' firm belief, therefore, that once they secure funding from a foundation, that funding should be perpetually renewable, as long as they are doing a good job. Given this preoccupation with starting up and this expectation that securing a grant from a foundation is the functional equivalent of "until death do us part," it is no surprise that continuation is hardly ever mentioned in proposals.

When first asked for a continuation plan, the applicant is likely to react initially with frustration: "We haven't gotten the grant, the foundation says we might not get the grant at all, yet it wants us to do a lot of work to plan what we will do after the grant ends." Sometimes the realization that foundation funding is not forever elicits an answer that combines naïveté with brutal realism, as in this response to a request for a continuation plan actually received by a midwestern foundation: "We would hold on as long as we could pay our bills, while hoping for a miraculous rescue."

The first continuation plan submitted by applicants usually relies entirely on securing grants from other foundations. This is about the same thing as a personal retirement plan that relies on repeatedly winning the lottery: it *theoretically* can happen, but the odds are badly against it. As Michael Seltzer argues in his important book *Securing Your Organization's Future* (1987), two concepts must be stressed to the applicant: diversifying sources of support and gaining control over as many of these sources as possible. To be sure, grants from foundations, corporations, and government sources should be a part of any continuation plan, but not the only component nor perhaps even the main one. Earned income should have a prominent place, for it is not subject to the vagaries of foundation funding. Varieties of earned income include sales of products, fees for services, and contracts with other entities. The applicant could establish a for-profit subsidiary. Many have been very successful, the best example being the for-profit catalogue business of Minnesota Public Radio, which the organization sold to Dayton Hudson in 1998 for a reported $120 million. A supporting organization could be formed to enhance fundraising, for it offers excellent tax benefits to donors (and because individuals make up 90 percent of the charitable dollar, anything that makes an organization more attractive to individual donors will enhance the chances for continuation). The applicant could establish a "friends of" group and organize special fundraisers. The applicant could use the foundation's support as leverage to secure other investments, such as seed capital to start an endowment. And, getting back to grants: foundations, corporations, and the government are not the only sources. Some public charities are also grantmakers of significant size; the Fidelity Investments Charitable Gift Fund, for example, topped $100 million in grants in fiscal 1996 (Billiteri, 1998). Implementing any of these ideas would greatly diversify the base of support for the project beyond foundation funding. Many of the ideas, such as creating a supporting organization and producing earned income, are controlled by the grantee, which means that the organization is no longer held hostage to the whims of funders.

There are many other sources of ideas for project continuation. The National Center for Social Entrepreneurship, based in Minneapolis, has established programs to help nonprofit organizations adapt business standards and practices and thus become less reliant on foundation grants. Among the books that have been published on the subject are *Nonprofit Piggy Goes to Market* (Simons, Lengsfelder, and Miller, 1984), *Part of the Solution* (Union of Experimenting Colleges and Universities, 1988), and *Revolution of the Heart* (Shore, 1995). Applicants should be encouraged to avail themselves of these publications and services as quickly as possible. The time to develop a continuation plan is before the project starts, not, as typically happens, about thirty-two months into a thirty-six-month grant.

Evaluation

Evaluation is the cod liver oil of foundation work, as in "Take it: it's good for you." Of course it is, for evaluation teaches lessons both grantmakers and grantseekers can learn by no other means, and it provides much-needed evidence of project outcomes. But, like cod liver oil, evaluation can be tough to swallow. Grantmakers and grantseekers alike live in dread of a negative evaluation report that (they fear) could jeopardize the future of a project. Grantseekers complain that grantmakers often use the evaluator as a sort of academic gumshoe, keeping an eye on them from afar. And often, they say, the program officer uses a less than perfect evaluation report as a flimsy pretext to decline interest in further support.

Nonetheless, there is evidence that evaluation is becoming more accepted in the grantmaking world, which is undergoing a shift in the way evaluation itself is conceived. As explained in the report *Program Evaluation Practice in the Nonprofit Sector* (Fine, Thayer, and Coghlan, 1998): "In recent years there has been a growing debate between two broad approaches to program evaluation. In the more traditional model, an external evaluator is employed as an objective observer who collects and interprets quantitative and qualitative findings and presents the information to management. . . . In the participatory evaluation model, program staff, clients . . . and other 'stakeholders' of the program are engaged in the evaluation process to increase their evaluation knowledge and skills, and to increase the likelihood that the evaluation findings will be used."

So where do foundations stand on this question of the "old" (observer) versus the "new" (participatory) evaluation? The answer is that foundations are all over the map. Some are rigorous about evaluation, some less so, and others ignore it altogether. Moreover, there is no correlation between commitment level and style; that is, foundations that are committed to evaluation practice both old and new styles, as do those that are less committed. Although there is no unanimity, the new style seems to be gaining ground. And this style comprises four basic principles of best practice that can help grantmaker and grantseeker alike make wise decisions about conducting evaluation—decisions that will help make evaluation taste less like medicine and more like a plum. These principles are discussed in the paragraphs that follow.

PRINCIPLE 1: Good project evaluation is good grant management, and good grant management is good program evaluation.

Part of the reason that applicants (and many program officers) have regarded evaluation as distasteful has been their perception that it is something alien to, or different from, programming. If the evaluator is viewed as an outsider who sits in judgment of the project and its people, he or she will be feared. The "new" view sees the evaluator as part of the management team for the project. There is no "us versus them" if everyone is "us" and, more particularly, if everyone is focused on the same goal: the highest standards of project management.

PRINCIPLE 2: Project evaluation should be owned primarily by the applicant and designed primarily for the applicant's use.

If the project evaluation is owned by the foundation and designed by the foundation for its use, there is no way to prevent the grantee from regarding the evaluator as a spy for the foundation, and the evaluation itself as a form of social control imposed on the project by the foundation. When the applicants own the project evaluation and design it for their use, their perceptions change dramatically. The evaluator becomes a member of the team, and the evaluation a vital part of the project management plan. This is not to say that foundations cannot use or learn from project evaluations; it is to say that project evaluations are most useful to all when the foundation relinquishes control of them to the applicant.

PRINCIPLE 3: The most important decisions about evaluation need to be made by the stakeholders in the project.

If the stakeholders—the applying organization, its partner organizations, the people they are trying to serve, and the foundation—simply hand over decisions about evaluation to an outside consultant, they are doing a disservice to all involved. As the owners of the project, the stakeholders are best qualified, intellectually and spiritually, to make evaluation decisions. Allowing others to make them all but guarantees that stakeholders will get an evaluation plan that does not fit their needs, and it also guarantees that they will not learn how to create a useful evaluation plan for future projects.

PRINCIPLE 4: The stakeholders need to identify the important questions they wish the evaluation to address.

These questions may be focused on the *context* in which the project is being launched (What are the external factors that will affect this project?), on the *implementation* of the project (What can be learned about how to successfully manage such a project?), and especially on *outcomes* (What changes would the stakeholders like to see as a result of this project?). There need not be a plethora of questions—two or three for each of the headings should be sufficient—but they must be significant. These questions will determine nearly everything else about the evaluation. What sort of data will be required to answer the questions? The answer will determine the methodology to be used. What sort of expertise will be needed to gather the data? The answer will determine who should lead the evaluation process—someone internal to the project or an outside individual or firm. How will this information be used? The answer will determine the need for dissemination or marketing services as part of the project. Taken collectively, all these answers will determine how much the evaluation is likely to cost.

Working with Applicants on Evaluation

Keeping these four principles in mind, you will typically have a great deal of work to do on the evaluation portion of the proposal. Very few applicants will have taken ownership of project evaluation in the fashion described here. In fact, in many proposals, evaluation is not mentioned at all. Your first task, then, is to promote the notion of project evaluation as good project management and to convince applicants that they would be the owners of the evaluation component of the project. Depending on applicants' past experiences with and prejudices about evaluation, accomplishing this can be a very time-consuming process. It is essential to do it, however, or applicants will always regard evaluation as an imposition.

Once you have completed the task of promoting evaluation as a management tool, you will need to encourage the grantseeker to begin the process of making the fundamental decisions about the evaluation component, especially to decide about the important questions that the evaluation needs to address. These decisions should be made *before* the applicant decides which person or which firm will manage the evaluation of the project. For some projects, it may be appropriate to have a stakeholder take the lead on evaluation. Although this approach is generally the least expensive choice, the obvious conflict of interest involved means that it is best employed for smaller projects or for those in which the likely outcomes are fairly straightforward. If, however, the stakeholder is not skilled in evaluation techniques, the initial low expense might multiply, for it may be necessary to bring in others to clean up the resulting mess. The most expensive option is to hire a professional evaluation firm, which offers a high level of evaluation expertise. In-between options include hiring professors or other experts in the field, or engaging graduate students. In any case, in order to be done right, evaluation costs money. Whatever the cost, it is important to *add* it to the request. Nothing will sour an applicant on evaluation faster than insisting that the cost of evaluation be covered by taking it out of the originally requested amount.

Finally, it will be necessary for the applicant to choose a methodology. As mentioned previously, the methodology required will flow directly from the type of questions that the evaluation must answer. At one time, most methods of evaluation were classified under three broad rubrics: *impressionistic,* which was long on observation and short on data; *anthropological,* which was focused on the reactions of the people touched by the project; and *experimental,* which mirrored the rigor of the sciences, with baseline studies, control groups, experimental groups, and a heavy reliance on statistical techniques. More recently, evaluators have taken to using "mixed methods" that combine approaches from all three rubrics. Although the complexity involved with using mixed methods can be somewhat daunting, the move toward this approach is encouraging. Because each project is distinctive, evaluations *must* be as well. Evaluation components should never come "off the rack": they need to be custom tailored.

It makes little sense to attach a highly complex, million-dollar evaluation to a modest $10,000 project, nor is it any more sensible to select a basic $5,000 evaluation for a complex, million-dollar initiative. In fact, for some types of grants, there is no need for any formal evaluation at all. For instance, an annual "good corporate citizen" operating grant to a local arts council is highly likely to be repeated, unless the organization it supports becomes an outright failure. To rigorously evaluate the outcomes of such a project would be a waste of time and money. The key considerations in a case like this are flexibility and proportionality. You need to be flexible in applying rules about evaluation, and you need to make the evaluations proportional in size and scope with the projects they are assessing.

The cost of the evaluation, as mentioned before, will be largely determined by the questions that must be answered and by the methodology required to answer them. There is no counterpart to the health care concept of reasonable and customary fees when considering the cost of project evaluation. Evaluators have no established pay scales, and there is no generally accepted fee schedule among foundations themselves. The costs of an evaluation will vary with such factors as the number of sites, distance between them, number of people served, scope of the project, methodology chosen, and type of reporting required.

We can nonetheless derive a very rough guideline as to how much a foundation should pay to evaluate a project, by expressing the cost of evaluation as a percentage of the total cost of the project, using data collection and manipulation needs as key indicators. If very little data need be collected or manipulated in order to answer the important questions for the project, 1 to 2 percent of project costs is a reasonable price to pay for such an evaluation. If these data needs are significant but not enormous, and if the complexity level is not too high, 4 to 6 percent of project costs seems a reasonable range for such services. If it will be necessary to conduct a very large amount of research, data gathering, analysis, and publication of results, and if the complexity of these tasks is high, then 10 to 20 percent of total project costs would not be out of line for this work. It is worth noting that the price of an evaluator's service is always negotiable and that the first price he or she asks usually includes room for bargaining. It pays the foundation, therefore, to keep these guidelines in mind when contracting with an evaluator.

Formative and Summative Evaluation

The terminology of evaluation is also undergoing evolution. The "old" way of practicing evaluation referred to evaluations conducted during the life of the project as *formative;* evaluations conducted at the end of the project were called *summative.* Formative evaluation allowed for the project managers to get important feedback on the project's development and to make necessary midcourse corrections. Summative evaluation told what happened during the life of a project and explained why it happened. More recently, the distinction between these two terms has blurred. "New" evaluators point out that every formative evaluation has some aspect of summative evaluation in it, and vice versa. These terms have come to be defined mainly in terms of how the evaluation will be used. If the purpose is program improvement, it is formative; if the purpose is to make a go–no go decision regarding further funding or bringing to scale, the evaluation is summative.

It is important to understand that formative evaluation— undertaken for refinement and improvement of the project— should be started early. There is always value in evaluating projects at any stage in their life span, but the sooner it starts, the sooner feedback will flow to the project director, and the sooner midcourse corrections can be effected. And the sooner that process of refinement begins, the better the project outcomes are likely to be. In short, the best way to get a positive summative evaluation is to have an early formative evaluation, and in truth, both formative and summative evaluations should be regarded as a seamless whole.

Choosing the Evaluator

Another question is, Who should be the evaluator: an expert in the field or an expert in evaluation? The dilemma is that the person who really knows the subject at hand often doesn't know anything about evaluation methods, and the expert on evaluation methods often knows nothing about the subject of the grant. In an ideal world, the expert in the field would also be an expert in evaluation methods. Failing that, it would be useful, if finances allow, to hire as a team both types of experts, thus ensuring that the methodology is impeccable and that nuances of the knowledge base are appreciated and included.

If the applicant must choose between one kind of expert and the other, however, there are a few guidelines to follow. One is to consider who will be the primary audience for the evaluation. If it is to be others in the field, it may be best to choose the expert in that field. If the primary audience will include policymakers, it is best to have a methodologically unassailable evaluation, so the evaluation expert would probably be the choice.

Another guideline has to do with the people conducting the project and those benefiting from it. Often they are comfortable with someone who knows their field and their language, and especially with someone who shares their values; they are uncomfortable with those whom they perceive do not fit these criteria. Such facts might argue for choosing the person familiar with the field over the evaluation specialist.

The last guideline is the hardest to judge; it springs from the principle involved in the Hawthorne effect, which holds that the very act of observing a system stimulates changes in the output of that system. Evaluators, whether subject experts or evaluation specialists, need to do their work as unobtrusively as possible. If all other things are equal between the subject expert and the evaluation expert, their subtlety and discretion could become a deciding factor.

Who Hires the Evaluator?

The question of who hires the evaluator should be easy to settle. If the grantee owns the evaluation, then the grantee should hire the evaluator, and the evaluator should report to the grantee's project director. If the evaluator is hired by the foundation and reports to the program officer, the grantee will never get past the feeling that the evaluation is an imposition and that the evaluator is a spy. It is always useful for the foundation to retain veto power on the hiring of the evaluator, in case the grantee should wish to hire someone with whom the foundation has had a bad experience previously. This veto power, however, should be used as sparingly as possible. If employed more than once per applicant, it will feel to the applicant as though the foundation is trying to control the evaluation by denying the applicant's choice of evaluators.

The great challenge you will face in helping applicants to make all of these decisions about project evaluation is that all of the decisions must be made during the proposal review stage, while keeping everything conditional. Until a proposal is actually funded, no one can be hired to evaluate the proposed project. Yet it is important to launch a formative evaluation simultaneously with the start of the project, for the lessons begin to arise immediately. The challenge, therefore, is to work with the applicant to *conditionally* select the evaluation questions, design, methodology, and evaluator (and estimate the cost), so that the evaluation will be ready to launch should the project be funded.

A number of excellent primers on evaluation have been published. Among the best are *Practical Evaluation* (Patton, 1982); *Program Evaluation Practice in the Nonprofit Sector* (Fine, Thayer, and Coghlan, 1998); and the *W. K. Kellogg Foundation Evaluation Handbook* (Millett, 1998).

The Budget

Assessing the proposal's budget is far more an art than a science. There is no set standard as to how expensive any project should be, and costs do vary from place to place. There are, however, a few useful assessment methods. The first is to check the budget against the proposal's narrative. If the proposal says that the lion's share of the project's resources will be concentrated on providing mentors for impoverished youth, then the preponderance of spending should come out of the Mentoring line item. If the line item for buying computers is by far the largest, there is a problem: both of these propositions cannot simultaneously be true.

The second method is to follow the doctrine of proportionality. Although costs will vary from project to project for many reasons, they usually vary within a predictable range. If, for example, one proposal budgets personnel costs at three times higher than those of roughly comparable projects, the disproportionately expensive budget should, to say the least, excite some concern on your part.

The third method is to seek clarity. Are the line items clearly labeled, or are they so vague that they could be interpreted in virtually any way? A line item called Meeting Costs is clear enough, but what about line items labeled Capital Expenditures or Expense Recovery, or that perennial favorite, Miscellaneous? You will need to ask the applicant for clarification before you can recommend such a proposal for funding.

You need to be ever watchful for line items that your foundation does not allow (such as for endowment or general operating support), and especially for line items that have been padded. Some long-suffering applicants, who have repeatedly endured grantmakers arbitrarily cutting their line-item requests, routinely budget for more than they need, with the expectation that their request will be cut back at some point during the process. This is a no-lose proposition for the grantseeker, because if the request is cut, they will still get about what they need, and if it is not cut, they will get a windfall. Of course, mistakes can be made in the other direction; sometimes applicants estimate too low. They frequently do so with the line items for meetings and transportation. In such cases, you should not hesitate to suggest increasing the amounts for such anemic line items.

You will need to be vigilant for line items that should appear in the budget but do not. Applicants sometimes omit activities that would enhance the outcomes of a project; they do so perhaps in an effort to save money or possibly because they are unaware of them. Examples include specialized training for project staff, technical assistance, dissemination, evaluation, and policy education. Again, you should not hesitate to suggest adding these activities to the request (but if and only if the foundation is prepared to pay the additional cost of the added line items).

It is often helpful to ask the applicant to submit two budgets. One would be the total budget for the project, including grants from other sources and earned income. The other would be the budget dedicated solely to the amount requested from your foundation, showing exactly how the applicant proposes to spend the dollars being requested. These two budgets allow you to understand the full scope of the project.

Assessing Organizational Capacity

There is a final test that every proposal must pass: Can the organization submitting the proposal truly pull it off? Do they have the capacity to make their ideas work in the real world? Unfortunately, the only way to know for sure is to fund the idea and find out, but there are a few clues to look for in the proposal that may fore-shadow the answer. The first lies in the tone of the language. Ex-travagant or grandiose prose is often a fig leaf used to hide an organization's substantive shortcomings. The second clue is found in the match between the narrative and the budget of the proposal. Is the applicant promising boutique outcomes for bargain-basement prices? Conversely, is the grantseeker grossly overestimating what its outcomes will cost? Either type of discrepancy suggests that the applicant might be inexperienced in this subject area and may not be able to pull off the project. The third clue is to check the inter-nal logic of the proposal. A lot of contradictions or inconsistencies suggest that the grantseeker may be making things up as it goes along. The fourth is to check the internal logic of the proposal against external reality. How realistic is it to believe that the appli-cant can do what it claims as compared to what others in the field have been able to do in related projects?

Beyond these clues, you need to look at the applicant's audited financial statement, IRS Form 990 tax return, and human resources. If a grant proposal requests an amount that represents multiples of the organization's current budget, it should raise questions about the applicant's capacity to absorb, manage, and sustain such a proj-ect. Is the organization burdened by a heavy load of debt? Does it have an operating reserve that would allow it to carry on if it should experience a temporary cash flow problem? Is the staff large enough to tackle the project? Do the staff seem to possess relevant skills and training? Does the proposal ask for funds to fill any "ex-pertise gaps" the organization may have?

All of these are sensible ways of detecting organizations that lack the capacity to do what they say they will do. You must recog-nize, however, that a powerful intangible factor may be at work that could change the entire equation. Every veteran program officer is able to tell stories about how he or she has witnessed grantees over the years do the highly improbable, even the seemingly impos-sible. Any purely cognitive assessment of a proposal ignores the fact that what drives grantseekers is their spirit, not their logic. And what the spirit can drive people to achieve sometimes defies all con-ventional calculations. From time to time, therefore, the essence of good grantmaking lies in taking a leap of faith: funding some-thing based on belief in the *potential* capacity of the applicant, not on its actual track record. Such a leap of faith provides a good example of what is meant when people talk of grantmakers needing to take risks. By all means, carefully and rationally calculate the odds, but you must also consult the still, small voice of the spirit. You should not take risks willy-nilly, but unless you venture out on a high-wire from time to time—and even fall off now and again—you are not doing the job right.

Conclusion

The proposal is many things to many people. For the grantseeker, it is a means of telling a story and a plea for assistance. To you, it is an application to be scrutinized, a potential contract to be weighed, and, sometimes, a wild dream that might be made possible. And to people who benefit from the idea it describes, the proposal could be a ticket to a better way of life. Because so much depends on the proposal, you are obligated to scrutinize it in the most rigorous and thoughtful manner. But proposals also deserve to be given another look, through the lens of the spirit. Certainly, this involves taking risks and occasionally backing long shots. When you consider the potential reward of backing the improbable winner, however, you can appreciate the merits of taking the leap of faith required. Although these leaps sometimes end badly, they often end transcendently, and the only way to that transcendence is to jump. As the great hockey player Wayne Gretzky once reflected, "You miss 100 percent of the shots you don't take."

Chapter Five

Declining Proposals

I'm just a gal what cain't say no
I'm in a terrible fix
I always say "c'mon, let's go"
Just when I oughta say "nix"

So sang the acutely self-aware Ado Annie in the musical *Oklahoma!*
Whatever Annie's subsequent career path may have been, it is a safe
bet that she did not become a program officer, for one skill indispensable to that position is the ability to say no, both often and
well. It is an inescapable fact of life that foundations receive many
more proposals than they can possibly fund. Although the proportion varies from institution to institution, it is not unusual for
the decline-to-fund ratio to stand at five to one. At some larger
foundations, it exceeds ten to one.

When asked what they do for a living, grantmakers often say,
"I give away money." Invariably, the response from the new acquain-
tance is, "It must be great to give away money for a living." Indeed,
it *is* wonderful to call someone with the good news that a grant request has been approved. Far more often, however, it is necessary
to deliver the bad news that the request has been denied. Doing
so with clarity and compassion is a core skill for a grantmaker: you
must be someone who *can* say no.

Saying no, and the way in which you say it, serves as yet another
test of character. As mentioned elsewhere, grantseekers often criticize the way these messages are delivered. They complain of learn-

ing the bad news via an impersonal form letter, which leads them to wonder if their proposal was ever seriously considered—or read at all, for that matter. They report exasperation when the letter does not share the foundation's reasons for declining the request or give feedback on how the proposal might be improved. They decry the program officer's reluctance to give them leads on approaching other funders. Perhaps most frustrating of all, sometimes the foundation returns neither a yes nor a no answer, but instead defers making a decision for months—sometimes for more than a year—leaving the applicant in "proposal purgatory." If there is any place where the relationship between grantmaker and grantseeker is often rubbed raw, it lies in the manner and the mode of rejection.

These complaints have varying degrees of merit, but there is plenty of fire underneath the smoke. For example, there is no legitimate excuse for a grantmaker to drag out a decision on a grant request. Different foundations, of course, have different response times, depending on their proposal volume, staffing patterns, and review processes. Barring extraordinary circumstances, however, an applicant should expect to get an unambiguous yes or no in response to a proposal, preferably within six months' time and certainly in less than a year.

To be fair, the applicant must help by also being responsive. When you send a list of questions and concerns, for example, it is incumbent upon the grantseeker to quickly turn around these requests for information. The grantseeker can hardly complain of slow response time on the part of the foundation if it is guilty of the very same thing. Grantseekers, too, have some less than exemplary behavior to answer for; it is also the case that not all of their complaints are wholly reasonable. For example, it is not fair to expect program officers to do extensive free prospect research for applicants.

Given the tensions on both sides, it is accurate to say that, like crowded lifeboats, the process of declining proposals tends not to bring out anyone's best qualities. Program officers and applicants alike could benefit from resolving to improve their behavior in this arena. A good place to start is for both parties to gain a better understanding of the process and display more sensitivity toward each other's needs and feelings.

The Four Reasons to Decline a Proposal

Every year, U.S. foundations decline proposals quite literally by the millions. Yet all these decisions are made for one or more of only four basic reasons:

1. The proposal requests a much larger amount than the foundation is willing to pay—or is even capable of paying.
2. The proposal describes an idea that lies outside the scope of the foundation's funding guidelines.
3. The proposal describes an idea that is within the scope of the guidelines but is clearly of inferior quality.
4. The proposal describes an idea that lies within the scope of the guidelines and is competitive in terms of quality but is marginally less promising than those that are chosen for funding.

Each of these reasons for declining a proposal is quite distinct, and each requires a somewhat different approach to the delicate art of notifying the applicant.

The easiest proposals to decline are those that are too expensive, that are out of scope, or both. No matter how clear a foundation is in writing its guidelines, and no matter how widely it disseminates them, it will still receive a steady stream of proposals requesting much more than the maximum amount the foundation has said it will consider, and for precisely those things that it specifically says it will *not* fund. These errors can occur because the grantseeker did not read the guidelines, or did read them but misunderstood them, or sent out a generic proposal to dozens of funders without first doing sufficient homework. At any rate, if a foundation says it funds only requests under $1 million, that it supports projects solely in the United States, does not support the performing arts, and does not consider endowment requests, it will no doubt receive a proposal requesting $10 million in endowment funds for the Pyongyang Opera House. Such proposals are simple to decline because they lack all ambiguity: you can cite the foundation's publications, state exactly what guideline the request violates, and decline interest clearly and completely.

You can also decline such requests expeditiously because they are so obviously unfundable that no feedback from your colleagues is required in order for you to make the decision. These proposals can, in fact, be declined by return of mail, but it is wise to avoid being quite *that* efficient. Many grantmakers report that when they have declined proposals the very day they have received them, they occasionally get irate calls from the disappointed applicants, who, having become accustomed to dilatory foundation decision making, accuse them of declining the proposal without having taken the time to read it. The better course is to wait a decent interval (perhaps a week) before declining out-of-scope proposals, so that the grantseeker does not suspect unprofessional behavior where in fact none exists.

Proposals that are within the general guidelines of the foundation but clearly of inferior quality pose a different set of challenges. Guidelines must of necessity be rather broad in scope. You will receive many more proposals that fit under their umbrella than can be supported. Those that fit in general but have significantly less merit than others must be declined, but because they violate no specific guideline, the decision will be necessarily subjective. For example, an educational request that generally fits the foundation's guidelines but is fundamentally a mediocre idea must be declined, not because it is not a good fit but because it just is not very good. The challenge is to convey to the applicant the hopelessness of the situation without being gratuitously cruel. You will probably find that the comparative approach works best—that is, stating that the idea described in the proposal simply was not competitive with the excellent ideas that were funded. This approach clearly conveys the no answer without heaping unnecessary insult on injury. You can share with the applicant specific weaknesses in the proposal or flaws in the basic idea, but there are potential pitfalls in doing so, about which more later.

Most agonizing of all to decline are the proposals that meet the guidelines, describe a good idea, and are competitive with others received, but that ultimately fall victim to the superfluity of good ideas received by the foundation. There are always a substantial number of these, and they are declined ultimately by judgment calls that are often based on razor-thin calculations. Perhaps the idea seemed to have slightly less potential for impact than others, or the organization appeared marginally less capable than others in the pool, or the portfolio of projects needed geographical diversity. However the judgment was made, there really is very little of substance that can be shared with the applicant, except to say that it was a judgment call. This lack of substantive feedback causes frustration all around. You might like to provide more feedback than this, but there truly is not much more to give, for the decision might easily have gone the other way. The grantseekers naturally want to know why, if their proposal was so good, the decision was made to decline it. Because you can neither pinpoint any major flaws nor offer any significant suggestions for improvement, the applicant inevitably comes away disappointed in the outcome and sometimes angered by the decision process.

Rhetoric Versus Reality

We might add a fifth reason to decline proposals: rhetoric that is not descriptive of reality. Whenever a foundation publishes its interest and priorities, grantseekers tend to write proposals that tailor their rhetoric to fit these interests. This behavior is entirely appropriate so long as the idea being described truly fits with the foundation's expressed interest. The temptation for grantseekers, however, is to use the rhetoric to make it appear as though ideas that don't match foundation interests at all really are a good fit.

This gap between rhetoric and reality is occasionally evident in the proposal. Sometimes, for example, the outcomes desired by the foundation will be stated as the project's goals, but the work plan will use methods that are highly unlikely to produce the stated result. More often, however, you cannot find the discrepancies simply by reading the proposal; it is often necessary to visit the applicant's offices and to discuss the proposed project with those who would be running it should it get funded. Even then, it is not always possible to detect rhetoric gaps before funding a project.

When you do detect such a gap, however, the best course is to decline the request. Although it might be possible to negotiate an agreement for a grant that more closely adheres to the foundation's interests, it is clear that the applicant does not really share these interests and really wants to work on other pursuits. It is best in such cases to acknowledge such differences and decline the "rhetorical" proposal.

Traps for the Unwary Program Officer

Most people who become grantmakers start as grantseekers, which is as it should be. After switching roles (Russ Mawby, former CEO of the Kellogg Foundation, quipped that he "swapped his academic robes for a foundation garment"), nearly all of them vow that they will not practice the annoying habits of program officers to whom they have submitted proposals. Specifically, they resolve that they will be completely forthcoming with applicants as to why their proposals were declined. It does not take long, however, before they discover that artless transparency is not the wisest policy. There are often legitimate reasons for keeping confidential some of the factors that contributed to the decision. Unscrupulous grantseekers (a tiny minority of the species, to be sure, but they *do* exist) can and will turn naive openness against you.

Grantmaking is essentially the art of placing bets on people. Therefore, the character and ability of the applicants truly matter. And because the grantmaking and grantseeking universe is a relatively small one, there will be occasions when you know from firsthand experience that, for example, the CEO of an applying institution has a history of being dismissed from positions of authority because of concerns about his financial probity. Fiduciary responsibility demands that the proposal therefore be declined, but artlessly telling the organization's director of development "We declined the proposal because your president is a crook" is not a legitimate message to convey. Even if true, it can land the foundation in court, and there is always at least a chance that the allegation is *not* true. Far better, in such a situation, to cite other legitimate reasons for declining the request and to omit mention of the fiduciary concern.

Many a new program officer has been burned by the small but damaging unscrupulous element among grantseekers. For instance, when the program officer calls to say that the proposal has been declined, a conniving grantseeker will ask for the reasons, which the program officer obligingly supplies. This applicant promptly edits the proposal to respond to the objections, then resubmits it, along with a cover letter stating that all of the changes *demanded* by the program officer have been made, and closes by asking when the applicant might *expect* the check to arrive. If you should choose to share the reasoning behind the foundation's decision, it is vitally important to stress that the decision is final and not subject to resubmission. That conversation should be followed up immediately with a letter to the same effect. Unless this message is clearly delivered and documented in writing, a manipulative grantseeker has an opening to try to beat the system. And good but inexperienced applicants, who truly do not understand that the reasons for a decline are being shared to help them sharpen their presentation to *other* funders, unwittingly may go to the work of resubmitting a once-rejected proposal, innocently believing that it now has a chance.

Character and Clarity in Declines

When you are declining a proposal, it is enormously tempting to blame "them" for the negative decision. It is also cowardly and grossly unprofessional. All of that notwithstanding, "they" may indeed be to blame. As discussed in Chapter Four, most foundations require a group decision for the approval of funding requests, whether that group be a council of program officers, an internal committee including officers of the foundation, or the institution's board of trustees. Sometimes you will champion an applicant's proposal to the bitter end, only to have the group decide against funding it. It then falls to you to deliver the bad news—a decision that you vehemently opposed—to the applicant. This system is somewhat peculiar, rather akin to requiring parents at a piano competition to inform their child that he or she is a loser. It would be literally true in such cases if you were to say, "I fought for you, but my colleagues insisted that I decline the proposal." Nevertheless, it is the coward's way out. You always represent the foundation, and the foundation is not the Supreme Court: no minority opinions about funding decisions are allowed. The foundation's decisions must be presented as coming from a united front, and thus you must say "we" and avoid saying "they" when communicating the verdict. If pressed by the disappointed applicant, you must explicitly say, "I concur with the decision." If you cannot bring yourself to handle declines in such a fashion, then the only course left is to resign as a matter of principle.

Ellis's Law (stating that grantseekers are optimists seeking affirmation and are therefore prone to misinterpret any communication from a grantmaker) holds just as true for declining proposals as it does for conducting meetings. Crystal clarity is essential in such communications; any ambiguity is likely to be seized on and to come back to haunt you later. Consider, for example, the language employed in this actual letter, which first declined interest in an idea, then mentioned several meetings in which foundation employees had participated that were also attended by employees of the applying organization. The letter ended with these words: "As a result of these interactions, in the future we may be in a position to provide programmatic assistance of various kinds such as you suggest. When it seems possible for us to do so, we will be in further contact with you to explore such possibilities." When the applicant read this letter, there could be little doubt but that the "no" in the first paragraph was negated by these two sentences. Although the first sentence is qualified to some extent, the second is virtually a promise. Such mixed messages serve only to stoke applicants' natural optimism, building them up for a cruel disappointment later. There can be no substitute for clarity. Of course, clarity need not be synonymous with cruelty; it is important to say no without being callous or offensive. But the no must be unalloyed, or the grantseeker will think, to borrow the old line, "Your letter says 'no, no' but your tone says 'yes, yes.'"

Grantseeker Complaints, Grantmaker Responses

It is natural to be disappointed in general whenever a proposal has been refused, but grantseekers often cite specific reasons to be upset with the manner in which they are notified. Some of these complaints have real merit. To be fair, however, grantmakers also offer some countercriticism of grantseekers, some of which have real merit. Each side deserves a turn to air its grievances.

COMPLAINT 1: Rejections are often completely impersonal.

The notification letter fairly screams "form"; it is completely generic except for the salutation, and robotically informs the applicant that the proposal into which they had invested so much of themselves is defunct. Grantseekers assert that they deserve the civility of a telephone notification or, at the very least, a personalized letter.

Grantmakers respond that the sheer volume of the requests that they must read and act on precludes them from calling every applicant or even writing a completely personalized letter to each one. They need to be efficient with their declines in order to pay sufficient attention to those projects that they *do* fund.

Both sides have legitimate concerns. On the one hand, a form letter is soulless and insulting; there can be no arguing that a telephone call would be much more considerate. Some grantseekers, on the other hand, need to understand that once a decision to decline is made, it has been made by a committee, and the program officer who delivers the message is not solely responsible for it, nor can he or she reverse it. Shooting at the messenger only makes the messenger less likely to call the next time.

To call or to write—that is the question, and one way to answer it is through a doctrine of proportional response. If the applicant merely sent in a cold proposal, then a letter declining it should be sufficient. If the applicant called, then a phone response would be preferable, but a personalized letter would also still be appropriate. If there were extensive interactions, such as a visit or numerous calls, then a phone call should be mandatory. Of course, a call is also de rigueur if the organization to be declined is headed by a *personage:* a national leader in the field, for example, or a celebrity.

If you handle the decline by phone, then you should follow it up immediately with a letter confirming the substance of the phone call. This is good professional practice, for a letter officially notifies the grantseeker, serves as necessary documentation for the foundation's project file, and protects you. Should the declined applicant complain about the outcome, it is essential to have a letter showing what was said, to whom it was said, and when it was said.

Finally, you cannot write a letter of decline de novo for every proposal that is turned down—this would not be the best use of your time—but there is never any excuse for merely sending a mechanical form letter, either. You can and should personalize form letters with the name of the organization, the name of the proposal, and the foundation's main reason(s) for deciding to decline it. The applicant deserves, at the very least, to know that the proposal was read and seriously considered before the decision was made.

COMPLAINT 2: Program officers too rarely give substantive feedback as to why a proposal was declined.

The vague and general answers grantmakers give, such as "We get too many good proposals to fund them all," tell the grantseekers nothing about what they did wrong or how to improve their proposal writing in the future. "If they can't give us money," say the seekers, "they could at least give us advice."

Program officers respond that very often, it is literally true that the proposal being declined is within scope and competitive—of the type that has no "fatal flaws"—and was beaten out for funding by "just a whisker." In such cases, there really is no substantive feedback to offer. When a proposal is of the "within scope but inferior" type, program officers are often reluctant to offer substantive feedback for fear that it will come back to haunt them in a future submission or in a complaint.

There is no one-size-fits-all piece of advice on how much feedback is appropriate. Grantseekers are right in saying that vague and general responses do nothing to help them improve future submissions. It does make sense for them to try to get constructive criticism from program officers, but it is also true that many proposals are declined not because they are bad but because they were not quite good enough. In such cases, it does little good to offer tips for improvement precisely because there are so few tips to offer. And a small percentage of grantseekers are guilty of trying to use the feedback imparted to reopen a declined file or to complain to higher authorities about the decision. Such experiences make program officers understandably reluctant to provide feedback at all.

Nevertheless, it is good professional practice for you to share with the grantseeker as much of the reasoning behind the decision as is feasible. It is wise to begin the conversation by stressing that the decision has been made and that the foundation will not welcome a resubmission of the proposal. If the proposal was out of scope, the reasoning will be objective, but if within scope, the reasoning will be subjective, and it is best to admit from the start that the decision was based on a judgment call. Sharing the substance of the reasons for declining the proposal makes sense, so long as you remember not to impart any potentially embarrassing or insulting information.

COMPLAINT 3:   Program officers often refuse to give grantseekers referrals to other foundations.

This complaint has the least merit. It is natural for people whose request has been rejected to want to get leads to other funders, but it is wholly unreasonable to expect a program officer to run a no-cost fundraising consulting service. "Applicants seem to believe," remarked one grantmaker, "that program officers from one foundation know what every other foundation is interested in. Heck, I can barely keep up with the changes in my own foundation." It is true that busy program officers cannot possibly stay current with the constantly evolving interests of thousands of other foundations. Referrals offered by program officers are often based on outdated or incomplete information, so the applicant is sent on a fool's errand, and one or more colleagues at another foundation waste valuable time in responding to a request that is "dead on arrival."

This awkward situation is sometimes exacerbated by the way in which grantseekers handle referrals. Eternal optimists that they tend to be, they often inflate a bland referral into a strong endorsement. "Whenever someone calls me and says 'So-and-So at the XYZ Foundation enthusiastically suggested that your foundation would be interested in this exciting proposal,'" says a program officer, "I wonder: If this proposal is so damned exciting, why didn't she fund it?" When an ill-informed grantmaker recommends approaching another foundation, it is sure to cruelly raise—and then completely dash—the applicant's hopes. And it is bound to cause resentment among colleagues in other foundations, who have about as much admiration for grantmakers who fail to do their homework as they do for grantseekers who similarly shirk this duty.

There are some helpful rules to follow when asked for funding leads by a disappointed grantseeker. First, do *not* make a referral unless certain that you are absolutely up-to-date about another foundation's priorities and unless you can refer the applicant to a specific program officer at the other foundation. Second, dampen expectations by pointing out that the chances at the other foundation are probably about the same as they were at your foundation: in other words, the referral is no sure thing. Third, if you can offer no good leads, say so, and then refer the would-be grantee to the Foundation Center. After all, it is the grantseeker's job to do prospect research, not yours. Fourth, if you decide to make referrals, strictly limit the number you make and the amount of time you spend on them. Your time is best spent on making grants and managing the resulting projects, not in making referrals to grantseekers. One grantmaker put it bluntly: "If you use your time working on behalf of rejected applicants, you will have no time left to work with the projects you funded."

COMPLAINT 4: Some program officers string grantseekers along, without an answer, for months at a time.

This complaint is the one with the most merit. Grantseekers can be left in limbo, neither funded nor refused, with no timeline for a response. Grantmakers respond by saying that it takes time to navigate some proposals through sometimes inhospitable institutional waters. They are playing for time until new funds become available or until policy shifts or institutional priority changes make the foundation more friendly to the proposal. This explanation is reminiscent of those who attempt to "time the stock market," buying just as it bottoms out and selling just as it reaches its top. In theory it is possible to do this, and one might even get lucky on rare occasions and achieve it, but as a long-term strategy, it is a proven loser. Foundations do change priorities from time to time, but the direction and timing of those changes is not readily predictable, so delaying a decision in the hopes of a policy breaking in the right direction is likely to yield a low percentage of success. Even if the strategy works, however, the grant that results may be a bad one. Proposals have a limited shelf life; as the months go by, the world changes, the applying institution changes, and eventually the proposal becomes obsolete. The simple fact of the matter is that if a proposal has not been approved within a year of its submission, chances are it will never be approved, and even if it is, it will probably no longer be useful to the applying organization. And in the meantime, the delay and indecisiveness has infuriated the applicant and achieved nothing in the real world.

The Problem of the Persistent Proposer

Every program officer can tell horror stories about the grantseeker who keeps applying, keeps getting declined, and keeps coming back for more. Some of these persistent proposers are as pugnacious as G.I. Joe, some as meek as Casper Milquetoast, but all endure repeated rejection while perpetually submitting doomed proposals. As mentioned earlier, the persistent person makes the best grantee, but when the ideas are not competitive, persistence crosses the line to fanaticism, and the virtue turns into a vice.

What are you to do? In most cases, it makes sense simply to treat the persistent proposer as one would treat any other applicant. Accept the proposal, read it, consider it on its merits, and if it is as bad as usual, decline it. Refusing to consider a proposal, even from a very quixotic applicant, usually causes more trouble than it saves. It tends to make the foundation look unresponsive and casts the perennial applicant in the role of the wronged victim. If, however, things take an ugly turn—should the applicant makes threats toward the foundation or its employees, for example—there is no reason why the foundation should not refuse further contact. Such a decision would encompass refusing to accept phone calls, returning mail unopened, and even, if necessary, referring the matter to the police. Foundation employees should not have to endure such assaults.

You also need to prepare for the inevitable day when a disappointed grantseeker complains to your superiors in the foundation. The best defense against this is to avoid giving offense, by interacting with all applicants in a professional and respectful manner. Most disappointed applicants will not complain, however unhappy they may be about the outcome, if they feel that they have been treated with respect and fairness. It is also vitally important to document all contacts with applicants, especially phone calls. Should an applicant file a complaint, you will then have a record to use in response. No matter how professionally you act, however, and no matter how thoroughly you document the records, there will still be times when your superiors are called. Here, too, professionalism will be an asset. If you have handled the relationship with efficiency and respect, and above all, you can document that behavior, then you are likely to get the benefit of the doubt in any confrontational situation. The file is always your best friend.

Conclusion

If ever in the grantmaking enterprise there is a place where there is plenty of blame to go around, it would have to be in the matter of declining proposals. No one (except a confirmed sadist) enjoys inflicting pain, and many grantmakers therefore tend to be guilty of not saying no quickly enough, clearly enough, or openly enough. No one (except a confirmed masochist) enjoys receiving pain, so a few grantseekers tend to be guilty of defensiveness, ill humor, and even mendacity in response to disappointing news. Unfortunately, these unpleasant reactions tend to encourage grantmakers to become more dilatory, more opaque, and more distant when saying no.

It is doubtful that this subject could ever be made pleasant, but it could be made less offensive if grantmakers would strive to be more decisive in their process and more open about their reasons for declining proposals, and if grantseekers would accept the decision with more grace and make fewer unreasonable demands of program officers. It is unrealistic to expect that declining proposals or having them declined will ever be pleasant for any of the parties involved, but if handled properly, it need not be a mutually miserable experience.

Chapter Six

Responding to Proposals

One of the tried-and-true aphorisms of foundation work is that no proposal arrives ready to fund. No matter how good the idea, there will be holes in one or more of the five plans that describe it: the implementation plan, the continuation plan, the evaluation plan, the dissemination plan, and the financial plan (budget). Your task is to decline proposals that will never be ready for prime time and to develop those that are not ready *yet*. As previously mentioned, the "never-will-be's" far outnumber the "maybe's," usually by a factor of five or more to one. Those few survivors will require a lot of your attention and nurturing before they are ready to face the internal funding committee or the board of trustees. Most of this work will be routine, but some of it will be delicate, and a surprising amount of it revolves around managing applicants' expectations.

Keeping Applicants' Expectations in Check

The bad news is that the longer applicants survive in the proposal process, the harder it becomes to rein in their aspirations. Just making the first cut when the vast majority of proposals do not is enough to send hopes soaring. Grantseekers' natural optimism bubbles up, and they begin to think in terms of *when* the grant will be made, not *if*. You must ride herd on such unrealistic expectations, constantly reminding applicants that grants are awarded by corporate decisions and that clearing one hurdle in the process by no means guarantees that all obstacles to funding will be surmounted.

There are many ways to do this, the easiest of which is to clearly explain the foundation's decision-making process. There are a series of steps that a proposal must negotiate in order to be funded; the applicant should be made aware of each, and be made *very* much aware that, at each step, the proposal can be declined. It sometimes helps to point out that there is only one way in which a proposal can be approved but many ways in which it can be rejected. You should also disclose the approximate timelines involved in proposal review; however, you should stress that these *are* approximate, otherwise the applicant will become anxious if they are not met or, worse yet, will come to rely on them as firm.

Once grantseekers learn that in some foundations the gestation period of a grant approximately matches that of a human (and that in a few foundations it approaches that of an elephant), they will begin to understand that the applicant's folk wisdom "The longer they review, the better it is for you" does not always apply. Then too, it makes sense to prepare grantseekers early on for the iterative process—the cycles of responding to questions and rewriting their proposal—that is likely to lie ahead. In this process, you are the one who coaches change, but it is the applicant who must be the inkslinger.

Initial Review of Proposals

Foundations have almost as many ways of initially reviewing proposals as there are proposals themselves. Some rely on individual program officers to read and respond quickly to submissions. Others, particularly larger foundations, have intake offices that do an initial sort, declining the clearly out-of-scope and uncompetitive proposals and sending the rest to the appropriate department for consideration. Some foundations have program officers working as individuals; others form them into teams. Many foundations have clear deadlines for proposal receipt and decision making, but some have a "rolling admissions" policy and no deadlines.

Whatever their approach, however, all foundations require program officers to read, analyze, and recommend disposition of proposals. In smaller foundations, this may be a one-person task, but in many foundations of varying sizes, this is a group effort that ultimately involves, in addition to program officers, officers of the foundation and often members of the board of trustees. The reasoning behind this team approach is simple: it guards against arbitrary decision making by any one person. A single program officer in a bad mood (or with a particular bias) can decline a lot of good ideas in a single day. The group decision-making process prevents this (and similarly prevents any one program officer afflicted with, as Alan Greenspan might say, "irrational exuberance" from turning bad ideas into bad projects).

These group decision-making mechanisms can also take on many guises, from formal meetings in which the merits of proposals are debated and votes are taken on decisions, to informal "round robins" in which each program officer reads the proposal and comments on it, leaving it to the lead program officer to weigh the input and decide on a course of action. (Most proposals in most foundations are assigned to lead program officers, but sometimes teams are formed to handle them.) Typically, the lead program officer is the first to read the proposal. In those foundations that employ a team approach, if that program officer feels the proposal has potential, he or she passes it along to other members of the review team. A point of etiquette should be mentioned here: nothing disgusts colleagues on review teams quite as much as receiving from the lead program officer proposals that are obvious declines. It wastes their time and casts them time and again in the role of the "heavy." It is important, therefore, that lead program officers decline nonstarters rather than circulate them for consideration.

Once all the reviews are in, they are rarely unanimous. Therefore, most foundation review teams operate by consensus, with a majority of reviewers (but not 100 percent of the reviewers) needed to support a particular course of action. The lead program officer then usually handles the next step. Should that be a decline, the course of action is obvious. If the decision is to further consider the proposal for funding, the wicket gets stickier. Responding to a proposal is a delicate art; the main purpose is to gather information needed to make a final decision, but this must be done without unduly encouraging or discouraging the applicant before a decision is finally made. This is anything but an easy task.

The Questions and Concerns Letter

There may be a few foundations that respond to proposals with either a yes or a no answer. Most, however, employ as initial responses maybe or no. The former answer is usually accompanied by some sort of request for additional information. Different foundations will have different names for the documents they use to secure the needed information. No matter what the name, however, the document shares the foundation's questions and concerns with the applicant, so the term *questions and concerns letter* (Q&C letter, or simply Q&C) will be used in this book. The form of the Q&C depends, of course, on the issues contained in—or omitted from—the proposal. It is safe to say that all Q&Cs are sent because the program officer is considering recommending the proposal for funding. Because so much of the chaff has already been separated from the wheat by this point in the process, in many cases a Q&C letter will eventually lead to funding. It is not particularly unusual, however, for the Q&C to reveal so many weaknesses that the proposal ultimately will be declined. That is precisely the function of the Q&C: to gather vital missing information that will be needed in order to make an informed decision about the request.

Because proposals are so diverse, and because the questions raised in their review are so distinctive, most foundations do not have a prescribed format for the Q&C, leaving its length, tone, and form to the program officer's discretion. Whether the Q&C places emphasis on the *Q* or the *C*—on posing questions or stating concerns—depends largely on where the foundation falls on the 4-P continuum and on whether its program officers tend to see themselves as stewards or sentries. If the foundation is somewhere in the proactive range, or if its program officers are stewards, the Q&C is likely to focus on questions; if the foundation lies more to the prescriptive side, or if its program officers are sentries, the Q&C is likely to focus on a more directive stating of concerns.

The proactive foundation is likely to believe that a Socratic method of questioning will lead to an improved proposal and project. Because the questions do not necessarily reveal the foundation's position, the answers the applicant gives are less coerced and more revealing. These questions do more than gather information for the grantmaker; they also impart information to the grantseeker. The Hollywood director Gregory Ratoff is reputed to have remarked, "Let me ask you a question, for your information," and this malaprop actually makes sense in the realm of the Q&C. Of course, there is more ambiguity involved in gathering information via Socratic questioning than there is by making straightforward demands for changes, and it does take some time for grantmaker and grantseeker to come to a mutually agreeable position.

The prescriptive foundation is likely to believe that the best way to develop a proposal is to identify flaws and to instruct the applicant to fix them. The Q&C will contain specific criticisms, along with clear directions for fixing the problems. This directive approach reveals the foundation's position, which adds an element of coercion to the grantseeker's response. It also eliminates ambiguity, however, and tells the applicant exactly what must be done to change the proposal.

Most often, the Q&C is a hybrid of both open-ended questions and more directive concerns. Even proactive foundations have certain rules that they will expect grantseekers to follow, and even prescriptive foundations have questions they will want grantseekers to answer. A good rule is to ask questions when there is some flexibility and to state concerns when there is no flexibility. For example, when the point under consideration is the best way to conduct a rural development project, the appropriate tool is a question. If the applicant has requested a line item that the foundation is unwilling to support, then the proper response is a directed statement of concern.

The Q&C Format

In many ways, a Q&C letter is reminiscent of Pat O'Malley's observation that "Speeches are like babies—easy to conceive, but hard to deliver." To coach without dictating and to inform without promising are much easier said than done. In order to stay on track, it is helpful to follow a formula in writing Q&C letters. The formula that will be discussed in the following pages is one that works well, but it is by no means the only one that you could employ. You can "mix and match" the elements it contains, and you may want to omit some for certain requests. You could use a completely different format. The important thing is to create a general template so that you can maintain consistency and remember to ask important questions.

Opening Paragraph

The Q&C should begin with a paragraph identifying the proposal to which it is a response. This identification includes the date of the proposal, the name of the applicant, the amount requested, the purpose of the proposal, and its identifying number (if the foundation assigns one). All of this information will eliminate any ambiguity as to the purpose of the letter or as to the proposal to which it refers.

Second Paragraph

This paragraph should identify the status of the proposal. Keeping always in mind the need to manage grantseeker expectations, you should tell the applicant that the proposal has been reviewed and that there is interest in considering it further as a *candidate* for *possible* funding. Further underscore these qualifications by saying that the Q&C is requesting information that will allow the foundation to make a final decision, and that it is very possible that the proposal still may be declined.

Third Paragraph

This paragraph should convey to the applicant the format in which the foundation expects a response. If there is a deadline by which the Q&C must be answered, it should be stated clearly in this paragraph. There are essentially two types of responses: the addendum or the rewritten proposal. The addendum allows the original proposal to stand and merely adds information to it. A rewritten proposal requires the grantseeker to start over from scratch. You should request an addendum when the original proposal was basically sound, but there are a few points that require clarification. Requesting a rewritten proposal places a hardship on the applicant, and such a request may create in the applicant's mind an implied contract. ("Since I am being required to do all this work, the foundation should be willing to fund the rewritten proposal.") You should request a rewritten proposal only if there are major issues that need resolution or if it is a classic good idea–bad proposal situation.

There is no simple guideline for making the choice between requesting an addendum or a rewritten proposal. A crude but generally effective consideration is to estimate how long the addendum might be. If it is likely to be more than half as long as the original proposal, you almost certainly need to ask for a rewritten proposal. And if the rewritten proposal is likely to be significantly longer or more complex than the original proposal, probably the better course would be to decline the proposal altogether. The choice frequently boils down to a matter of instinct and experience, and it is appropriate for you to make the call based on which of the two—addendum or rewrite—would make it easier to see the idea through to funding within the foundation.

Fourth Paragraph

This paragraph should list any special requirements for answering the questions. Some foundations prefer, for example, to have applicants copy the questions and then provide their answer to them, so that the program officer does not have to toggle back and forth between a copy of the Q&C and the response. If the foundation wishes the applicant to go into greater detail on any particular question, you should also disclose such information in this paragraph. In any case, you should specify that the questions be answered and numbered so as to correspond to the order and numbering of the questions and concerns sent to them. Applicants have been known to answer questions randomly or to respond in essay form, making it difficult to tell exactly which questions they are answering or whether they are in fact answering the questions at all.

List of Questions and Concerns

Having presented this preparatory material, you now list the questions and concerns. There are a number of effective ways to organize such questions and concerns in the letter. If there are only a few issues, it makes sense simply to list them in the order in which you encountered them in the proposal. If the number is larger, it might make sense to arrange them by proposal section; that is, you would create subheadings for the implementation plan, the continuation plan, the evaluation plan, the dissemination plan, and the budget. Other methods are possible, such as listing the questions and concerns in order of descending priority. No matter what organizational method you use, it is good practice to label the questions and concerns with either a letter or a number, so that both you and the grantseeker can refer to them later without ambiguity or confusion.

If the questions and concerns are many in number or higher in complexity (as is often the case when requesting a rewritten proposal), it usually makes sense to divide the questions and concerns into two classes: overarching and specific. Overarching questions and concerns pertain to fundamental issues that undergird the entire project, such as, "Were young people consulted about this youth serving project?" or "Does the omission of formative evaluation make sense? If so, why?" Specific questions and concerns are those that pertain to only a limited area of the proposed project, such as, "Is the amount budgeted for meetings adequate?" or "Might video be a more effective means of dissemination than a book?" Generally speaking, the number of overarching questions should be smaller than the number of specific ones. If there are more than five or six overarching questions about a proposal, the sheer number of troubling "big issues" suggests that the proposal should probably be declined. There is no ideal figure regarding numbers of specific questions (ten to twenty are not unusual for a complex proposal), but if the number rises above thirty or so, you might wonder if there are simply too many questions and consider declining the request.

Final Paragraph

The final paragraph in the Q&C letter should serve the function of a reminder; because the questions and concerns can be rather lengthy, it is wise to restate the deadline, the format, and the special requirements for answering the questions. Most important, the last paragraph should contain one more disclaimer, stating that even if the applicant satisfactorily answers all the questions posed in the Q&C, there can still be no guarantee of funding. This disclaimer will serve both to control expectations and to document that the applicant was not unduly encouraged, should questions arise in the future.

Information Worksheet

If there are pieces of information that the foundation needs to share with virtually every applicant to whom a Q&C is sent, it often makes sense to create a separate worksheet on that topic and enclose it with the Q&C letter. Doing so avoids the necessity of retyping budgetary or evaluation requirements, for example, which can be quite involved and lengthy, in every Q&C. Finally, if you are the program officer taking the lead on responding on behalf of a review team, it is good practice to share a copy of the Q&C letter with all members of the team, so that they can be kept abreast of the progress of the request.

Crafting the Questions and Concerns

The number of questions that *could* be asked in a Q&C, of course, is virtually limitless. The only questions that *should* be asked are those that will elicit information needed to write the funding document and to defend it before the internal committee or the board of trustees (or both). If you will not need data for these purposes, then the Q&C should not request such data. This simple test will save time for all involved, both you and the grantseeker.

Most of the questions in a Q&C will be strictly factual, designed to gain information: "How many people will the project serve? What will be the cost per person? How will the project's outcomes be evaluated?" There is also, however, a need for occasional leading questions, designed to make the grantseeker defend a position: "Do you believe that the best approach to promote a childhood vaccination campaign is through advertisements in periodicals? If so, why?" Leading questions can also be very pointed, so as to help the grantseeker fix mistakes in the proposal: "All studies of which we are aware suggest that your conclusion regarding the first point on page three is in error. Could you provide additional support for your position? If you are unable to provide additional support for this conclusion, would you consider withdrawing it?"

Concerns, like questions, could be offered in virtually infinite numbers. It is best, however, to limit them to major issues on which the foundation has policies—or strong opinions, at least. For example, if the proposal has no evaluation section and the foundation requires that projects be evaluated, then you should state as a concern the need to include an evaluation plan in the addendum. Similarly, if the line item for personnel is higher than the foundation considers reasonable, then you should state that fact as a concern—and counter with an amount that is considered reasonable. An important rule to remember is never to ask a question when the answer is not negotiable. If the proposal contains a line item titled Contingency and the foundation's policy does not allow for such a line item, then that fact should be stated. There is no point in asking the grantseeker to justify something that will be disallowed anyway.

Coaching the Applicant

A well-crafted Q&C will elicit the information you need and will also help the grantseeker strengthen the proposal. It will *not*, however, rewrite the proposal for the grantseeker. Unless you work for an unabashedly peremptory foundation, you should subscribe to the belief that a proposal should ultimately reflect the will of the applicant or, at any rate, the joint will of the applicant and the foundation. If the proposal is merely a series of statements signed by the grantseeker but dictated by the grantmaker, then it loses its legitimacy with the applicant. You must therefore be a coach without becoming the author of the proposal.

The questions in the Q&C become the cornerstone of the coaching process. They raise issues without prescribing answers and give applicants a chance to craft solutions (as opposed to your foisting solutions on them). In fact, as one grantmaker says, "Program officers are often better at analyzing shortcomings in a proposal than at suggesting improvements. I find that, once I have identified the problems, the grantseekers usually come up with better solutions than I would have."

The concerns, in contrast, raise issues *and* prescribe answers. They tell the grantseeker what to do or not to do. Generally speaking, then, the goal of the Q&C should be to maximize the Q and minimize the C. The exact proportion will vary from proposal to proposal, but it is safe to say that if the number of concerns ever exceeds the number of questions, then you are actually writing the proposal.

Another of the key considerations around coaching the applicant has, due to its crucial importance, already been mentioned: the management of expectations. We have covered only one side of that task, however: that of preventing optimism from running away with the applicant. Although much rarer, the opposite reaction can also occur: the grantseeker can become unduly discouraged upon receiving a Q&C. Typically this happens after the applicant receives a long letter of questions and concerns. The number and complexity of the queries seem overwhelming, and the applicant concludes that it would be too big a job to respond or, worse, that the foundation has concocted such a complicated letter specifically to talk the proposal to death. It is useful when sending along a Q&C to reassure the applicant that there is real interest, all the while remembering to continue to manage expectations. This is a neat trick, something akin to telling a date that you are deeply in love but not at all sure about making a commitment.

Language something along these lines may be helpful: "My colleagues and I recognize that the number of questions and concerns raised in this letter may seem overwhelming. We would not have gone to the trouble of reading your proposal so carefully, or of analyzing it so thoroughly, if we were not serious about considering it as a candidate for funding. However, we must make it very clear that this does not mean necessarily that the proposal will be funded. Even if you satisfactorily answer all of our questions and concerns, it is entirely possible that the foundation will decide not to fund the request." This statement will, with luck, guard against the applicant becoming unduly pessimistic or unrealistically optimistic upon receiving the Q&C.

In a related vein, you can inadvertently do a poor job of coaching by creating a Q&C letter that is technically accurate in its queries but so negative in its tone that the grantseeker becomes too offended or too frustrated to respond. You need to strike a delicate balance in coaching, making problem areas clear without descending into nastiness or irritation. It can be handy to have a colleague read a draft Q&C specifically for a "tone check" before sending the letter to the applicant.

The final coaching consideration centers on management of timeline expectations. Unless a foundation has specific deadlines for making decisions, it is likely that the applicant will assume that a decision will be made sooner than is actually the case. Grant-seekers are often operating under tight deadlines themselves, and they hope that foundations will quickly give them a thumbs up or a thumbs down. Given such hopes, it is better to let them know sooner rather than later that the decision is likely to come later than they want.

Sample Q&Cs: Serious and Humorous

Q&Cs, as the foregoing discussion demonstrates, can be of many different lengths and written in many different styles. The sample Q&C offered here, therefore, should not be construed as the only way in which you can write such a document. It is offered merely as an illustration of the general format described in the preceding paragraphs. All names mentioned are fictitious, as is the project.

Dear Ms. Applicant:

My colleagues and I have now had the opportunity to review your letter and proposal of December 8, 1999, requesting assistance from the PDQ Foundation in the amount of $950,000 over three years for a project to systematically improve access of low-income youth to educational computer technology. This proposal has been assigned PDQ Foundation ID no. 1234.

After carefully reviewing your proposal, my colleagues and I have come to the conclusion that we are interested in further consideration of your idea for possible funding. I hasten to add that this is not a positive funding decision; it merely means that we require more information before we can make that funding decision, which could be positive or negative.

Therefore, we would like you to respond to the questions and concerns listed below, and when we receive this response, we will treat it as an addendum to your December 8 proposal. Because this information will help us to make our funding decision, it is important that you respond as fully and completely as possible to our questions, and that we receive a response by March 1, 2000.

Please number your responses to correspond to the numbers of the questions and concerns in this letter. We ask you to pay particularly close attention to the "overarching" questions below. My colleagues and I recognize that the sheer number of questions and concerns raised in this letter may seem overwhelming. We would not have gone to the trouble of reading your proposal so carefully, or of analyzing it so thoroughly, if we were not serious about considering it as a candidate for possible funding. However, we must make it very clear that this does not mean necessarily that the proposal will be funded. Even if you satisfactorily answer all of our questions and concerns, it is entirely possible that the foundation will decide not to fund the request.

During the course of our review, the questions and concerns that were expressed resolved themselves into two types, overarching and specific. We will begin with the overarching questions:

1. Reviewers expressed confusion about which organization would be the grantee, should the PDQ Foundation decide to fund this request. The proposal refers to Computers for Kids (CFK) as the grantee, but all of the correspondence pertaining to the request comes from CFK's Southern Regional Office. Which of the two organizations would be the grantee? If CFK South is to be the grantee, is the national CFK aware of this project, and do they support it? In any case, no matter which organization might be the prospective grantee, we will need a letter from the chief executive officer of that organization, expressing support for the request; a photocopy of the organization's IRS determination letter; and a photocopy of the organization's most recent IRS Form 990 tax return.

2. The reviewers also raised a question as to just how "doable" this project is. The plan requires CFK to run a national information campaign, to transform the high-tech products of an entire industry, and to provide information and training to ten million youth. Does CFK have the capacity to do all of this? Can it be done for $950,000 over three years? What is the deliv-

ery system that would be used? We will need a persuasive "business plan" to convince us that all of this can
be achieved in the time allotted, and within the budget
requested.

   3. The proposal discusses a number of partnerships, but it was unclear to the reviewers as to whether
these partnerships are in fact firm, or whether they are
hoped-for partnerships that CFK will attempt to consummate once a grant is secured. Quite frankly, the
PDQ Foundation is very skeptical of "build it and they
will come" approaches to partnerships. Please detail
for us exactly what partnerships are consummated and
which are in the formative stages.

   Let us turn now to the more specific questions,
which follow in no particular order of priority:

   1. On page four of the proposal, you mention
graduate student stipends but do not tell us exactly
what the graduate students would be asked to do.
Could you be more specific on this point?

   2. On page five of the proposal, you mention that
you are seeking approximately $100,000 to undertake
a feasibility study related to expanding Web-based
delivery of accessible information. Obviously, this is an
important first step, but it leads us to wonder when the
actual improvement of the website would begin, and
who would fund it?

   3. On page six, it is stated that CFK will ask the
PDQ Foundation for approximately half of the
$500,000 that CFK anticipates spending over three
years to jump-start technology training for youth.
Where will the other half of the funding come from?

   4. Still on the subject of technology training, do
you anticipate that this can be made self-funding? If so,
how long would it take to reach the break-even point?
Is it feasible to consider that it might even become a
profit center for CFK at some point?

   5. On page seven, on the subject of specialized
technical assistance, you mention regional seminars.
How many of these do you plan to hold, and where
would they be located?

6. Still on page seven, you make the point that employers are unaware that a great number of jobs can be performed by young people who have had appropriate technology training. It would be helpful if you could share with us a few concrete examples of such jobs, and how technology training can help make young people eligible to perform such jobs.

7. On page nine, it is mentioned that CFK means to undertake a public service announcement (PSA) campaign. The reviewers were highly dubious that PSAs alone would make for an effective public information campaign. It misses those who do not watch TV, and it even misses many of those who do, for PSAs are notoriously aired in the 1:00 A.M. "graveyard" time slot. Would it not make more sense to consider a more comprehensive campaign that would include print as well as broadcast media, and that might also include direct mail, the Internet, or other creative technologies?

8. Still on the subject of the PSA campaign, you mention on page ten that CFK has conducted similar campaigns in the past. What evidence of impact for these campaigns can you offer us? We would also be interested in knowing what the $200,000 requested from the PDQ Foundation for the PSA campaign would purchase. Would this be creative work, air time, or some mixture of the two? What in-kind assistance could you get for the campaign?

9. It will be important for us to know what other funders have supported this effort, what other funders have been approached to support it, and what they have been asked to contribute.

10. The PDQ Foundation has specific expectations with regard to project evaluation. I have enclosed a worksheet that will explain those expectations in detail. Please read it carefully, and provide all of the information it requests.

11. The same worksheet that explains our expectations with regard to project evaluation also explains our expectations regarding the preparation of the project budget. Again, please read it carefully, and send us a project budget in the format requested.

We remind you that the deadline for receipt of your answer is March 1, 2000. Once we receive this information from you, we will attach it to the proposal as an addendum, and if you have fully responded to our questions and concerns, we will be able to come to a final decision as to whether to recommend this proposal for funding. Even if we should recommend it for funding, however, it will go into a very competitive process in which a limited pool of funds is available. Therefore, you should not consider this letter as an assurance that your request has been selected for funding.

Thank you for your patience, and all the best to you as you prepare your response. [If you are open to receiving a phone call, you could insert a sentence to the effect of "Call me if you have any questions" here.] I will look forward to receiving your addendum.

Sincerely,
Ima Major Donor, Program Officer

"And now," as John Cleese of Monty Python used to say, "for something completely different." Some years ago, a grantseeker (who has preserved his or her anonymity for reasons that will shortly become obvious) imagined what would have happened if the Declaration of Independence had been a grant request, and if Great Britain's King George III had been a program officer. The pointed humor found in King George's Q&C should be self-evident to grantmaker and grantseeker alike:

The Court of King George III
London, England

September 10, 1776

Mr. Thomas Jefferson
c/o The Continental Congress
Philadelphia, Pennsylvania

Dear Mr. Jefferson:

We have read your "Declaration of Independence" with great interest. Certainly, it represents a considerable undertaking, and many of your statements do merit serious consideration.

Unfortunately, the Declaration as a whole fails to meet recently adopted specifications for proposals to the Crown, so we must return the document to you for further refinement.

The questions which follow might assist in your process of revision:

1. In your opening paragraph you use the phrase the "Laws of Nature and Nature's God." What are these laws? In what way are they the criteria on which you base your central arguments? Please document with citations from the recent literature.

2. In the same paragraph you refer to the "opinions of mankind." Whose polling data are you using? Without specific evidence, it seems to Us that the "opinions of mankind" are merely a matter of opinion.

3. You hold certain truths to be "self-evident." Would you please elaborate? If they are as evident as you claim, then it should not be difficult for you to locate the appropriate supporting statistics.

4. The goals of your proposal seem to be, "Life, Liberty, and the Pursuit of Happiness." These are not measurable goals. If you were to say that "among these is the ability to sustain an average life expectancy in six of the thirteen colonies of at least fifty-five years, and to enable newspapers in the colonies to print news without outside interference, and to raise the average income of the colonists by 10 percent in the next ten years," these could be measurable goals. Please clarify.

5. You state that "Whenever any Form of Government becomes destructive of these ends, it is the Right of the people to alter or to abolish it, and to institute a new Government." Have you weighed this assertion against all of the alternatives? What are the trade-off considerations?

6. Your description of the existing situation is quite extensive. Such a long list of grievances should precede the statement of goals, not follow it. Your problem statement needs improvement.

7. Your strategy for achieving your goal is not developed at all. You state that the colonies "ought to

be Free and Independent States" and that they are
"Absolved from All Allegiance to the British Crown."
Who or what must change to achieve these objectives?
In what way must they change? What specific steps will
you take to overcome the resistance? How long will it
take? We have found that a little foresight in these
areas helps to prevent careless errors later on. How
cost-effective are your strategies?

8. Who among the list of signatories will be
responsible for implementing your strategy? Who
conceived it? Who provided the theoretical research?
Who will constitute the advisory committee? Please
submit an organizational chart and vitae of the
principal investigators.

9. You must include an evaluation design. We have
been requiring this since Queen Anne's War.

10. What impact will your solution have? Your
failure to include any evaluation of this inspires little
confidence in the long-range prospects of your
undertaking.

11. Please submit an organizational chart,
itemized budget, and continuation plan.

We hope that these comments prove useful in
revising your "Declaration of Independence." We
welcome the submission of your revised proposal. Our
due date for revised proposals is December 31, 1776.
Ten copies with original signatures will be required.
                Sincerely,
                George III, By Grace of God
                Chief Program Officer of the United Kingdom
                of England, Ireland, and Scotland

Grantseeker Responses to Q&Cs

The way in which the applicant answers the Q&C tells you almost as
much as the answers themselves. If the applicant answers a complex
Q&C by return mail, it suggests that the applicant is desperate to get
the money. If, in contrast, the applicant takes many months to
respond to a straightforward Q&C, the implication is that the proposal is not high on the grantseeker's priority list. Parenthetically, it

is almost a given that the applicant who has taken months to respond will telephone the day after the foundation finally receives the long-awaited response and ask if the foundation has made a decision on the proposal yet!

After the response has arrived, you must decide whether the proposal-cum-addendum or rewritten proposal is satisfactory. If not, is another Q&C letter called for, or has the response to the first Q&C revealed that the proposal should be declined? Each possibility requires a different strategy.

If the addendum or revised proposal satisfactorily answers most questions, then you must determine the next step. Is a site visit in order? Are there a couple of minor questions that could quickly be answered by a phone call? Did the response in fact answer all major questions, so that the funding document can now be drafted? These are very straightforward alternatives, and it is usually easy to determine the appropriate next steps.

If the response answered only some of the questions (or if the answers raised new questions), then you must decide whether the proposal should be declined or whether another Q&C is in order. If you should decide to send another Q&C, it will then be useful to set a limit on how many Q&Cs the foundation will be willing to send. With every Q&C sent, the likelihood increases that the applicant will conclude that it is being made to jump through hoops, and accordingly both annoyance and expectations rise. A direct correlation also sets in: the more Q&Cs the foundation shares with a grantseeker, the harder it becomes to decline the proposal should that become necessary. Although there is no ironclad rule, anything beyond two Q&Cs usually triggers diminishing returns. The chances of funding the proposal drop with each successive iteration, while the expectations of the applicant continue to rise. Therefore, if the second Q&C comes back inadequate, the proposal should, in most cases, be declined.

Any time you must decline a proposal after having sent a Q&C, you must be prepared for a difficult reaction. No matter what pains you have taken to manage expectations, no matter how many disclaimers you have made, the receipt of a Q&C will stoke the fires of grantseeker optimism. And it is highly likely that the grantseeker will feel that it has answered all the Q&C questions very thoroughly, so that getting the grant can only be a matter of time. Under such circumstances, it is *imperative* to inform the applicant of the negative decision by telephone, followed up, of course, by a letter. The good news for you is that it is possible to cite definite reasons for the decision, namely the applicant's failure to adequately respond to the questions and concerns posed in the letter. The bad news is that the grantseeker is certain that the responses were adequate, will probably want additional opportunities to respond, and may become angry when informed that such opportunities will not be forthcoming. Nonetheless, given that the grantseeker has made the effort to send in the proposal and respond to the Q&C, it is an important courtesy to share the sad tidings in a personal fashion.

Conclusion

Q&C letters are important both for what they say and for what they might imply. They specifically convey to grantseekers what must be done to make their initial proposals fundable, which is obviously a matter of real importance. They also have an intangible but nonetheless profound impact on the applicant's expectations, often inflating them unrealistically but sometimes deflating them unduly.

In these communications, as in meetings, the same elements are of vital importance: clear communications, management of expectations, and careful documentation of activities. These principles are even more important with Q&Cs, however, for the Q&C comes later in the process, and to the grantseeker, each step takes on a greater significance as time goes by. For you, the Q&C is the essential information-gathering and decision-making tool that separates the grantees from the wanna-be's. Q&Cs must be written carefully, thoughtfully, and well, or they do more harm than good.

Chapter Seven

Site Visits

No matter how well written a proposal might be, no matter how carefully you read it, and no matter how thoughtfully it is negotiated between you and the grantseeker, the fact remains that the idea embedded within the proposal is still seen through a glass, dimly. Proposals can give you only a glimpse of what a project, once funded, might be like. A proposal cannot convey the personalities of the people who will be responsible for the project, their passion, their spirit, and their dedication. It cannot convey a sense of the physical setting where the project would play out, nor does it tell much about the partnership (or lack of same) between the applicant and those whom it is trying to help. The best way for you to gain a greater understanding of these important considerations is to visit the offices of the applicant, the places where the project would be implemented, and the people whom it would affect.

To Visit or Not to Visit, That Is the Question

In an ideal world, you would conduct a site visit for every project that the foundation is seriously thinking of funding. Interrelated factors—distance, expense, and time constraints—make that impossible, however. When considering a grant to an organization thousands of miles away, you will need to face the fact that conducting a site visit would take days to accomplish and would be very costly. Because program officers are chronically short of time, and because every dollar spent on travel and lodging is a dollar that the foundation cannot pay out in the form of a grant, it is impractical to visit every prospective project. Given this conundrum—that it would be ideal to visit all candidates for funding but not responsible to do so—it is useful to consider some guidelines to determine when a site visit makes sense and when one does not.

1. Site visits usually should be reserved for projects that the foundation is leaning toward funding rather than for those that it is leaning against funding. If the proposal review process left you with serious qualms about an idea, laying out cash for a site visit generally becomes a case of throwing good money after bad. It is always possible, of course, that a site visit will reveal hidden gems that the proposal did not, but this does not happen frequently enough for the rate of return to justify the investment.

2. Site visits should aim to maximize learning. If a proposal under consideration would fund the twelfth project in a series or cluster of grants, it would make less sense to visit the site than if it were to be the first project in a cluster.

3. Site visits should be cost-efficient. If it would cost $2,000 to conduct a site visit for a $5,000 request, any benefits derived would not outweigh the expense. Even if the request is for a large sum or the trip would be inexpensive, you should not automatically elect to make a visit, but rather should weigh its potential benefits against its potential costs.

4. Site visits must have a value that outweighs the foundation's opportunity costs. When you are on a site visit you are not doing other valuable and useful things, such as reading proposals or managing funded projects. A site visit that is not potentially valuable enough to justify these opportunity costs should not be conducted.

5. Site visits should improve the quality of and the support for the proposed project and should verify the claims of the proposal describing that project. The site visit provides opportunities for you to fine-tune proposal ideas, make sure there is presidential and board support for the project within the institution applying for funding, and double-check on the reality of claims of competence and partnership.

The Inevitability of Rising Expectations

There is another hidden cost of visiting a site: it inevitably sends the expectations of the applicant soaring. The grantseeker's reasoning goes something like this: "The foundation wouldn't take the trouble, or go to the expense, of making a visit unless it had already decided to fund this project. No matter what our program officer says, the grant is 'in the bag.'" Once such a belief settles in, it is well-nigh impossible to dislodge it. This assumption alone is a very good reason to avoid frivolous visits, for they raise expectations that may well be dashed later. Even a few of the serious prospects you visit will ultimately have to be declined. There is no reason to put anyone through this kind of disappointment unless absolutely necessary.

Although you cannot control the applicant's expectations, there are at least a few ways to manage them. Before the visit, when finalizing arrangements, you should include a written disclaimer explicitly stating that the visit does *not* mean that the proposal has been approved and that in fact it might still be declined. This message should be followed up with a similar disclaimer in a thank-you note after the visit. Even if grantseekers discount such disclaimers, it is very useful to cite them later, should it become necessary to decline the request. During the visit itself, it is important to repeat this warning in a very straightforward manner to the leaders involved. The message sometimes has more impact when delivered face-to-face.

Foundations occasionally like to send more than one program officer to conduct a site visit. In many institutions, grantmakers work in teams, so it is sensible to make the visit as a team. It might also be the case that a senior program officer is mentoring a junior colleague, so both make the visit. The grantseeker, however, reads a very different meaning into this practice. By their calculus, if a foundation sends three program officers to conduct a site visit, it must be because the foundation is three times as interested in the proposal as if it had sent only one person. If one of the members of the team visiting the site happens to be an officer of the foundation, the grantseeker will turn as giddy as Scrooge after the third spirit departed. The best way to contain these unrealistic expectations is simply to send one person. If, however, there are compelling reasons to send more than one, it will be essential to spell out the reasoning to the applicant beforehand and to specifically state that the extra visitors do not signify deeper interest on the part of the foundation.

Timing of the Site Visit

Most grantmakers agree that a visit should come later in the process rather than sooner—making a site visit the day after meeting a grantseeker is rushing things a bit—but there is less agreement about which point in time is ideal. Many grantmakers feel that the perfect time is after they have read the proposal, sent a Q&C letter, and received a response to the Q&C. According to this school of thought, the site visit can then focus on resolving the few outstanding issues before a funding document is prepared.

Others in the field argue for site visits earlier in the process. Early visits are particularly helpful, they say, for community-based organizations that do not have a lot of experience or sophistication in grant writing. An early visit allows the program officer to coach the applicants on proposal writing, and helps build a relationship of trust between the grantmaker and the grantseeker. Providing intensive help at the front end of the process, they say, reduces problems later on.

There are even a few advocates of *multiple* site visits throughout the process. They operate on the theory that good grantmaking is a hands-on enterprise and that the more interaction between applicant and program officer, the better for the final product. In fact, they say, multiple visits allow program officers to truly add value to the process by providing coaching and technical assistance, and such an intensive regimen results in projects ultimately having positive impacts that would, without intervention by the program officer, likely turn in disappointing results.

There are also a small number of grantmakers who take precisely the opposite position from those who favor multiple site visits; they hold that site visits should not be done at all. They claim that the many expenses associated with site visits, whether measured in dollars, time, or opportunity, divert essential resources from grantmaking. Far better, they say, to define foundation interests clearly, read proposals rigorously, and spend money on grants, not on airline tickets or hotel rooms.

Clearly, as with so many other aspects of grantmaking, there is no single right or wrong answer to the question of timing site visits. Although it usually makes sense to conduct a visit near the end of the process, each process is distinctive, and for some requests, a site visit earlier on is highly sensible. For still other requests, especially smaller, recurring, or late-in-a-series proposals, it is probably best to do no site visit at all. Multiple visits are desirable under certain circumstances, but probably are not ideal as a general policy due to their high cost in time, money, and opportunity. Eschewing all site visits will surely reduce administrative overhead and get more grant dollars out of the door, but it will also likely lead to isolation for the grantmaker. One of the important fringe benefits of conducting site visits, after all, is the direct contact with real leaders grappling with real problems. Program officers can provide these leaders with valuable consultation, and the experience keeps grantmakers current with the latest issues in the field. Over the long run, if a grantmaker avoids this sort of contact, he or she is likely to lose touch with external conditions and issues, which will lead to impaired performance.

It should be mentioned, as well, that there may be occasions when it is sensible to delay a site visit until *after* a project has been funded. This approach is generally reserved for those organizations with which a foundation has had one or more past grant relationships, or occasionally for an organization that has an absolutely stellar track record. Typically, the foundation makes the grant for reasons of opportunity or timeliness, and the site visit is conducted a few months after the project is up and running.

Setting the Agenda

Once you have decided to make a site visit, you must create an agenda for the visit. This process will reveal both parties' common—and divergent—interests. You have in common the desire to come to an agreement so that the project can go forward. Your interests diverge, however, in one crucial way. It is in the grantseeker's interest to impress you, and it is in your interest to uncover any hidden problems that may potentially hinder the project. This urge to shine versus the urge to investigate makes for potential conflict and underscores the need—from the foundation's point of view—for you to control the site visit's agenda.

Your first imperative is to investigate any concerns that may linger after the initial review. The second is to conduct a general due diligence review, double-checking to ensure that the applicant is competent, honest, and financially sound. The third is to gather information needed to write and defend the funding document. (In most foundations, the funding document is the summary of the project that is sent to the internal committee or the board for discussion and, one hopes, approval.) All of these needs will come into some degree of conflict with the grantseeking organization's desire to impress you by putting its best foot forward. To avoid conflict, you should make it clear from the outset that there is certain information that you *must* gather in order to make a final decision on the request and that therefore the agenda must be designed to serve this purpose. In practice, this means that you should create a list of issues to cover and of people to meet, and share that list with the grantseeker early in the process. It will be normal for the applicant to resist this agenda to some extent, because it will not be completely compatible with the grantseeker's desire to roll out the red carpet. Strenuous resistance, however, could be a sign of problems. If, for example, you wish to see community leaders involved with the project, and the applicant strongly objects, it may well be that the applicant wishes to disguise the fact that there is not a real partnership in place.

You must recognize, too, that there may be people who are not on your list but with whom you must hold a meeting for reasons of protocol or politics. The key consideration is to completely satisfy the needs of program first; you can then deal with protocol and political issues as a secondary priority. Realistically, however, protocol needs cannot be ignored completely.

Public and Private Conversations

Projects have a number of stakeholders, and all of these stakeholders should be part of the site visit. The obvious ones are the foundation and the applicant organization, but others include partner organizations, community-based organizations in the areas that will be targeted by the grant, the people living in these areas, interested policymakers, and so on. For the most part, the conversations during the site visit should be open, or public, and be accessible to all of the stakeholders. There are times, however, when private conversations—with only one or two of the stakeholder groups present—are legitimate or even necessary. For example, there may be personnel issues surrounding the project, and it is appropriate for reasons of confidentiality under such circumstances for only you and the representatives of the applying organization to discuss such matters.

It is essential to have private conversations with such groups as community residents or youth advisory boards. Always the least powerful of the partners in any given grant proposal, these groups are often intimidated into silence, a silence that may be broken if you have a chance to speak privately with them. It is also a useful test to observe the reactions of the representatives of the applying organization when you request such private meetings. If they are exceedingly uncomfortable with the idea, it suggests that there probably are some issues with the partnership, such as power imbalances, that need to be explored.

Remember, however, that you should use private meetings sparingly. In any partnership situation, it is desirable to conduct as much of the business as possible as openly as possible. You should use private meetings only when confidentiality must be preserved or when you are unlikely to get at candor in any other way.

The final public conversation should provide a summary of the site visit, so that there are no misunderstandings about what has transpired. You should also use this opportunity to remind the applicant that there can be no assurances that the request will be funded, and then discuss the next steps (including an estimated timeline) leading to the foundation's decision on the request. The clearer you are at this point, the better for all involved.

Signs of Trouble

If all goes according to plan, data gathered during the site visit will reinforce the earlier judgment of interest in the proposal. One of the important opportunities offered by the site visit, however, is the chance for you to discover signs of trouble that you could detect in no other way. Perhaps the most visible of such signs can be found in the nonverbal communication of the applying organization's staff. If the staff members are glum and unmotivated, and wander about like extras from the set of *Night of the Living Dead*, it belies the enthusiasm expressed in the proposal and should raise concerns about the health of the organization and the energy with which the project would be managed. An office with no phones ringing should raise concerns, for inevitably proposals paint a picture of an organization in frenetic motion. Do the staff members model the values of the project? If not, how will they be able to pull it off?

The organizational culture of the applicant, as revealed in the site visit meetings, can be another source of warning signals. Do partners bicker and contradict each other? Is one partner doing all the talking, in fact jumping in to answer questions posed to another partner? Are community residents or youth advisory councils represented? If so, are they being treated respectfully or condescendingly? Do they seem to have a real role, and real power, in this partnership? Is the applicant reluctant to let you talk to certain people about certain subjects? Are key members of the applicant's board of trustees aware of the request and actively supportive of it?

The site visit also is an opportunity to measure how well reality stacks up against the claims made in the proposal. Does the physical plant, computer system, and other equipment resemble that described in the proposal? Is there anything that should have been mentioned in the proposal that was omitted?

Always remember that applicants have prepared feverishly for your visit. They will be on their best behavior and probably have papered over a few organizational cracks. It is reasonable to assume that a surprise visit would find them looking a bit different, but usually this is a difference in polish only—the shoe underneath remains the same. Therefore, although you should not necessarily believe everything you see or are told, there is no reason to suspect that it is all a fabrication, either.

There is also much to be said for gut instinct. Occasionally, although nothing appears to be overtly wrong during a site visit, you may come away with an uneasy sense that something is not right. Experienced grantmakers come to trust these instincts, which often can ferret out intangible factors, such as mistrust, dishonesty, and low morale, that can come back to haunt a funded project. This point underscores once more the importance of the spirit—the heart as well as the head—in grantmaking. Just because it is difficult to define some issues does not mean that they do not exist or that they are not important.

Field Notes and Follow-Up

The site visit is not completed until you have shared the field notes with your colleagues and placed them in the file. The term *field notes* implies a precision that the article itself only rarely possesses. Unless a foundation has a specific format for field notes (which few do), the style is left to you, and the result is as close as foundations come to Maoism (at least in the sense of "letting a thousand flowers bloom"). There are a number of effective ways to organize field notes, but perhaps it is best to start this discussion with a couple of methods to *avoid*.

The first method might be described as verbosity tempered by extraneous detail. This typically consists of a virtually verbatim transcript of every conversation held during the visit, including those with cab drivers, with details provided on every event, including a synopsis of plane flights. Copious detail and irrelevant information serve no one well. These kinds of notes do not provide a usable record for the project file, and bore readers long before they can extract useful information. They bring to mind Truman Capote's assessment of Jack Kerouac's work: "That's not writing—it's typing!"

The second method to avoid goes to the other extreme. It might be called the Joe Friday approach—an outline on a diet—which raises the laconic to an art form. Such field notes can be paraphrased as follows: "Arrived. Discussed. Succeeded. Left." The first method drowns information in trivia, the second desiccates important information. Neither type does the intended job of the field notes, which are meant to document the site visit and to persuade others of the value of the project.

How then should field notes be organized? If the visit itself was brief, a simple way to organize the notes is to write a narrative of the key points discussed, in the order in which they were discussed. For a longer visit, it makes sense to lay out the key points in priority order (regardless of the actual order in which they were discussed during the visit) and then record the outcomes for each. Some program officers favor an expanded outline; others like to flesh out the story with narrative. Still others create a template that they can fill in, so that their notes for different projects have a consistent format.

However you choose to organize the notes, they need to convey certain essential information. They must demonstrate that you met all the key players and judged them capable, assessed the applying organization's capacity and found it adequate, examined the partnerships and decided they were sound, and weighed the overall risks and concluded that they were worth taking. Moreover, if the site visit is made late in the process, the field notes must be persuasive to foundation colleagues who will be deciding whether a funding document should be written. Unless you receive permission to write a funding document, the proposal will never become a grant. The field notes should close, therefore, with a brief summation of why you believe that the idea described by this project is worthy of support by the foundation and ready to be funded. The field notes are a report on the facts, but they are more than mere reporting: they also rise to the level of advocacy. For this reason alone, they should be completed soon after the visit, written crisply, and most important, written with conviction.

Finally, remember that a part of the follow-up process for a site visit is writing a letter to the applicant thanking the participants for their hospitality. This letter, as previously mentioned, should be used to manage expectations—once again reminding the applicant that funding is not assured—and also reiterating the next steps discussed at the close of the site visit. It is important to have these documented in the file should any questions arise later about what was said by whom to whom.

Declining Requests After Site Visits

After a site visit, particularly a late-in-the-process site visit, applicants have, in Mark Twain's memorable phrase, "the serene confidence which a Christian feels in four aces." Nothing can disturb this unshakable belief that their request will be funded. Fortunately for all involved, due to the fact that most program officers visit only those projects that the foundation is seriously considering, most usually are funded. However, on those rare occasions when a site visit turns up too many troubling issues to support the request, it becomes necessary to trump those four aces (as it were) with a decline. You should expect anguish and anger whenever you have to make such a call. There are, however, a few things you can do to at least keep the situation from turning into a major incident.

The most important of these has already been discussed: the use of disclaimers in all before-and-after correspondence, as well as in the face-to-face discussions. Although it is probably true that these warnings have more value as documentation than as communications devices (as the innate optimism of grantseekers often causes them to discount such messages), disclaimers are invaluable should it ever become necessary to decline the proposal later.

You should always remember that there is an element of public humiliation in being declined so late in the process. To the applicants, being declined after a site visit is like being left standing at the altar, so they will want an explanation—and a good one—for this decision. Under the circumstances, it is imperative to call with the bad news and, if at all possible, to share a definite reason or reasons for the decision. For example, if the site visit revealed that the "partnership" was not really in place, you should cite this lack as one of the contributing factors to the decision. Above all, it is important to be personal and specific. Being jilted is bad enough, but getting the news from a vague form letter is galling in the extreme.

No matter what precautions you take, however, the applicant will be hurt and disappointed. The public nature of the refusal makes the post–site visit decline the hardest of all to take, and it behooves all grantmakers to be sensitive to this whenever such declines become necessary. The unpleasantness of such rejections makes a strong argument for excellence in proposal review and Q&C letter writing, so as to ensure that as many of the problems as possible are detected before you darken the applicant's doorstep.

If preventive measures do not work and you are faced with an irate "declinee," it is best to meet the situation head-on. The proper approach to take is that of being kind but firm. Remind the applicant of the disclaimers that were provided both orally and in writing. Express understanding of the applicant's disappointment, but make it clear that the decision was arrived at by a fair and thoughtful process and is final. Finally, you should document all conversations and be sure to alert your superiors in the organization so that they are not caught unawares should the applicant complain to them. You should always remember that the occasional unhappy rejection will occur no matter how carefully or professionally you behave toward applicants.

Using Consultants for Site Visits

Your schedule being what it is, you may not have the opportunity to conduct site visits in a timely fashion. The choice then becomes to forego site visits or to have a consultant conduct them. Although it would be ideal for you to conduct the visit personally, it is almost always better for there to be a consultant-conducted site visit than none at all. This is not to say, however, that a consultant-conducted site visit is without its own set of challenges.

First, you need to weigh the general pros and cons of working with consultants. These will be covered in detail in Chapter Ten. Second, it is unfair to all involved to simply toss a file at a consultant and expect that person to conduct a quality site visit. You need to debrief the consultant before the visit on key issues to be covered and desired outcomes to be achieved. Third, it is not realistic to expect that the consultant can do as good a job as you could. The consultant has not been immersed in the process of proposal review, nor is he or she as familiar with the general context of the foundation's grantmaking and how this request fits into that context. Fourth, it is not realistic that the leaders of the applying organization will treat the consultant in quite the same fashion as they would treat you. They will feel as if they are getting a second-stringer and will probably behave accordingly.

Nonetheless, there are also some real advantages to sending a consultant. Applicants are sometimes less guarded around consultants than around program officers. The fresh eyes of the consultant may see things that you, who are more immersed in the request, might miss. And it cannot be gainsaid that it is better to have a consultant-conducted visit than to have no visit at all.

Conclusion

The site visit serves as a dose of reality in the too-often surreal world of the grantmaker. There can be no substitute for seeing and hearing the people and the places in which the foundation is considering making an investment. No amount of writing, its quality notwithstanding, can ever convey all the dimensions of a complex idea. Visiting gives you a chance to judge the veracity of the grant proposal, weigh the capacity of the people and the organizations who will be doing the work, and gauge the potential of the project to change the world. Visiting also keeps you current with developments in the field. And, not least important, it gives you more evidence that you can use to persuade colleagues of the appropriateness of the project for funding. The site visit, if carefully chosen and thoughtfully planned, is truly a trip worth making.

Chapter Eight

Writing the Funding Document

One of the most common misconceptions among grantseekers is that the proposals they have submitted are read in full by the committee or board that makes the ultimate decision on grant requests. In the vast majority of foundations, this is untrue—what the committee or board receives and reads is a funding document, written usually by the lead program officer for the grant request. The funding document is typically a summary of the proposal received from the applicant, written in a standardized format, that gives the committee or board essential information about the request and makes the case for appropriating funds for that request. Although the name of this document varies from foundation to foundation, its contents are fairly consistent: a background section; a rationale for funding the project; information on project evaluation, continuation, and dissemination; and a budget. The length of the funding document varies among institutions but ranges from one to ten pages, with shorter ones being more common. In most cases they are the only documents that the committee or board sees—it is rare for them to request to read the original proposal.

This system, although pervasive in private foundations, is not perfect. Its main drawback is that the committee or board never gets to consider the proposal, which carries the authentic voice of the applicant. This difficulty is far outweighed, however, by the many advantages that the funding document offers over the original proposal. The funding document is written in a brief, standardized format and is shorter than the proposal, without addenda or other distractions. It distills the essence of the proposal and, if written well, makes a compelling case for supporting the ideas described within.

Writing the Funding Document

Those three little words, "if written well," cover a multitude of sins in the writing of funding documents. Getting it right is a challenge, even to a facile writer, for the funding document demands a distinctive and unusual blend of composition skills and styles. This level of sophistication, moreover, is demanded of grantmakers, who, by and large, do not enjoy putting pen to paper. Many things draw people to foundation work—the passion to change the world, a desire to help people, a yen to affect public policy—but rarely is anyone drawn to this calling by a burning desire to generate prose. In fact, many program officers will readily say that writing is the part of their job that they like the least.

In the case of the funding document, this disdain can easily evolve into outright hatred, for creating an effective funding document requires equal skill at two very different types of writing. It must be, on the one hand, a work of scholarship, well researched and carefully documented. If it is not, the committee or board will quickly shred it, and rightfully so. As program officer, you are requesting that the foundation make a considerable financial investment in an organization: you had better be able to document the need for and the wisdom of making that investment. It must therefore be as meticulously supported as any research paper.

Yet if the funding document is solely a collection of facts, figures, and statistics, it would have very little power to move people. Here again enters the spiritual element in philanthropy: committee members and trustees, just as much as program officers, were called to service in foundations by emotional and spiritual desires as much as or more than by cognitive interests. In order to appeal to this passionate side, the funding document must also be compelling and moving. It has to explain the opportunity the project presents and share a vision of how the world will be better if it is funded. The document must therefore be a first-rate piece of persuasive writing.

Finding a good writer of any variety is not an easy task, as professors of English will testify. But to find someone who is skilled at two very different prose styles *and* who is adept at melding the two into a single document is to find a rare bird, indeed. Most program officers have at least a basic level of skill at creating research papers. Many have, after all, earned advanced degrees in institutions of higher education where writing of that ilk is a core skill. Fewer have experience or ability in authoring persuasive compositions. And only a handful have any idea of how to marry the two into one well-supported, highly persuasive document.

Secrets of Successful Funding Documents

The greatest secret regarding the creation of successful funding documents is this: there is no secret. Most foundations have a format for composing funding documents: follow the format. Most have limitations on length: respect these limitations. All have a deadline for submitting copy: honor the deadline. Such glib advice is admittedly reminiscent of the recipe for making elephant soup— "Step one: Find elephant"—but it would surprise most people outside the foundation field to learn how often grantmakers violate these elementary rules. Funding documents are created that deviate from the approved format, go far beyond the prescribed length, and miss the stated deadline for submission. There is no secret about these rules, and it is no secret that they should be followed.

The second great nonsecret is to write for the ultimate audience. If the funding document will be judged by an internal committee, you need to know just how expert the committee members are in the field of the proposal. This will determine how technical the document should be. If it will be judged by a lay board, you would be wise to adjust the level of technicality accordingly. Whether an internal committee or the board makes the decision, it is very important to know at least the basics of each member's worldview. Although there is no need to pander to such views, there is no percentage in egregiously offending them, either. Most of all, there is no point in writing generically, in a one-size-fits-all mode. Funding documents are very much like suits: all of them follow a basic pattern, but each of them requires some custom tailoring for its ultimate wearer.

The third nonsecret is to follow the general rules for effective writing. These have been summarized, in a humorous form, by some anonymous scribe who compiled the "Twenty-Five Rules for Writing Good":

1. Verbs has to agree with their subjects.
2. Prepositions are not words to end sentences with.
3. And do not start a sentence with a conjunction.
4. Avoid clichés like the plague.
5. Be more or less specific.
6. Also, too, never use repetitive redundancies.
7. No sentence fragments.
8. Contractions aren't necessary and shouldn't be used.
9. One should never generalize.
10. Use words correctly, irregardless of how others use them.
11. Puns are for children, not groan readers.
12. Do not use no double negatives.
13. One-word sentences? Eliminate.
14. The passive voice is to be ignored.
15. Eliminate commas, that are not, necessary.
16. Eschew obfuscation; never use a humongous word when a diminutive one would suffice.
17. Kill all exclamation points!
18. Understatement is always the most superb way to put forth earthshaking ideas.
19. Use the apostrophe in it's proper place, and omit it when its not needed.
20. If you have heard it once, you have heard it a trillion times: resist hyperbole.
21. Go around the barn at high noon to avoid colloquialisms.
22. Even if a mixed metaphor sings, it should be derailed.
23. Who needs rhetorical questions?
24. Exaggeration is infinitely worse than understatement.
25. Proofread carefully to see if you any words out.

Do's and Don'ts

Besides the foregoing general rules for effective writing, there are a number of specific rules for writing funding documents. These can be summarized as a series of do's and don'ts. Even when you are operating within the rules, and even while you are staying mindful of the audience, you retain a fair amount of compositional leeway. You can use that leeway to write persuasively and help make the case, or to write foolishly and doom the requested project.

Do's

1. *Do share context.* As soon as possible within the approved format, it is important to include context that will help explain the requested project. What are the important societal issues that this project will address, and what is their history? Why is the recommended grantee the right organization to take on this project? What is the grantee's history? Without this context, the recommendation will exist in a vacuum, unconnected to important traditions or social needs. You must meticulously research and document this context.

2. *Do define the opportunity.* Once you have established a context, the next need is to define why this recommendation presents the foundation with an *opportunity*. What change will it bring about? What will be lost to society if the project is not funded? Why support it now? Why support it in the fashion requested? If a funding document fails to define exactly why the project it describes is too good to pass up, readers can infer only two possible explanations: (1) that the funding document simply is poorly written, or (2) that the funding document is accurately written, and the project is *not* too good to pass up. Neither inference bodes well for the fate of the proposal.

3. *Do anticipate and answer questions.* Members of the committee or board are bound to have questions. The funding document should, to the extent possible, anticipate and answer those questions. This is not to say that you must moonlight as a "famous psychic" for the *National Enquirer;* it is to say that some questions will be obvious, and the funding document should answer them. For example, if the recommended grantee organization is new, you might anticipate questions about its programmatic capacity. If the grant request is large relative to the grantee's current budget, you might anticipate questions about the organization's fiscal soundness or its ability to administer the grant. Ignoring such issues in

the hope that no one will notice them rarely works. It is far better to meet the issues head-on and provide answers before the questions are raised.

4. *Do make careful use of abbrevs.* It is always good to keep the funding document as brief as possible while still conveying the essential information. One very helpful way of doing this is to employ abbreviations and acronyms, especially in place of lengthy names. There are, however, several cautions to remember when employing these handy tools of the writer's trade. The first is to always spell out an organization's full name when it is initially mentioned, followed in parenthesis by the abbreviation; for example, the Salvation Army (SA). Doing this eliminates any ambiguity as to what the abbreviation refers to or actually means. The second caution is to use abbreviations sparingly, ideally for no more than three separate organizations in a single funding document. If you use more, the funding document will soon be swimming in a confusing alphabet soup. Third, reserve the abbreviations for those organizations that are mentioned repeatedly in the document. It makes little sense to go to the trouble of abbreviating an organization that will never again be mentioned in the document, and doing so could lead readers to wonder why it was never mentioned again.

5. *Do define terms* the first time *they are mentioned.* In the course of reading proposals, writing Q&Cs, and conducting site visits, you become *the* expert on a given proposal. After you have worked on the project for months, it becomes all too easy to assume that "everyone knows" about the terms describing the ideas in the proposal. Because members of the internal committee or board will have less familiarity with these terms than you do, and because they may well be lay people, it is very important to define terms that are not used in everyday discourse. These definitions should be concise: one line, if possible. The only thing that is deadlier than an undefined term is a definition sprawling over a paragraph or more of text. There is also an iron rule of definitions, and that is to define the term the *first* time it is used in the document. Program officers are sometimes tempted, for reasons of narrative flow, to postpone the definition to the second or third time that the term is used. Resist this temptation at all costs. Readers are puzzled when first encountering an undefined term, then usually become annoyed when it is defined subsequently. Defining it the first time prevents puzzlement and annoyance.

6. *Do use data judiciously.* Despite Benjamin Disraeli's assertion that there are three types of lies: "lies, damned lies, and statistics," data have their place in every funding document. It is hard to conceive of making a truly defensible case without using statistical and anecdotal data to support the positions taken. Data, however, make a better relish than an entree; nothing is less palatable than endless strings of numbers. Facts and figures should be used to prove points and should not be allowed to become the points themselves. Data presented should be as complete as possible and be drawn from sources known for their soundness and fairness. The importance of consistency and accuracy can hardly be overstressed: figures that vary or contradict each other, or percentages the sum of which is more than 100, will invariably be spotted and questioned by readers. Finally, take care to avoid citing "tie your own noose" statistics. For example, if 20 percent of the young people receiving an intervention in a pilot program experienced a successful outcome, and you proudly cite that fact in the funding document, it also means that 80 percent did not experience success, and that fact is sure to be raised by members of the committee or board. Statistics should be brief, to the point, and highly supportive of the argument you are making.

7. *Do end with a bang, not a whimper.* The narrative portion of the funding document is your opportunity to make the case for funding the project. The narrative should begin by explaining context and opportunity, and it needs to end in that way, too. The last paragraph should *not* merely repeat the earlier narrative, but it should find a shorter and punchier way to reinforce the points you have made. Often a carefully chosen quote from an authority will serve the purpose nicely. In any case, the worst thing you can do is end a funding document with a housekeeping item or a run-on sentence dripping with jargon. The final words should inspire, not tire, your readers.

Don'ts

1. *Don't ignore the format.* If you work for a foundation that has a format for preparing the funding document, take care to actually follow the format. Again, this may seem painfully obvious, but when you are immersed in writing a funding document, it is all too easy to stray from the appointed framework, especially if it does

not seem congenial to your expressive style. Even if the resulting document is well written, it is sure to raise the hackles of readers who are expecting to read it in a different format. Freelancing on the framework simply borrows trouble; it is far safer to exercise creativity *within* the prescribed approach. A worthwhile check, when you have completed the funding document, is to give it a final review expressly to ensure that it adheres to the expected format.

For those foundations without a funding document outline to follow, the field is obviously more open, but probably not *wide* open. Even in such institutions, there are more than likely informal rules, or at least traditions, associated with how funding documents are written. Often the unwritten rules are just as rigorously enforced as the written ones. Rather than assuming that the absence of a formal outline means that anything goes, you would be far safer to read past funding documents to get a feeling for the style and range of acceptable approaches. Once again, you *can* exercise creativity, but it makes sense to exercise it within the established—or implicit—rules.

2. *Don't condescend to readers.* Although you are the expert, and need always to take care to explain technical terms, it is also important to avoid erring in the other direction by talking down to readers. This is often a subtle distinction, and there is no infallible rule that you can apply in all situations. Some foundations make life easier for you by providing guidelines about what must be defined and when. Absent such guidelines, however, there are a few tests that can be helpful. The first is the "tone test." Ask a friend not connected with the foundation to read the prose and determine if the tone appears about right. Is it too technical? Too glib? Too know-it-all? Avoid constructions like "as is generally known . . ." or "everyone agrees that . . . ," which are guaranteed to annoy readers who do not know or who do not agree. Above all, avoid being dismissive of conventional wisdom unless data can be produced to back up the position. Sacred cows are often dearly loved, so if you are going to kill one, the job needs to be done very carefully and very thoroughly.

3. *Don't filibuster.* The grand old tradition of holding the floor for hours to block passage of legislation may be considered appropriate in the U.S. Senate, but it is not a good idea to employ that tradition in funding documents. The logic that two pages are twice as persuasive as one, and that four pages are twice as persuasive as

two, simply does not apply. Brief is better. Naturally, it is necessary to write enough to make the case, but if you cannot make the case in short order, chances are that you cannot make it simply by piling up the page count.

4. *Don't write like Joe Friday.* The laconic star of the classic television series *Dragnet*, Sergeant Joe Friday, was fond of reminding witnesses that he wanted just the facts—nothing but the facts. Good advice, this, for detectives, but not so good for program officers. Dry-as-dust writing is highly in vogue in some quarters, prized for its safety and security. (No one is ever offended by the lifeless drone of factual information.) It is also true, however, that no one is ever inspired by such tedious prose, and in philanthropy, the spirit still matters. If you can offer no compelling rationale to fund a project beyond presenting a mountain of statistics capped with a snowy crown of densely packed verbiage, you are unlikely to inspire the members of the committee or the board to believe that this is a peak worth scaling.

5. *Don't write like a romance novelist.* If "just the facts" makes for an inadequate funding document, so too does its polar opposite, "just the emotion." You must give readers a reason to care about the proposed project, something that goes beyond the purely cognitive and fires the spirit. If, however, the cognitive is entirely thrown over in favor of sentimental appeals and stirring calls to action, the readers are likely to conclude that their emotions are being manipulated. If, coupled with this, there is a paucity of data and research results to back up the assertions, the funding document will likely get about as much respect from its readers as Harlequin romances get from the *New York Times Book Review*.

Lest the rules become overwhelming, it is worth repeating that there is no good reason to lapse into formulaic writing on funding documents. You can follow the rules, write for your audience, and still produce a funding document that includes passion and persuasion, one that moves the heart even as it informs the head.

Conclusion

The funding document is an odd mixture of documentation and inspiration. It must support its assertions as completely as any doctoral dissertation, and it must stir its readers to action as effectively as the most eloquent polemic. Combining the two styles into a single document can be done, but it makes for a merger as challenging as any ever consummated on Wall Street. No formula can be absolutely guaranteed to turn out the perfect document every time. Perhaps the best way to approach the goal is to study exemplary funding documents written by others to learn how they managed the trick, and then consciously seek to glean the best elements of their styles.

Still, no one should expect to hit the mark every time. Some proposals lend themselves better to the factual approach, whereas others are more attuned to the emotional and spiritual appeal. Striking the best balance between the two approaches in writing the funding document is one of the most essential skills any program officer can develop. Those who learn to do it well deserve praise for mastering this most challenging task of the grantmaking calling.

Chapter Nine

Presenting the Funding Document

When hiring program officers, few foundations consider prospects' thespian talents as one of the employment criteria, but perhaps they should, particularly those foundations that require oral presentations of funding documents. Not all foundations have such policies, and even those that do usually do not require that every funding document be presented. When there is an oral presentation, it is typically conducted by the lead program officer or sometimes by the entire team that has worked on the project. The audience is the internal funding committee or the board of trustees. As one program officer has remarked, "It is exactly like the theater, except that there is no makeup."

It would not be theater, of course, without a good deal of stage fright. Numerous surveys have demonstrated that the number one fear Americans have is of public speaking, and that level of dread is inspired by the prospect of innocuous after-luncheon speeches to local service clubs. Imagine how much greater the anxiety becomes when thousands or even millions of dollars are on the line, not to mention many months of hard work. Program officers are haunted by the thought of wrecking the chances for funding of a potentially superb project by making a lousy presentation to the ultimate arbiters of funding.

Like most fears, this one is considerably overblown. Among the foundations that require presentations, few make them into adversarial affairs. Indeed, most go out of their way to make the experience as collegial as possible. Still, the fear persists, perpetuated by the folklore dispensed by some veteran program officers, who occasionally regale colleagues with stories of gaffes that doomed grant requests. These stories may well be true, but they belie the fact that in most foundations, most of the funding documents brought before committees or boards are approved. The percentage of approvals varies from institution to institution, but it would be a rare foundation indeed in which less than half of those proposed are funded.

The reason for this high success rate is most emphatically *not* that committees or boards are rubber stamps for funding requests. It is rather due to the careful preparations undertaken by the program officers. The committee or board has approved priorities for the foundation's grantmaking. Everything that is sent forward, with only rare exceptions, will match these approved priorities. Moreover, program officers carefully monitor reactions to funding documents as they are submitted. If a committee or a board expresses reluctance to see another funding document on a topic, it is certain that no more documents will be sent forward on that topic. In short, the high success rate is largely due to a rigorous process of self-selection. Although grantmakers take risks from time to time, mostly they send forward documents that *should* get approved. None of these facts, however, seem to cure the stage fright of the grantmaker who has been asked to make a presentation before a committee or board.

Strategies for Presentations

One of the things that program officers find daunting about presentations is that they often feel as though they are standing alone before the world. Indeed, one program officer clutching a sheaf of note cards does make for a rather solitary spectacle in a board room. Therefore, an excellent way to calm the jitters is to go beyond the usual "talking head" presentation. There are a number of ways to do this, each of which offers both great advantages and some risk of backfiring.

If the funding document under consideration describes a project that creates something tangible, and if a sample is available, it makes sense to bring it to the meeting for "show and tell." Museum professionals have long recognized that physical objects possess an authenticity that can be only imperfectly described in print, and if the object can be handled, so much the better. For instance, if the project under consideration would dramatically expand the work of a center to teach entrepreneurial skills, and if one of the center's star students is already producing a product, you could share an example of this product as a tangible demonstration of the project's potential. A product literally in the hand makes an abstract request seem much more real.

This approach can backfire if you bring in too many products. An embarrassment of riches might raise the question, "If they are doing so well, why do they need our help?" Exercise caution if the applicant suggests making a gift of a product to each member of the committee or board. Most foundations place dollar limits on the gifts that employees or trustees might accept, but even if the product's value is under this limit, the recipients still may feel as if the applicant is trying to bribe them. All in all, it is probably better to refuse such offers.

Another approach to avoiding the talking-head syndrome relies on the bounty of modern technology. Slide shows have illustrated presentations for years, of course, but advances in technology make it possible for slide shows to include zooms, fades, and even motion, which will enliven any discussion. Videos can be made to illustrate the request, videoconferencing can bring the applicants right into the board room, and the Internet allows for real-time simultaneous communications around the world. In the not-too-distant future, it will be feasible to use virtual reality to spice up presentations. When used well, these technologies allow for committee and board members to experience the proposed project on an almost firsthand basis.

All grantmakers, however, should remember a simple correlation before totally embracing the electronic revolution in communications: the more complex the technology, the greater the risk of failure. A presentation built on a videoconference collapses whenever the satellite loses its signal. Even less catastrophic glitches can be troublesome, throwing the presentation off its pace. Human failure can plague these visually aided talks, as well. There are eight possible ways to insert a slide into a slide projector, seven of which are incorrect. A person can easily push the wrong button during any computer-controlled presentation, leading directly to chaos.

Prior preparation, and lots of it, is essential to making the presentation go smoothly.

You should also be concerned about whether you are adept at simultaneously handling the speaking duties and operating the technology. Too frequently, fumbling with the controls disrupts the speech, or concentration on the talk prevents you from pushing the proper buttons in a timely fashion, either of which results in a disjointed presentation in which the cadence is erratic and the pictures are out of synch with your words. If you have any concern along this line, it makes sense to have someone else operate the machinery while you speak. Finally, it is well not to get carried away by technology. If the multimedia show becomes too slick, the committee or board members may well begin to wonder if there is any substance behind all the glitz.

Another highly effective strategy to banish the single talking head is to bring in *multiple* talking heads: one or more people from the applicant organization or from the population that the applicant is attempting to serve. Try as you might, you will never be able to fully capture the authentic voice of the project or to convey the energy and excitement it generates. Bringing in these leaders allows committee or board members to hear that voice and experience that energy firsthand, and this often has a profound effect on decision making.

Yet even this powerful approach presents many potential pitfalls. It creates an expense that someone must pay, and the expense could be significant if the applicants are at a great distance from the foundation. It also presents a risk, for you have no control over what the representatives might say. One grantmaker tells of an experience in which a guest unexpectedly chided members of the foundation's board for their stinginess in considering a grant of such a modest amount. There is also the danger that the grantseekers will seize the opportunity to make the most of their moment on the stage, and carry their presentation far beyond the allotted time. This, in turn, cuts into the committee or board members' time to ask questions, which might make some of the members wonder if the presentation amounted to an attempt to close off debate and force the request through without its being seriously examined. In fact, some members may feel that the presence of the guests precludes them from raising the tough questions they would like to ask, causing them to resent the whole situation. For these reasons, it may be wise to set aside discussion time with the committee or board without the representatives present, and to guard that time jealously.

For the sake of accuracy, it is important to note that only a minority of private foundations allow program officers to bring in applicants to present to a committee or a board. Even among these foundations, such presentations tend to be unusual events, typically reserved for exceptionally large or complex requests or for those that launch new directions in a foundation's programming.

Presentation Home Runs and Third Rails

Whether you give a straightforward talking-head presentation or one embellished with one or more of the approaches just discussed, there are a number of things you should strive to do—and a number of things you must strive at any cost to avoid—in making the oral presentation. These can be divided neatly into "home runs" (do it and you have scored) and "third rails" (touch it and you are dead).

Home Runs

1. *Recalling that brevity truly is the soul of wit—for board presentations anyway.* Comedians have an excellent rule that all program officers should memorize: leave while they're still laughing. It is good practice to take no more than the allotted time, but it is even better practice to take less time. The presentation should be brief, crisp, and delivered in plain English. Should it appear that the committee or board members are losing interest, it is time to wrap up the presentation immediately, no matter how much longer it might be scheduled to run. The greatest wisdom on this subject comes from the pen of Louis Nizer: "A speaker who does not strike oil in ten minutes should stop boring."

2. *Making the presentation a talk as opposed to a verbatim reading.* A presentation of sorts can be made with eyes glued to the paper and voice firmly set on "monotone," but it is not a performance likely to stir people's souls. You may speak from notes, but you must make eye contact, not just with some fixed point in the middle distance

but with each and every person on the committee or board. After
the presentation, a question-and-answer period is sure to follow,
and it would be better for all concerned if that session were to be a
conversation, as opposed to an interrogation. A conversational presentation, with each member of the committee or board feeling
that you are talking directly to him or her, can help to set the scene
for such a give-and-take session afterwards.

Unless you are a naturally gifted speaker, achieving a conversational presentation will require a good deal of rehearsal. Some
grantmakers disdain rehearsals on the grounds that they are too
busy or that it savors too much of show business. The benefits of
an excellent conversational presentation, however, far outweigh
the costs of the preparation.

3. *Convincing through enthusiasm.* During the presentation, you
become the salesperson for the proposed project. Here, unfortunately, is where your stage fright can come into play. For some
program officers, it is all they can manage to force themselves to
do a workmanlike job of presenting while concealing their unease.
Asking them to whip up some enthusiasm is asking a lot, indeed.
Nonetheless, enthusiasm *matters.* If the salesperson for the project
cannot demonstrate the great opportunity that the project offers,
there are certainly other salespeople and other projects for the
foundation to support. All of this is not to say that you must be a
cheerleader during the presentation; it is to say that you should not
project the gravitas of a Supreme Court justice. Enthusiasm truly
is contagious, and when you are presenting a funding document,
an epidemic of enthusiasm is a welcome affliction.

4. *Using humor—but very sparingly.* Foundations are all over the
map when it comes to the atmosphere of the committee or board
room. In some, the favored mood is one of hushed solemnity; in
others, the preferred atmosphere is informal and light. Obviously,
humor should be banned from presentations to mirthless committees or boards. Even in the less formal settings, you should use
humor only with great care. One program officer remarked, "At
my board meetings, seven people are allowed to be witty, but I ain't
one of them." In less colloquial terms, behavior that is considered
appropriate for an officer or a trustee of the foundation may not
be considered appropriate for a program officer. Humor is best

used strategically, as a change of pace or a tension releaser. Whole categories of humor are off-limits, including anything in questionable taste, of course, but also ad hominem jibes. Never, never do you wish to give the impression that you are laughing at the question being asked or, especially, laughing at the questioner. Even the use of self-deprecating humor is a dicey proposition, for it might call into question your competence or credibility.

What, then, might you use to leaven the presentation? About the only safe type of humor concerns something that bears directly on the requested project. Often an anecdote from a site visit will provide the comic relief needed. For example, one program officer told of how he had been pressing corps members in a youth service program to tell about the program's drawbacks. After several attempts, one young woman finally said she had one to share. She stood, pointed at her pants, and said, "It's these uniforms! They are drop-dead ugly!" This anecdote not only is amusing but also reinforces the recommendation, for it tells the members that the youth being served are happy with the program—they must be, for their biggest complaint is sartorial, not programmatic. Even with "safe" humor, however, it is best to limit yourself to a single use per session, for the worst thing you can do is to project a frivolous or clowning image.

5. *Anticipating questions.* When preparing your presentation, ask yourself, "Were I a member of the committee, what questions would I have about this project?" Then be sure to include the answers to the two or three most important questions. For example, if the request is to make a grant to a new and small organization, trustees will surely have questions about the organization's ability to successfully administer the project. Or if a proposed grantee is controversial, you should address this issue up front. It is better for you to raise such issues, if for no other reason than to prove that you are aware of them and have considered them.

Third Rails

1. *Going on too long.* This is one of the most serious mistakes you can make. Unfortunately, writing a short talk is no easier than writing a short funding document. There is so much that you could

say, and probably should say, that it is difficult indeed to pare it down. Yet pare it down you must, for the longer the presentation, the more restless becomes the audience. One grantmaker relates that when he presented his first funding document, his stage fright caused him to speak too rapidly and for longer than he had planned. After he finally finished, the first thing one of the officers of the foundation said was, "You should look into a new twelve-step program I recently heard about. It's called 'Onandon-Anon.'"

2. *Rehashing information found in the funding document.* The most deadly of all mistakes is simply to read a passage of the document, verbatim, to the committee or board, each member of which has already read the material. Your doing so is very much like saying to members, "You cannot read, so I'll do it for you." Use the presentation to give committee or board members project-related information *not* included in the funding document. Or the presentation can be topical: you can relate the request to a recent news report or journal article. The presentation is an opportunity to offer additional information in support of the requested project. If you use this opportunity to repeat old news, it is simply an opportunity lost.

3. *Ignoring body language.* It is ironic that in an oral presentation, the nonverbal communication often counts as much, if not more, than what is actually said. No matter how eloquent or sensible the words, if you deliver them with a scowl, or if your stance is closed and standoffish, the verbiage is not likely to be heard. You can project feelings of hostility, defensiveness, or unease through nonverbal cues just as easily as through verbal ones, and with the same disastrous results. Always remember to smile, open your stance, and physically relax whenever you are making a presentation.

4. *Dropping names.* Quoting experts to support a point is good practice when used in moderation, but when a parade of authorities, celebrities, and personages wend interminably through the presentation, name dropping ceases to be persuasive and starts to become annoying. Such as approach begins to say to the members of the committee or board, in effect, "People more intelligent, eminent, and important than you support this proposed project, so it would behoove you to do likewise." Great names are like Great Danes: a couple are probably all that can be handled at one time.

Fielding Questions

Once you have made the presentation, there will be time set aside for the committee members or trustees to ask you questions. Typically, any question is fair game, so you need to have done plenty of homework prior to the session. The importance of preserving this question-and-answer (Q&A) period cannot be overstated. Officers and trustees have one job to do in such meetings, and that is to decide whether to fund or decline recommendations. In order to make this decision, they need to have all of their questions answered, and the Q&A period is their only opportunity to get those answers. As mentioned previously, it is wise for you to ensure that they get these opportunities—in fact, that discussion time is maximized.

Once the Q&A session begins, it is important for you to *welcome* the opportunity it presents and to project that feeling to committee or board members. Acting as if you are facing the Spanish Inquisition will immediately create the wrong atmosphere and will probably invite harsher questioning. The Q&A truly is an opportunity for you, for it allows unfiltered communication with the foundation's decision makers. It is a wonderful chance to educate, to experiment, and to test approaches for the future. If you both feel *and* project this attitude, chances are the Q&A session will be a pleasing and productive experience for all involved.

Just as for oral presentations, there are home runs and third rails for Q&A sessions.

Q&A Home Runs

1. *Treating every question as a good one.* Whether it is obvious or subtle, simple or complex, off target or dead on, every question should be treated with respect and answered with care. Starting off the answer with a construction like "I am glad you asked that" lets everyone know that you relish open give-and-take and *want* to answer the question.

2. *Presenting positive body language and facial expressions.* A thoughtful look or a smile telegraphs an engaged, positive program officer. Any other expressions send the wrong messages. Your

standing erect, making eye contact, and being relaxed tell committee and board members that you have confidence in the proposal you are presenting. Again, the nonverbal cues can be more powerful than the verbal messages.

3. *When necessary, disagreeing with committee and board members in a tactful but honest way.* Inevitably, a member will take issue with something found in the funding document or the oral presentation. In responding to this, it is essential that you avoid appearing combative. Obviously, if the member is correct, it is wise to openly and graciously acknowledge that fact. If the dispute is over an interpretation or a matter of opinion, it is usually best for you simply to yield the point. Winning a public argument with an officer or a trustee over a trivial matter is for you the very definition of a Pyrrhic victory. If, however, the dispute is over a matter of fact and the member is clearly mistaken, then you cannot leave the error uncorrected. You should, however, find a tactful way to handle the correction. For example, you might say, "I am glad you raised that point. It is true that the consensus of opinion for many years has been in agreement with the position that you just mentioned, but the most recent research by X and Y indicates that just the opposite is the case." This tack avoids such hot-button words as *wrong*, *incorrect*, and *error*, and lets everyone know that you are both respectful of others and conversant with the latest research.

Q&A Third Rails

1. *Appearing defensive.* No matter how pointed the questions, you must field them with openness and good humor. A single roll of eyes ceilingward suggests contempt for the questioner and can sink even the most lucid presentation. A tone of anger in your voice will cancel out any number of well-made verbal points. You should always drive defensively, but you should never behave that way during a Q&A session.

2. *Making up an answer when you are stumped by a question.* The temptation to do so is enormous. No one, especially one who is supposed to be an expert on a topic, ever wants to admit ignorance. Because officers and trustees make up the audience, doing so seems tantamount to admitting to the boss that you have not

done the necessary homework. And because the audience members are not experts on the subject, chances are that they would believe a plausible fib. Tempted though you may be, you must resist the urge to be "creative" in this fashion. Should you actually be caught in such a fabrication (which will happen sooner or later if you make up enough responses), you will have placed yourself in the unenviable situation of admitting to being either a dissembler or a sloppy researcher. Whether losing one's credibility or losing one's reputation for intellectual rigor is worse can be debated, but what cannot be gainsaid is that neither does you any good. When you are asked a question to which you don't know the answer, it is well to remember Mark Twain's celebrated advice: "Always do right. This will gratify some people, and astonish the rest." A response might be, "That is a very good question. I am embarrassed to say that I do not know the answer to it. However, I will find the answer as soon as I can and get right back to you." You need to do this follow-up and do it as soon as possible. It is a far, far better thing to own up to ignorance on a particular point than to give people grounds to question your integrity and character.

3. *Disrespecting the questions.* This is, by extension, disrespecting the questioner, and it is a very bad move indeed. To indicate, whether verbally or nonverbally, that the question is elementary or that its answer is obvious is to telegraph disrespect. The inappropriate use of humor is equally deadly; seeming to make fun of the question or questioner offers a certain path to alienating people who will shortly be voting on the funding request. You must approach each and every question with courtesy and dignity, as though the passage of the request depends on your response—which it very well might.

After the Q&A Session

After the presentation and Q&A session are completed, you will not likely know for a few hours or even for a few days how it has all come out. Committees or boards at most foundations vote in executive session, and the outcome is relayed to the grantmakers later by various means. Put this time to good use by immediately finding answers to any "stumper" questions and following up on any other requests for information made during the meeting. If these pieces of data can be conveyed to members before the final vote is taken, they can do nothing but make it more likely that the request will pass.

Should the vote go against the proposed project, you must swallow disappointment and seek to discover all you can as to the reasons for the decision. Learning if the problem was in the funding document, the presentation, the response to the questions, or in some other area entirely will improve your chances for success the next time. You need to do this research without betraying anger or defensiveness at the decision; otherwise you are projecting the image of a whiner, not a professional.

Once you have completed this research, you are faced with the distasteful and delicate task of informing the applicant. No matter how heroically you have worked to keep the grantseeker's expectations in check, inevitably the applicant's hopes will be soaring. Having cleared every hurdle up to the final one, the applicant expects that surely committee or board approval is a mere formality, so the bad news will be not just disappointing but also shocking. Clearly, a telephone call is required (or if the applicant is nearby, a visit), for the impersonality of a letter would add egregious insult to what is bound to be considerable injury. This call is likely to be the severest test of your professionalism, for at this late date in the process, everyone knows that you were an advocate for the request and that it must have been voted down by the committee or the board. Yet you must represent the foundation and present the decision as a corporate one. In fact, in order to convey that corporate decision, you must explicitly affirm that you agree with it. You must do this, moreover, while being respectful of the applicant's dignity and sensitive to its disappointment. Given the difficulty all around, it is well that this is not a task that you must often undertake.

Relationships Between You and the Board Members

Presentations, of course, require personal interaction between you and the members of the foundation's board of trustees. Foundations vary widely when it comes to policies about contact between staff and trustees. Some encourage such interactions, on the theory that staff and board can bring mutually useful ideas and experiences to the common enterprise. More common are those foundations that build a veritable Berlin Wall between the two, on the theory that board members should set policy and not get involved in day-to-day operations. The majority of foundations operate between these two extremes, allowing episodic but not consistent contact between board and staff members.

Whatever stance a foundation chooses, it is imperative that it make the rules governing such mixing as straightforward as possible; otherwise, awkward situations will inevitably arise. The classic example occurs when a foundation board member receives a proposal and forwards it to you for disposition. Should you give such a proposal priority attention, or can you place it into a queue with all the others? Has a decision already been made to fund the proposal, or can you place it into the regular review process? Should you work with the board member in responding to this request? Should you merely keep the board member informed? Or does the board member want nothing more to do with the proposal? In the absence of clear rules or instructions, you are placed in a very awkward—and fundamentally unfair—position in having to handle such a request.

No matter what the rules that govern the interaction between board and staff members, you should take care to scrupulously observe them. In those foundations where never the twain shall meet, nothing will make a CEO more nervous than the suspicion that a program officer is "freelancing" with a board member. This kind of situation underlines yet again the crucial importance of creating clear rules to govern such interactions. Here truly is a case where policy ambiguity leads directly to problem superfluity.

Conclusion

The day of the silver-tongued orator belongs to history. Gone is the era when William Jennings Bryan could win a presidential nomination by vowing that mankind shall not be crucified on a cross of gold, or when Winston Churchill could save a nation by offering nothing but blood, toil, tears, and sweat. Nevertheless, you can still do much to boost the chances of passage for the request by making an effective presentation and by satisfactorily answering questions. Any grantmaker can become a first-rate advocate by embracing brevity and enthusiasm, and shunning defensiveness and dissembling. Perhaps the best advice is to avoid making a presentation that fits the *Liberty* magazine definition of a speech, which it likens to cattle horns: "A point here, a point there, and a lot of bull in between."

Chapter Ten

Managing the Project

"When the gods wish to punish you," advises the old proverb, "they make your dreams come true." Many a program officer has learned the truth of these words after the committee or board has funded a project that he or she recommended. The moment you receive approval, your role as program officer once more changes dramatically, and that new role can seem rather punishing compared with that of championing a request. Recall that you begin as a sentry, protecting the foundation's resources from unworthy ideas. Then, when you encounter a good idea and become convinced of its worth, you transform into an advocate for the applicant: a steward. Now, after that advocacy has succeeded and the proposal has become a project, you must shift gears once more and become a manager of the funded project.

Almost inevitably, program officers find management to be the most challenging aspect of their jobs. Part of this, of course, is because management is hard under any circumstances. Squeezing the most out of resources and inspiring people to give their best are challenging even when the manager has authority to attempt these things—and you do not have that authority. What you do have is a distinctive management challenge with which to contend; and with numerous projects in your portfolio, that challenge is multiplied many times over.

What makes this style of management so distinctive is that you are partially responsible for delivering results from an organization of which you are neither an employee nor a board member. Another complication is that frequently the project for which you are responsible represents only a single facet of a very complex organization, and this facet is sometimes far from the top of the organizational priority list. Further, the project may be dependent on "soft money"—other grants from other sources—to fully operate, and these grants will start and stop on a schedule over which you have no control. Small wonder, then, that grantmakers find project management such a challenge: without authority to make things happen and in the midst of many competing priorities, they must somehow manage for results.

It would seem that you have available at least one "big stick" to get these results: the leverage of money. Everyone wants foundation dollars. Everyone wants to stay on your good side. Therefore, even if you have no direct authority, even if the project is not the organization's top priority, and even if soft money comes and goes unpredictably, you can still use the power of the purse to make things happen.

There is some truth to this analysis, but it considerably overstates the case. Although grantseekers need foundation money, grantmakers also need good grantseekers, so the power of the purse is far from absolute. The influence of money, moreover, is always strongest in *prospect*. That is to say, you have maximum influence *before* a grant is made, while the request is still under consideration. The reason for this is simple: although foundations routinely decline grant requests, they only rarely demand that grantees refund the money granted to them; this step, due to the expense, complications, and embarrassment involved, is usually reserved for only those very few grantees that are, like Tom Terrific's nemesis Crabby Appleton, "rotten to the core."

The new grantee knows that disagreements over management of the project almost surely will not lead to the grant's being revoked. If the commitment is for only one year, the foundation has lost nearly all of its leverage; if it is a multiyear grant, you still have some clout in that you can delay or even deny future installments of the commitment. Even in the case of multiyear grants, however, you would much rather see the commitment completed than not. Ironically, then, you have plenty of clout before a project is funded and very little after it is funded, which is naturally when you need it the most.

Despite all of these daunting challenges, you can become a surprisingly effective manager of projects for which you are responsible. You cannot control, but you can influence. You cannot demand, but you can persuade. You cannot buy loyalty, but you can use the power of the purse for positive ends. And, most important, you cannot hire and fire people, but you can promote the growth of a true partnership.

Project Management: The Possible and the Practical

It is possible, at least in theory, for project management in the foundation world to be a model of communication and cooperation. In this scenario, you would be in frequent touch with the project director, not necessarily on a weekly basis, but probably monthly. That communication would not be limited to the written word but would include occasional telephone discussions and at least one site visit during the life of the project. During the visit, you would meet not only with the leaders of the project but also with the top leadership of the institution of which the project is a part. If the project has an advisory board, you might sit on it, and could even help its members raise money in support of the project's activities. It is possible that you would be so engaged that you would not merely react to crises but rather anticipate problems and proactively move to resolve them before they became significant. You would strive to be helpful without being overbearing or dictatorial, and would seek to be engaged, alert, and accessible.

So much for what is theoretically possible. What is practical is usually a different matter. As any grantee who has ever directed a project will testify, program officers rarely, if ever, achieve—or sustain—this level of engagement in managing projects. There are a number of reasons for this, not all of which are under a grant-maker's control. In fact, blame for the leading cause of program officer inattention to management can be laid at the doorstep of America's favorite scapegoat: the U.S. Congress. It was not that Congress, in passing the Tax Reform Act of 1969, meant to crimp program officers' ability to manage funded projects, but the law of unintended consequences took over. As previously mentioned, the Act mandated a minimum payout requirement for private foundations, which has been adjusted a number of times and stands as of this writing at 5 percent of the foundation's net asset value. Failure to meet this yearly target triggers a penalty tax of 100 percent of the shortfall. Although some wiggle room is built into the regulations, the fact remains that the law imposes a "use it or lose it" imperative on private foundations. This is good in that it requires private foundations to fulfill their charitable purposes by making a substantial number of grants. The downside, however, is that a great deal of work is required to ensure that these funds are paid out responsibly. There is always pressure to "get the money out of the door" in a timely and effective way; there is no comparable pressure to provide proactive management for projects that are already funded. Harried program officers, therefore, are often tempted to defer the important but less urgent demands of grants management. One long-time applicant and grantee summed up the situation well in noting wryly, "We would all have been better off if Congress had mandated a 3 percent payout rule, along with a 2 percent grants management rule."

Congress is deserving of a brickbat for this unintended outcome, but there is truly enough blame to go around. Some program officers are very much like entrepreneurs in the business sector. They enjoy the developmental aspect of their job far more than the managerial aspect. If given a choice between developing a promising new project or managing an existing project, they will follow their hearts and pay attention to the new opportunity. A business entrepreneur can use this approach at will, for he or she can sell off interest in an established concern and concentrate on new ventures. Grantmakers do not have that luxury; they are responsible for funded projects even as they are developing new ones. There is a happy balance to be struck between developing and managing, but the combination of the pressure to get money out of the door and the natural entrepreneurial tendencies of some program officers ensures that project management in foundations sometimes fails to achieve that balance.

Although many grantees bemoan this situation, it is fair to note that some find it very much to their liking. Far from missing the coaching, technical assistance, and general hand-holding that a program officer can provide to a project, these folks enjoy operating without close foundation oversight. There is nothing *necessarily* nefarious about this (although it is possible for bad eggs to exploit such a situation), for the vast majority of such grantees simply prefer to operate with several degrees of freedom. Sometimes, in fact, they deliver far more than promised in their proposal. Nonetheless, by studiously refusing to request program officer assistance, they tend to "aid and abet" any grantmaker who is not naturally inclined to practice attentive management.

Management Pitfalls

Grantmakers soon discover that the art of managing funded projects is a difficult one, indeed. There are any number of snares for the unschooled or unwary, and while many could be mentioned, four stand out as the most dangerous.

Fire and Forget

In the U.S. military, there is a class of missiles that is so automated nothing need be done to guide them after they have been launched, hence the nickname "Fire and Forget." Some grantees complain that that is exactly what some program officers do: "fire" (make the grant), then "forget" (ignore the management of the grant). One long-time grantseeker even compares the situation to the rituals of courtship: "There is a first meeting, a few dates, then you are going steady. All this time, grantmakers pay you lots of attention, but after you consummate the relationship—boom! They never call, they never write." There can be no denying that some of this goes on in the relationships between grantmakers and grantees. The need to be thorough in front-end due diligence—to meet, read proposals, write Q&C letters, make site visits—takes time, and the need to meet payout makes these tasks urgent. There is no comparable urgency associated with managing existing grants.

You should always keep in mind, however, Stephen R. Covey's distinction between the urgent and the important (1989). Not all urgent things are important (the ringing telephone urgently demands an answer, but an aluminum siding salesperson may be calling), and not all important things are urgent (providing technical assistance to a funded project will result in greater impact at its close, but the technical assistance need not be delivered today). The fallacy arises when you begin to believe that if a task is not urgent, it is not important—and therefore the truly important task is not merely deferred but actually ignored. Active management is essential in order to maximize project outcomes. To fire and forget may be a good military doctrine (assuming you have the right missile), but it is a bad strategy for grantmaking.

Full Immersion

This is the polar opposite of Fire and Forget—much less common to be sure, but no less problematic. In fact, it is probably worse, because benign neglect is usually better than malign meddling. To continue to use the imagery of relationships, if Fire and Forget is the equivalent of "love 'em and leave 'em," then Full Immersion is the equivalent of an obsessed suitor. In this situation, the program officer becomes inappropriately involved in activities both directly and indirectly relating to the grant. He not only sits on the advisory board for the project but also begins to compete with the project director in the day-to-day management of the project. He not only visits but visits repeatedly. He not only dispenses technical assistance but also delves into personnel issues and budgetary minutiae.

To be truly effective, you need to be, in the parlance of elementary education, "the guide on the side." In the Full Immersion mode, you are the "sage on the stage." It can be tempting, while dispensing technical assistance, to become impatient and finally to wade in and handle matters personally. This is the wrong thing to do on two counts. First, it wrongs the project director, whose responsibility it is to administer the project. Second, it wrongs the foundation, which is paying you to manage several projects, not focus like a laser on the daily operations of a single project. You need to maintain a healthy distance so that you keep the big picture in view.

Ignoring the Good Kids

All parents of a challenging child will recognize the problem: the child who is a handful absorbs all of their energy and attention, while the "good kids" get shortchanged. In the same fashion, problem projects urgently demand your attention, and you spend so much time fighting their fires that there is insufficient time left to manage the good projects. Although fighting fires is good, ignoring high-potential projects most emphatically is not. From the point of view of society, it is bad because so much potential is wasted.

From the point of view of your own portfolio, it is also bad, for the problem projects rarely return great outcomes—and neither will many promising projects if they do not get any of your help. But how can you ignore a plea for help from any funded project? The answer: sometimes it is necessary. It is far better to let a few projects stumble—better even to experience an occasional failure—than to consistently squander latent superb outcomes by allowing potentially great projects to lie fallow.

Moreover, if you have a portfolio full of problem children, it suggests that something is very wrong with the foundation's selection process or with your judgment. A few clinkers are inevitable, no matter how careful the vetting might be. (If a foundation is taking on the proper amount of risk and not simply funding unimaginative "safe" projects, the occasional problem-filled grant is unavoidable.) But a portfolio of grants that is overrun with duds means that poor judgment in selection has become the rule rather than the exception. The important thing is to do what you can for the problems without ignoring the needs of the good kids.

Avoiding the Average

If good kids often get the short end of the stick, the average kids often get no stick at all. One grantmaker put it this way: "Once you have gotten the grant, if you never want to see me again, just perform in a consistently mediocre fashion. If you louse up, I will be there to bail you out. If you excel, I will be there to work with you on expansion or on bringing the project to scale. But if you don't screw up and don't distinguish yourself either, I will be somewhere else: with a flop or a star." Unless you are making grants in the foundation-world equivalent of Garrison Keillor's Lake Wobegon—where all of the commitments are above average—it is true that in grants management, the bad is the enemy of the good, and both are the enemies of the average. The mediocre project is easiest to ignore because it is not itself on fire, nor does it appear as if it is going to set the world on fire. This is an understandable calculation for you to make, but it is fallacious on two counts. First, it shortchanges the project, which, if it was worth funding in the first place, is probably worth helping now. Second, it shortchanges society, for although troubled projects rarely can be elevated all the way to being high in impact, average projects often are not that far away from excellence, and sometimes a little technical assistance from you is just the missing ingredient. For these reasons, you should never ignore the average.

Techniques of Grants Management

As we have seen, grants management offers any number of opportunities to do a truly lousy job. Doing a superb job poses a tougher challenge, but there are techniques you can use in which to manage all the "kids": the good, the bad, and even the average. Perhaps the most important techniques are those with which the grant is launched: the notification of the grantee and the postaward conference call.

Notifying the Grantee

Nearly any grantmaker, when asked about a favorite part of the job, will surely say, "notifying applicants that they have gotten the grant." Typically, this is done by telephone (hence the grantseeker aphorism, "Bad news comes by letter; good news comes by phone"). The news is sure to touch off a celebration and possibly even headlines in the local press. In fact, notification is such an exhilarating occasion that it simply is not a good time to do much except give the good news. Some program officers attempt to review the legal conditions of the grant and the foundation's expectations during this initial call, but most find that the new grantee needs a time to celebrate before it is able to focus on the legal details of the grant relationship. For you it is probably not a good time to cover such weighty details, either, because bearing good news is a much rarer experience for you than delivering tidings of gloom and doom. Perhaps you and the grantseeker can be forgiven your giddiness at the moment of notification, which is surrounded before and after by so much hard work, uncertainty, and risk.

You might wish to consider, from time to time, allowing others to share in this moment of joy. Associates, assistants, and secretaries often must be the ones to deliver bad news to an applicant, so it is appropriate that, now and then, they get a chance to pass along tidings of great joy.

Making the Postaward Conference Call

Once the euphoria has subsided, anywhere from a day to a week after notification, it will be useful to conduct a postaward conference call. A grant agreement is a legal and binding contract between the foundation and the grantee. The terms of the contract will be spelled out explicitly in the commitment letter, but you should not count on the grantee closely reading, understanding, or acting on what is often a long, dry, and legalistic communication. Some do not read it all, others read it and do not take it seriously, still others do not understand it, while yet others understand it but later forget about it. A postaward conference call, during which you can explain the arcane provisions of the commitment letter in detail, will get everybody off on the right foot. The next paragraphs cover a number of key issues that should be discussed during the course of this conversation.

1. *Acceptance of the grant.* Foundations vary in their requirements on this subject. Some insist on a formal letter from the grantee's CEO, stating that he or she has read the foundation's commitment letter, understands its terms and conditions, and accepts them. Others require that the CEO or the project director countersign and return a copy of the foundation's commitment letter. Still others say that, by cashing the foundation's check, the grantee agrees to abide by all of the foundation's grant terms and conditions. Whatever the policy in effect, the first step in the conference call is to make sure that the grantee understands the terms of the commitment letter and makes the proper acceptance.

2. *The budget and its line items.* Most foundations stipulate that any deviations from the approved line items require prior approval from the program officer. Over the course of the project, the grantee will probably find it desirable to make some such adjustments, so it is well to emphasize the need for the grantee to get permission *before* doing so. Other budgetary issues to cover, depending on the policies of the foundation, might include whether new line items can be created, whether money earmarked for one funded project can be transferred to another, the minimum expenditures required by the foundation during any given grant period, and whether the foundation will allow the grantee to employ offsets

(diverting organizational funds that would have been spent on the project to other needs because the foundation has made the grant). Finally, you should also discuss the foundation's policy regarding carry-forward amounts. If the grantee does not spend all of the funds allotted during the first year of the commitment, does the foundation allow the grantee to carry these funds forward to the next year of the commitment, or must the organization return unexpended amounts? Alternatively, will the foundation allow the grantee to carry the funds forward but then reduce the next year's payment by that amount? Settling these issues at the start will prevent budgetary mayhem down the road.

3. *Management ground rules.* Reviewing the project's management structure and reporting lines with the grantee is sensible. You should reach an agreement with the grantee as to how much technical assistance the project can expect to receive from you, how accessible you will be by telephone, and whether the project can expect a visit during the life of the commitment. You also need to make it clear that you *must* be notified about changes in the project's management. Nothing is quite so mortifying to the grantmaker as to be the last to know about major changes in the leadership of one of his or her projects. As one grantmaker remarked, "The only surprise I have ever liked in my entire life was when my husband threw me a surprise birthday party. And I didn't even like that surprise very much."

4. *Reporting requirements.* Grantees deserve to know exactly what is expected of them in regard to reporting on project progress. Exactly what kind of reporting—narrative, financial, other—is expected, and by what deadlines? What essential information must be included in the reports? What are the sanctions for being late with the reports? In particular, can failure to report lead to a decision to postpone or cancel subsequent payments? Might the foundation even demand repayment of a grant? How will the evaluation feedback system be fine-tuned so that everyone is benefiting from the lessons learned?

5. *Timelines.* The grantee should be given unambiguous instructions regarding the timelines according to which you expect the project to unfold. If a project falls behind schedule, is it possible for the grantee to request an extension of time (without receiving additional funds) before reporting? Is there any deadline that,

if missed, will cause subsequent payments to be deferred or canceled? Will it be necessary to renegotiate project benchmarks or evaluation plans?

6. *Renewed or second-stage funding.* It is good practice to address this nettlesome issue at the beginning of a grant relationship, because many grantees firmly believe that getting a grant is very much like passing the bar examination: get over that hurdle, and you are qualified to practice for life. They truly feel that, ample evidence to the contrary notwithstanding, the grant should be perpetually renewable, so long as they return satisfactory outcomes. The message here needs to come in two parts. First, poor performance will doom any chances for second-stage funding. Second, good performance, even stellar performance, provides no guarantee of second-stage support. The foundation may, for any number of reasons, including poor portfolio growth or shifts in priorities, decide to refuse requests for further support. You need to stress this up front so that the project can quickly seek to diversify sources of funding.

These are the six major issues, but there can be others as well. Some program officers prefer to cover every provision in the commitment letter during the call; others prefer to cover only the most important ones. In any case, the overarching message you deliver should be one of encouraging open communication. Bad news should be shared just as quickly and just as openly as good news. One of the leading causes of rotten project outcomes is the fact that project directors are often afraid to share little problems with their program officer; these problems can then metastasize into big problems before the program officer learns of them, and by then it is too late. You need to explain to grantees that sharing bad news will not be held against them; in fact, doing so will be *helpful* to the relationship. You must resolve never to shoot the messenger but instead to accept the bad news professionally and calmly. Both you and grantee must resolve to work as a team in order to maximize the possible outcomes.

Types of Technical Assistance

All projects need technical assistance (TA) at some level. All program officers are (or at least should be) qualified to provide some type of TA at some level. In most cases, however, program officers possess neither the time nor the qualifications to provide all the TA that a project needs. Deciding what is needed, how much of that you can provide, and how much must be provided by others, is one of the ongoing challenges of project management.

This challenge is exacerbated by the fact that the grantees often do not know—or perhaps do not want to admit—their needs. During the proposal stage, many grantseekers feel that any admission of shortcomings could be seized upon by the grantmaker as an excuse to decline the proposal (and more than a few have experienced such treatment). Once the proposal is funded, this belief carries forward, transforming into a conviction that any admission of need could be seized upon by a program officer as a pretext for not renewing support for a grant (and more than a few have experienced this treatment, too). Both before and after funding, then, many applicants and grantees feel a strong need to bluff their way through. You must keep a wary eye on the situation, respond promptly to any calls for help, and be watchful for opportunities to offer help without waiting to be asked.

The types of TA needed by grantees are many, but among the most commonly encountered are assistance with personnel management, strategic planning, fundraising, strategic communications, public policy work, and networking. How much of this TA you can personally provide depends on your expertise and available time. If you were a fundraiser before coming to the foundation, for example, you might give the grantee invaluable assistance on that subject. In areas where you are not qualified to help, you might call in consultants to fill the gap. The key shortage here is not one of expertise (there are plenty of consultants to choose from) nor even necessarily one of money (it is usually sensible to include a line item for TA consultants from the beginning). The key shortage is that of your time. In fact, even when you are an expert on a given topic, the needs of the grantee may be so profound that they overwhelm the time you can devote to them. In such cases, you must call a consultant. Similarly, sometimes what seems to be a simple TA issue becomes, once you begin delving into it, a time-burner that requires consulting help. Generally speaking, money spent on TA consulting is money well invested, and it will pay dividends in improved project outcomes.

Use and Misuse of Consultants

Changes in the management of corporate America during the last two decades of the twentieth century have loosed a veritable army of consultants upon the land. At the same time, there has grown up an industry of consultants-by-choice, both in firms and as solo practitioners. Never before has it been possible to find so much "rent-a-talent" and in so many different areas of expertise. With so many consultants to choose from, it is inevitable that their skills and abilities are all over the map. Hiring a consultant, therefore, requires that you exercise due diligence first, just as if you were hiring an employee. Consultants have many legitimate uses but can also be misused in the management of projects.

As previously noted, consultants are needed to fill expertise gaps, which occur when neither you nor the project staff possess certain essential skills. Because they are not "too close" to the project, consultants bring fresh perspectives and new ideas. Like hired guns in days of yore, consultants can bring instant firepower to any project. Because they have many clients, they can bring to the table both wide experience and a ready-made network. And because they are not employees, they can be rapidly brought on and moved out as the needs of the project evolve.

There are many problems, however, associated with overreliance on consultants. Perhaps the most serious is the problem of mobile capacity. When the staff rely too much on consultants, they do not get adequate opportunities to absorb lessons and grow. Then, when the consultants leave, they take the capacity with them. Another problem is that of divided attention. Even when they are physically on location at a project, consultants are sometimes not fully "there." Trying to keep multiple clients happy, they occasionally have to give one short shrift in order to adequately serve another. Consultants can also be used to evade responsibility. "I only did what the consultant suggested" is a plaintive cry program officers hear all too often. The consultant has long since decamped, the project director blames the consultant, and no one is willing to take responsibility for the action. A final problem associated with consultants is that, because consultants are not employees, difficulties may arise due to lax supervision of their work or job assignments that are not clearly defined. Consultants, in short, are very much like dynamite: powerful, but useful only when handled carefully.

Withholding Payments and Terminating Grants

As mentioned previously, once a grant is made, you lose a lot of clout. If the commitment is for multiple years, however, you retain some measure of leverage because subsequent payments are scheduled. The transgressions that could trigger withholding those payments include budgetary improprieties, reporting irregularities, and failure to achieve satisfactory progress toward outcomes. It is necessary to spell out the consequences for such transgressions during the postaward conference call. You need to discuss a number of key questions with grantees. What are the exact rules regarding the budget? What reporting is required, and by what deadlines? What benchmarks of progress must be achieved, and according to what timeline?

Should the grantee violate these agreements, you will need to follow up swiftly, for if the grantee can break the rules once and experience no consequences, chances are that the first transgression will not be the last. When you withhold payment, you will need to be quite clear to the grantee as to why you are doing so; you will also need to be very explicit as to what the grantee must do, and according to what timeline, in order to release the payment. Nothing motivates a grantee to make changes quite as quickly as experiencing a payment being held in abeyance.

Terminating a grant is the foundation equivalent of a thermonuclear weapon. It is a tremendous deterrent, but one that should never be used, except as a last resort. The reason for this is simple: it is an admission that the project has irretrievably broken down. This situation makes no one proud and makes no one look good, so everyone would like to find some other honorable solution. Needless to say, termination should be reserved for the most egregious offenses—for example, the project director has absconded with money—or for situations in which repeated warnings have been flouted.

If a decision is made to terminate a grant, the unexpended grant dollars must be returned to the foundation. A thornier question is whether the foundation should demand the return of the grant dollars that have already been expended. Generally, foundations avoid making such a demand, due to the complications involved. The erstwhile grantee often does not have the means to repay the funds, and legal action to force a refund might cost more than the amount to be recovered. In fact, any return of funds is a surprisingly difficult and costly thing. Foundations are set up as essentially one-way financial streets, designed for moving money out of the door. Moving money back through that door is expensive and time-consuming, which is therefore another good reason to be circumspect about terminating grants.

Exit Strategy

Some sage once remarked, "It is easier to put your hand into a machine than it is to remove it." Grant relationships are much like that machine. A foundation should never get into one without an idea of how it will get out. More strictly speaking, a foundation needs exit strategies tailored to fit the many different kinds of grants they make. For some grants, the commitment is for a single year for a defined project, and that is that. For others, the commitment is the first in a series that may stretch for dozens of years, with the exit occurring only when a significant societal change has occurred. And there are all types of exit strategies in between these two extremes.

The most important piece of advice when it comes to exit strategies is "Do not promise to buy frogs when you are shown tadpoles." A tadpole may develop into a frog. It also may die, get eaten, or disappear without a trace. Foundations should be very careful about making long-range commitments before they have even short-term outcomes to guide them. In fact, it is wise always to leave the exit door ajar in case the hoped-for results come a-cropper. This is not to say that a foundation should abandon a project just because it gets off to a slow start; it is to say that no foundation should ever put itself into the position of perpetually supporting a project that will never deliver the desired outcomes.

The exit strategy usually consists of a number of coordinated substrategies. Among them might be a substrategy for promoting financial sustainability of the project; a substrategy for communicating news of its accomplishments to key audiences; a substrategy to help the grantee develop its leadership; or a substrategy to develop supportive public policy. The total exit strategy should be developed in consultation with the grantee and should be monitored constantly for progress.

The foundation should have an actual date of exit in mind, but it is not always necessary, or even wise, to share this date with the world. If a set date is announced prematurely, it can cause panic among the grantee's employees and other funders. A date set quietly can just as quietly be extended if the project is not ready for the transition, or it can be moved up if the project is successful in diversifying its support sooner than expected. But it is always wise to have an exit date in mind. The longer a foundation supports a project, the more it discourages the grantee's attempts to broaden its funding base. The exit strategy thus helps the foundation to avoid fostering a dependence that will hamper the development of the project.

Conclusion

What separates exemplary management of funded projects from merely adequate management? In a word, *anticipation*. Those program officers who merely react to events are better than those who practice fire-and-forget grantmaking, of course, but they are still guilty of failing to get the most out of a project. If you anticipate needs, head off troubles, and foresee opportunities, you will succeed in converting more of the project's potential into actual outcomes. Your anticipating in this way is the ultimate in adding value, for doing so costs the foundation nothing that it would not be spending anyway. The grant is already made. You will receive your salary in any case. But if some of your time is devoted to anticipatory management, then the impact of the grant dollars can be maximized—perhaps even multiplied. Here truly is a practical way to achieve the foundation ideal of "helping others help themselves."

Chapter Eleven

Closing the Project

The story is told of a king who called in a wise elder and issued a command to devise a sentence, using only four words, that would be true at all times and under any circumstances. After much deliberation, the elder spoke the following words: "This, too, shall pass." The elder's wisdom certainly applies to funded projects; sooner or later they all must pass into closure. You are faced with deciding when to come to closure, then with the bigger task of maximizing learning and multiplying impact. This chapter will discuss how to close the project in such a way as to maximize learning; the next chapter will concentrate on multiplying impact. You need to do these tasks while maintaining a good relationship with the grantee and while paying attention to other important duties, such as developing new projects and managing funded ones.

To Renew or Not to Renew?

Very few foundation grants are made for terms longer than four years, and fewer yet are made renewable on an indefinite basis. A small number are made with the explicit understanding that after the term of the commitment has expired, the grantees can never again request a cent's worth of support for the project. The great majority of all foundation grants, then, are made with the implicit or explicit understanding that the foundation reserves the right to renew the grant and also reserves the right to decline interest in funding the project again. The logic behind this open-ended approach is unassailable. When the grant is made, it is impossible to predict whether a project will be a success or a failure, and it is equally imponderable as to whether the value of the foundation's corpus will rise or fall. Given the project's uncertain prospects for success, and given the unknowability of how much money the foundation will have available to give in the future, it would be folly either to give the grantee a perpetual blank check or to set an arbitrary drop-dead point. It is sensible to monitor results as the project unfolds, then to decide later whether or not it is logical to renew the commitment.

As reasonable as it is for the foundation to take this position, one must remember that its attendant uncertainty makes the whole experience very hard on grantees. It is best for all concerned to make this policy, and the logic behind it, explicit very early in the foundation's relationship with the grantee. In fact, even before the grant is made, you should make it clear to the grantee that even *if* the grant is made, there will be no guarantees of future support. It should be *mandatory* to include language to this effect in the commitment letter sent after the grant has been made. If the policy is left unstated or implied, the grantee will almost surely believe, as has been mentioned, that as long as it is doing a good job, it should expect ongoing renewals of the foundation's financial support for the duration of its project. This attitude is understandable. After all, it is usually difficult, costly, and time-consuming to secure the foundation's support, and it is disheartening for the grantee to think that, in a mere year or two, the process will have to be started all over again. This is a misunderstanding between foundation and grantee that can and should be avoided, assuming that the foundation communicates its position clearly enough and often enough.

As discussed in Chapter Ten, it is highly useful for a foundation to have in place an exit plan well before the grant comes to an end, and preferably before the grant starts. The exit strategy should not be carved in stone, however. Many a project experiences a slow start but is nonetheless laden with potential to deliver tremendous outcomes. One of the sins of foundations is the tendency to give up too early on funded projects. Just as CEOs in the commercial sector are often guilty of focusing only on the next quarter's profits, so do some program officers focus only on the short-term results. If these are not spectacular, such grantmakers refuse to provide additional support. In the grantee's world, however, it is a tall order to produce instant success. The organization must gain trust, it must form and nurture relationships, and both people and institutions must change their habits and behaviors. All this takes time, which is, it seems, the one thing that some foundations are unwilling to give.

This problem is exacerbated by a tendency on the part of applicants to overpromise in their proposal in order to get the grant. As one program officer put it, with tongue in cheek, "Some proposals guarantee to deliver water from the Fountain of Youth in the Holy Grail, and place it for safekeeping into a perpetual motion machine." If you do not challenge these unrealistic projections and undeliverable promises, they will become the official goals of the project. Then, when the project inevitably cannot deliver on such goals, it is easy for observers to conclude that the project is a failure, even if what has been achieved is worthwhile or even impressive. In his book *Paper Lion*, George Plimpton (1966) reported that it was said of the great Detroit Lions quarterback Bobby Layne that he never lost a game—it was just that, on a few occasions, he ran out of time. The same could be said for many grantees, but for them the loss of foundation support often means the end of the game.

With this in mind, the foundation's exit strategy should be flexible, so that you have the ability to give late bloomers a second chance and to take into account the practicality of the project's goals when assessing performance. After all, it is better for the grantee to achieve 75 percent of an unrealistically high goal than to achieve 100 percent of an unrealistically low goal. It is not unusual for a project to require five to ten years of support in order to really take off and, by dint of its impressive outcomes, to begin to attract other funders. Patience is a virtue when it comes to considering second-stage funding—or even third- or fourth-stage funding in some cases—and this virtue is often rewarded with excellent outcomes. This is not to say that a foundation should continue to throw good money after bad for projects that are clearly failing; it is to say that premature withdrawal does no one any good. It certainly does not help the project, but it is also bad policy for the foundation, which will soon find it is developing a pattern of funding promising ideas that always seem mysteriously to fizzle before reaching their goals.

Making Sense of Grantee Reports

Your program officer's toolbox contains four implements that will help you make the right decision about whether to continue funding or to cut the foundation's losses. Although all are not equally valuable, each has its merits, and each should be used as appropriate.

Interim Reports and Site Visits

Most foundations require at least one interim narrative and financial report during the course of a funded project. Typically, these are required on an annual basis. One such report provides a valuable insight into how the project is developing, but multiple interim reports allow for a better sense of how the project is improving (or deteriorating) over time. The site visit to the funded project, of course, is an invaluable firsthand opportunity for you to assess how the grantee's efforts are faring. If you study the interim reports assiduously, paying particular attention to the progress of the project in answering the important evaluation questions, and if you make the site visit, chances are that you will form a very good notion of whether renewal of funding is merited even before the term of the grant has expired.

Final Financial Report

This report offers a wealth of precise data, but the meaning of that data is notoriously difficult to discern. For example, let us suppose that during the course of the project, the grantee requested permission to make numerous shifts of grant funds from one line item to another, and even secured permission to create new line items. The final financial report, therefore, bears little resemblance to the originally submitted budget. What does this mean? Does it signify that the grantee is a poor planner and an indifferent financial manager? Or might it be that the grantee is wonderfully flexible and adept at seizing unforeseeable opportunities? Another example: the final financial report reveals that the grantee still has a balance of grant funds left unspent. What does this mean? Does it signify that the grantee lacks energy and is not competent to complete the project according to the agreed-on timeline? Or might it be that the grantee is a careful financial manager, has found ways to economize and leverage funds, and is getting maximum bang for the foundation's buck?

The answers to these questions, of course, are a matter of interpretation, and the basis for making the judgment must come from the interim and final narrative reports, from site visits, and from the project evaluator's assessment. There are, however, a few things you can learn unambiguously from final financial reports. If the numbers do not add up, especially if there are big discrepancies, it means trouble. If the numbers reveal a series of unrequested and unauthorized line-item changes, it means trouble. If a *huge* amount of grant funds remain unspent, it raises many concerns. Is the grantee using the award as a de facto endowment? Why is the grantee asking for a second grant if it is nowhere near completing the first? Would not the more appropriate course be an extension of time without any additional funds at present? Finally, it is a good precaution to check that the financial report has been signed by two people, preferably the CEO and the chief financial officer of the grantee organization. This reduces (but does not wholly eliminate) the likelihood that one dishonest person is "cooking the books."

Final Narrative Report

This is an important tool for making the decision to renew or not to renew, but it is a flawed tool. Simply put, the project director, who is writing the report, has a vested interest in putting the best face on things. As a program officer notes, "Final narrative reports are a lot like corporate annual reports. Every year is always a 'very good year.'" The final narrative report, unlike the final financial report, does not need to add up, so it is highly likely that the project director will make every effort (borrowing from Johnny Mercer) to "ac-cent-tchu-ate the positive, eliminate the negative."

It should be acknowledged that there are many project directors who are very conscientious about writing balanced final reports. Even in the case of the majority who accentuate the positive in their reporting, not all is lost; in fact, there are several useful items of information to be gleaned from such reports. First, what outcomes did the project director decide to highlight? How do these compare to the original goals of the project? What might explain any discrepancies? Second, disappointing outcomes may sometimes be simply omitted from the report. What was left out and why? Third, does the narrative report agree with the financial report? If the narrative touts the outcomes achieved by intensive work in one area and the line item for that area is badly underspent, what explains the apparent contradiction? Fourth, is the narrative report generally consistent with the interim reports and your own observations from the site visit? If not, what explains the inconsistency? Fifth, how well does the project director's assessment of outcomes match that of the project evaluator? Presumably more objective than the project director, the evaluator should be able to render a more dispassionate judgment on the outcomes. If the two reports do not agree, it certainly suggests that you should investigate the discrepancy before making a decision on renewal of funding.

Final Evaluation Report

This is the most useful tool in the box. The evaluator is being paid explicitly to observe the project and assess its outcomes. As a third party formally employed by neither the foundation nor the grantee, the evaluator should not have any particular ax to grind. Of all the reports, therefore, the evaluator's is likely to be the most objective and the most useful for determining next steps. This is not to say, however, that the evaluator is a *completely* disinterested party. Two factors, one human and the other financial, make pure neutrality impossible.

The human factor springs from the fact that the evaluator has worked with the grantee during most or all of the project. This means that the evaluator has forged either good or poor working relationships with the project's leaders and thus has become either attached to or disaffected from the project. Obviously, attachment is likely to bias the evaluator in favor of positive outcomes (he or she likes the people or believes in the project); disaffection is likely to bias the evaluator in favor of negative outcomes (he or she dislikes the people or has lost faith in the project).

The financial factor enters the picture because the evaluator, whether paid directly by the foundation or indirectly by the foundation through the grantee, probably wants to continue the relationship should the grant be renewed and also probably wants to be the evaluator for other foundation-funded projects in the future. Some evaluators fear that a negative evaluation report would not be appreciated by the grantee or the foundation and might result in their getting replaced as the project goes into second-stage funding. Similarly, the evaluator may fear that a negative report could land him or her on a foundation "list" of proscribed evaluation consultants. Such fears are usually groundless, for most grantees and foundations recognize the value of constructive criticism, but every evaluator of any experience has a horror story to tell about the dangers of being too frank in his or her evaluation report.

Usually the human and financial biases, if evident at all in a report, are very subtle in nature. Only rarely do they get as blatant as those related by a program officer for a large midwestern foundation: "I had a project about which everyone in the state, from the governor's office to neighborhood groups, was bitterly complaining. Everyone was very vocal and very public about their dissatisfaction with the project and its director. Yet the evaluator, in his summative report, raved about how wonderful the project was and about how well respected its director was. I was stunned—it was as if the evaluator was the only one in the state who didn't know—but of course, he had gotten an earful from some of the same people who had complained to me."

Fortunately, that sort of outright prevarication is an extreme rarity. Nonetheless, it is important to recall that evaluators, third parties though they may be, cannot be completely impartial. Yet even after you have taken this caveat into account, the evaluator's report truly provides the sharpest tool in the box. The evaluator may have biases, but they are generally milder than yours or those of the project director. Although it is true that a summative report done by an evaluator brought in exclusively for that purpose may be more objective than one done by the project's formative evaluator (the purely summative evaluator would not have had the chance to become either attached to or disaffected from the project), it is still acceptable to have one evaluator do both. After all, the formative evaluator knows more about the project after having worked on it for so long.

Summative evaluations are of more value to you if they are clearcut as opposed to equivocal. It is difficult to decide on a course of action if the report offers mostly ambiguous conclusions. Summative evaluators are most valuable when they offer lessons that can be learned by both grantee and foundation alike, so that the grantees may improve their future performance and the program officers may sharpen their grantmaking skills. You are wise to cultivate a candid and open relationship with evaluators, the better to encourage them to tell the whole story in summative evaluation, whether that story be good, bad, or indifferent.

If there is no external evaluator, and the evaluation is being done by the project management team themselves, there is an obvious danger of the report being tainted by self-interest. In such cases, it is important for you and the grantee to clearly agree on the key evaluation questions, milestones, and targets in advance, before the grant commences. If you have this agreement, both interim and final reports can be used to measure progress or to explain why expected goals are not being met.

Closing Summary Statement

Once all of the reports are in and read, and once you have settled on a course of action—to renew or not to renew—it becomes desirable to document the closing of the file (or at least the closing of this phase of the project, should funding for it be renewed). Some foundations do not require such a step, but others do, under a variety of names. I will use the term *closing summary statement* in this book, but other terms, such as *program officer final assessment*, would do just as well.

In essence, the closing summary statement is meant to achieve three things. First, it should communicate your assessment of the key outcomes of the project, including any products it may have produced. Second, it should cite authorities for these judgments. Third, and most important, it should consider the lessons learned from this project and apply them in order to make recommendations for future action, whether for this project specifically, for the foundation's programming in general, or for policymaking.

These are all fairly straightforward propositions, excepting the third one. Some program officers tend to shy away from the advocacy implied in making recommendations for future action. Their distaste is revealed in tepid or weak suggestions. This failure to market strong project outcomes is an error that could cost the grantee, and the field, dearly. You should write a recommendation for future action in much the same way as a funding document: there must be clarity and enthusiasm, and the emphasis must be placed on the *opportunity* offered to the foundation by its renewing grant support for the project or by pursuing other approaches to programming suggested by this project. You should also make the case with adequate documentation to lend substance to the enthusiasm. It should be a clarion call to action, not a whimper for additional money.

In the creation of every closing summary statement, you will encounter a vexing conundrum. Unlike a funding document or a set of field notes, which focus on future activities, the closing summary statement focuses on things that have already happened. In writing it, then, you are essentially rating your own performance as a grantmaker. And because your superiors in the organization will be reviewing the closing summary statement, it becomes a de facto performance review document. Hence the conundrum: the closing summary statement is valuable only if it is filled out candidly, yet too much candor might come back to haunt you later. You may also wonder, What if my colleagues are turning in glowing reports in all of their closing summary statements, and I am the only one honestly reporting problems?

In tackling this conundrum, one school of thought descends from Oliver Cromwell's admonition to a portraitist to paint him "warts and all." Be bluntly honest, say program officers of this persuasion, and leave performance review to the foundation's officers. Another school says, in effect, that program officers should not be expected to braid the rope that will later be used to hang them. Devotees of this school therefore resolutely imitate the project directors of their grants and accentuate the positive in their closing summary statements.

Perhaps the best response steers a course between these two extremes but veers far closer to the warts-and-all approach than to the "praise the Lord and braid no rope" camp. It is a bad policy to repeatedly claim perfectly satisfactory outcomes for every project. Officers soon note this Pollyannaish approach and begin to doubt the credibility of the creator of such consistently glowing closing summary statements. The truth is always the best policy, but it makes sense to smooth off the bluntness. For example, how one chooses words becomes very important. If a project did not achieve all of its goals, you should note that fact in the closing summary statement, but you need not describe it as a "failure," "breakdown," or "disaster." If the project achieved 90 percent of its goals, note that first, before candidly discussing the 10 percent shortfall. Give explicit credit for all the project's accomplishments and explain the missteps. Take great care to make the reporting emphasis proportional to the outcome. For example, if the project was 75 percent successful and 25 percent less successful, then you should spend about three-quarters of the report on the successful items. Dwelling endlessly on what went wrong can make even the most effective project appear to be a dud. There is no reason why honesty must be tactless; candid assessments need not be wrapped in "red flags."

Making Use of Lessons Learned

Learning is important for its own sake, but lessons reveal their real power when they are put to use. First, the lessons learned from the conduct of a project can be disseminated to practitioners, academics, and policymakers, and can also be used to expand the project into a program with multiple locations—perhaps even to bring the program to a national scale. In the longer run, these lessons can inform and improve the way grantmaking is done at the foundation.

Harvesting the lessons learned closes the loop on program work. Grantmaking begins with scanning and priority setting, continues with strategic planning, goes through the phases of funding and evaluating projects, and after the lessons are learned and tested by dissemination, their full meaning is reflected on. Finally, the lessons learned are fed back into a new round of scanning and priority setting. Indeed, the entire cycle can be depicted as a circle, or wheel, as shown in Figure 11.1.

Although many metaphors could be applied to describe this wheel, perhaps the best one is agricultural. Starting with scanning and priority setting, and moving clockwise, the first four activities

Figure 11.1. The Grantmaking Cycle.

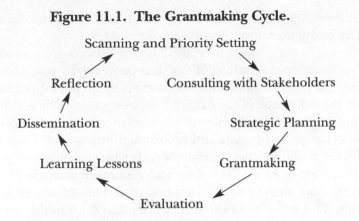

represent a sowing of ideas and dollars. The last four represent a reaping of lessons and outcomes. Because the process is circular rather than linear, there is no single starting point, but for purposes of description, we'll begin at the top.

1. *Scanning and priority setting.* Activities under this rubric include the first three found under the heading "The Five Steps in Setting Priorities" in Chapter One: niche identification, literature reviews, and scans of other foundations' programming. These steps establish the intellectual underpinnings of any grants program.

2. *Consulting with stakeholders.* This heading contains the two remaining priority-setting approaches discussed in Chapter One: consulting with those who will be affected by grantmaking in a particular area, including the disenfranchised, and possibly making a few small experimental grants (sometimes referred to as program testing). These efforts guarantee that the program will be designed to meet the needs and desires of the people it is intended to help.

3. *Strategic planning.* Armed with data, responses from stakeholders, and lessons from the learning grants, the foundation enters a formal process of structuring the grantmaking program, including setting goals, establishing timelines, and allocating resources.

4. *Grantmaking.* Once the strategic plan is in place, the program of grant investment can proceed in earnest. Although the initial direction of the grants will be determined by the three previous steps, midcourse corrections will be made as lessons are learned

from the projects. Included here as well are such activities as formative evaluation and networking of grantees.

5. *Evaluation.* Midcourse and closing lessons are provided by the summative evaluation of funded projects, by evaluations of clusters of projects, and sometimes even by meta-evaluations that assess the full range of the foundation's programmatic activities. It should be noted, however, that evaluation is best understood as a process for gathering data and recommending action. Final *responsibility* for making action decisions rests with the program staff.

6. *Learning lessons.* The data and recommendations provided by evaluators must be read, discussed, and then translated into decisions. This act of synthesis and leadership does not occur spontaneously; time must be set aside for it, and the foundation must budget resources to ensure that it happens.

7. *Dissemination.* Once the lessons have been digested, they can be further refined by sharing this valuable information with practitioners, academics, or policymakers. This information is often used to support an expansion of the project to other sites, but preliminary lessons should be shared widely with all who can use them. Taking a proprietary attitude toward lessons learned is not only fundamentally selfish but actually counterproductive, for a foundation's impact is greatly limited if the lessons it has learned remain unknown.

8. *Reflection.* Once disseminated, the lessons will be commented on, criticized, refuted, validated, or amplified by outsiders. For the foundation, this process will provide new lessons to be learned, as some of the old lessons will be disproved, many more will be validated, and most will be modified in some fashion. It is important for you to consider the meanings of these lessons and their implications for how you do your job. Again, opportunities for reflection do not occur spontaneously. Time and resources must be specifically budgeted so that foundation staff can consider what has been learned from past programming and apply these lessons to future activities. It is especially important to conduct deliberate and systematic reflection, for the highly tested and refined lessons learned during this eighth stage on the wheel will be invaluable in informing the next round of priority setting and scanning.

And so it is that information, data, and lessons flow around the wheel, with experience informing new ventures, and new knowledge improving on old practice. Unfortunately, some foundations do not fully maximize the power of the wheel. Too few take the time to systematically harvest their lessons, fully reflect on the meaning of those lessons, and energetically share them with the outside world. These are all opportunities lost, for it is good professional practice to become very intentional in maximizing the foundation's ability to capture, assimilate, and broker information.

Conclusion

Closing a project obviously marks the end of a relationship. But it also marks a beginning, for ideas and lessons extracted from the now-closed project will be inserted into the continuous process of renewing the grantmaking program. All foundations should understand and appreciate the circular process illustrated by the programming wheel and explicitly take the time to fully harvest lessons and thoughtfully reflect on their meaning. Failing to embrace every function on the wheel, especially those of harvesting and reflection, is akin to making shrewd investments in the stock market and then refusing to cash the dividend checks. The wise elder said, "This, too, shall pass," but it appears that this statement really is not true at all times and under every circumstance. At least one exception can be found in the work of programming: the lessons learned from projects never really pass away; they are "plowed back into the soil" to enrich the next crop of projects.

Chapter Twelve

Leveraging Impact

Foundation grants, each and every one, have some impact, somewhere, somehow, on the world in which we live. For the majority of grants, that impact is relatively modest: a few jobs created, several people helped, some social changes for the better, all in a local area. For some grants, the impact is much greater: hundreds of jobs created; thousands of people helped; significant social, systemic, or even public policy changes for the better—impacts that extend statewide, perhaps even across the nation. For a few grants, the impact is truly significant: thousands employed; millions helped; deep and lasting social, systemic, and policy changes; influence that spreads beyond the national to the global arena. Examples of foundation grants that generated huge impact are support of the research leading to the formulation of a vaccine to prevent polio; the development of the *Sesame Street* television program for children; the creation of the 911 emergency response system; the initiation of the hospice and elderhostel movements; and the widespread development of community colleges across the country.

In some ways, impact is what happens *after* the project is completed. Foundations no longer fund 911 systems; the impact has occurred with the spread of such systems all over the nation. Of course impact can begin before a project is closed, but in nearly every case, the greater impact is felt after the project has been institutionalized: after the funding and sometimes the governance have been assumed by other entities.

To a great extent, the impact of a grant lies beyond your control, or indeed the control of any person or institution. It depends on many factors, including the actions of the grantee and its partners, the reception given by the public to those actions, and the state of society at any given time. For example, had the Children's Television Workshop attempted to launch *Sesame Street* in the early 1950s, before there was widespread concern about violence on children's television programs, the *Sesame Street* idea may well have failed. There are, however, many things you can do to increase or magnify impact. Some can be done before the project is funded, others while the project is active, and still others after the project has been closed.

Increasing Impact Before the Project Is Funded

Since most of the impact will occur after a project is funded, it seems counterintuitive to consider that impact can be increased *before* a project is funded. It is nonetheless true that even before your foundation has decided to support a project, you can take steps that will greatly increase the splash it makes later on. These steps require foresight, strategic planning, and sometimes a little luck.

Coordinate Funding with Other Foundations

One way to magnify impact before a project is funded is to seek to coordinate your own foundation's funding of the project with support from other foundations. This is no mean feat, comparable in some ways to building the international space station, in that it must be done under conditions of zero gravity and without benefit of an atmosphere. As program officer you often have zero gravity (leverage) because you are attempting to interest other funders in supporting that which your own foundation has not yet supported. (It should be noted, however, that in some foundations, program officers are given budgets with discretion on how to expend them; in these cases, grantmakers do have the leverage to make commitments.) You have little air (breathing room), for you are attempting to coordinate many different institutional schedules and requirements so that all begin funding at about the same time. The complexities are daunting, but the payoff in terms of broader impact is potentially enormous. The obvious benefit is that several foundations will be able to grant much more money to the project than could any one. More subtle impact-increasers also come with such a package deal, including access to the other foundations' networks, dissemination channels, and policy clout. There is also a certain credibility—a sort of "good grantmaking seal of approval"—that comes with funding by multiple foundations. It adds believability and respectability to a project that it can get in no other way.

There are two methods by which foundations can work together to fund a single project: cooperatively and collaboratively. The distinction between the two lies mainly in the level of integration. In cooperative funding, a number of different foundations back the same project, each for its own reasons. A job training project for youth, for example, might be funded by Foundation A because the project fits the foundation's education criteria, by Foundation B because the project fits that foundation's youth development guidelines, and by Foundation C because it is interested in job creation. They are funding the same project, but without a common goal or plan. In collaborative funding, the level of integration is much higher. Multiple foundations coordinate their funding with a common plan and timetable, seek a common goal, and agree on a common evaluation plan.

Of the two approaches, the cooperative is obviously easier to implement, although it is still not easy to achieve. Cooperative funding is often orchestrated by the applicant organization without any of the foundations involved actively attempting to participate in a cooperative venture. The applicant organization is successful in securing multiple sources of support, and the cooperative venture—for the foundations, at least—happens by serendipity. On other occasions, program officers at the participating foundations are the organizers of the cooperative venture. These grantmakers work across institutional lines, sometimes with official organizational blessing, sometimes informally, to coordinate funding as best they can so that it will arrive at about the same time, to be used for closely related purposes. Coordinating events so that the processes at multiple foundations (each with its own requirements and set of deadlines) lead to approximately the same results at the same time is a high-wire act to rival that of the flying Wallendas.

The collaborative approach is much more formal and hence much more complex. Although it is theoretically possible for program officers at the various foundations to organize a collabora-

tive venture, formal alliances between or among foundations ultimately require approval by the foundations' officers and boards,
and in practice, collaborations are usually driven by leaders at the
highest levels of these organizations. Such agreements are complicated and take a great deal of time and effort to negotiate, so
are best reserved for large, complex, and expensive projects or programs that have the potential to repay all this effort with profound
societal impact.

Budget Adequate Funding for Evaluation

Evaluation, of course, is invaluable for the lessons it can teach grantee and grantmaker alike about how to sharpen their level of practice. But evaluation can also do much more, particularly when it
comes to leveraging impact. Before anything else can be done about
a project—before the good news about its achievements can be disseminated to interested audiences, before the project can be expanded until it is brought to scale—it is necessary to have evidence
that the outcomes of the project were actually positive. In order to
get that evidence, it will be necessary, before the project is supported, to adequately fund formative and summative evaluation.

How much is "adequate" will depend on many factors, but it is
an inescapable fact that hard statistical data are usually the most
valuable and persuasive. It is one thing to say that "Many wom-
en were helped by this project"; it is quite another to say that "75
percent of the eight hundred women participating in this project
found full-time employment, and nearly 80 percent of these had
retained their jobs after six months had passed." Gathering these
data, crunching the numbers, and drawing validated conclusions
from the data make for a rather expensive proposition. It is a common error to underfund evaluation on the front end and then to
suffer disappointment at the conclusion of the project, when the
evaluators cannot produce the hard data needed to leverage more
impact out of the project.

If a project is funded for mainly localized impact, you should
usually add 4 to 5 percent of the total programmatic project cost
for evaluation. If, however, the goal is to extensively disseminate
information about project outcomes or to undertake social marketing or, especially, to bring the project to scale, then you will

need a much beefier evaluation component. In such cases, 10 to 20 percent of the total programmatic project cost is not out of line, and even more may be justifiable.

Budget Adequate Funding for Dissemination, Strategic Communications, and Social Marketing

Just as evaluation needs to be adequately funded up front, so too do dissemination, strategic communications, and social marketing. A quick definition of these three terms is in order. Dissemination is a long-standing concept in the foundation field, and as its name implies, it focuses on spreading information widely. When a project returns encouraging outcomes, foundations have traditionally been willing to add funds to spread the word about these outcomes to potentially interested audiences.

Strategic communications is a relatively recent tool added to the foundation toolbox. Unlike the old conception of public relations, which was to promote general goodwill and to respond to criticism of the foundation or its programs, strategic communications is a component of programming. Its purpose is to identify the most important messages of a project and to deliberately deliver these messages to the most important audiences for the project. Public relations was essentially a passive tool; strategic communications is very much an active tool.

Social marketing is also a recent addition to the foundation toolbox. As its name suggests, it borrows practices and concepts from for-profit marketing and applies them to the needs and opportunities in the nonprofit sector, in which foundations and their grantees live and work. Traditional foundation dissemination was essentially a report on findings: its most typical approaches were a conference to discuss outcomes and a book to share lessons learned. Social marketing is essentially a call to action and an attempt to alter behavior. Its approaches are many and varied, including conferences and publications, but it also uses film, video, public service announcements, the Internet, popular culture venues (for instance, printed tray liners at fast food restaurants), inserts in mailers, and a host of other informal media. One of the tools borrowed from for-profit marketing is the concept of market segmentation: zeroing in on selected audiences to deliver information and calls to action. The practitioners of social marketing hold that it is not enough simply to inform people through dissemination; it is necessary to persuade them to act—or not to act.

Traditional dissemination is usually relatively inexpensive but also generally has little demonstrable impact. Strategic communications efforts often have little direct impact but lay the groundwork with key audiences for social marketing efforts that can truly magnify impact. Social marketing can significantly leverage impact, but its reliance on multiple forms of media to get the message out and to alter people's behavior is inherently expensive. Effective social marketing campaigns can easily match the expense of fully funded evaluation programs, and cost 10 to 20 percent (or more) of the programmatic cost of a project.

Just as with evaluation, the tendency is to try to do social marketing on the cheap, and, just as with evaluation, this is a mistake. If a full-blown marketing campaign is beyond the reach of the project budget, it is probably better to forego doing one at all and to conduct a dissemination program instead. In any case, deciding on which approach (or combination of approaches) to use and funding them adequately up front will set the stage for multiplied impact when the project comes to an end.

Increasing Impact While the Project Is Active

After a project has been funded, many opportunities unfold to multiply the impact it can achieve. The most effective of these revolve around the power of networking, both internal and external, using both evaluation and strategic coummunications vehicles.

Internal Networking

There are two major methods of internal networking: project networking and cluster evaluation. Project networking is the more straightforward of the two. It is simply a convening of projects, usually similar projects in a cluster or program, but sometimes dissimilar projects from different clusters that have things to teach each other. The foundation provides a venue for representatives of the funded projects to meet and learn together.

These networking meetings can be facilitated by you, by an outside consultant, or even by one of the grantees in the network. Generally speaking, an outside facilitator is preferable, for a program officer facilitating often defeats the purpose of developing leadership among the grantees, and if one of the grantees facilitates, she or he will not be able to fully participate in the meeting. It is important that whoever handles the facilitation does so with a light touch.

Program officers universally report that the most valuable aspect of networking meetings is not the formal program but rather the mutual learning that occurs between and among the grantees. Grantees share problems they have encountered, solutions they have devised, and opportunities they have seized. They form lasting attachments, and the network created at the meeting usually survives and develops afterwards, as the individual activities evolve into an informal mutual aid society.

The second method of internal networking is more formal and more expensive; it uses evaluation as its vehicle. When a cluster of similar projects has been funded, and each has its own project-level evaluation attached to it, there is a need to compare progress and outcomes of the individual projects. An excellent way to do this is to hire a cluster evaluator and to organize one or more cluster evaluation conferences. As in project networking, the cluster evaluator will convene project representatives (including, of course, the project evaluator) at a venue to share learnings. The difference is that the main focus of these convenings is to compare evaluation learning results, with only a secondary emphasis on programmatic dialogue. By networking project-level evaluators, it is possible both to improve their individual work and to create a team that can perform a first-rate evaluation of the lessons and outcomes of the cluster of projects itself. If finances permit, it would be ideal to hold a project networking meeting first, followed by a cluster evaluation conference afterwards, so that both the project staff and the evaluators are well networked and have their specific needs met. The W. K. Kellogg Foundation has been a leading exponent of cluster evaluation and has produced an excellent primer on the subject (Millett, 1998).

With both types of internal networking, it is possible to leverage considerable additional impact with the investment of relatively few additional dollars. This is particularly true of project networking, the costs of which are mainly limited to those of the meeting itself. In the case of cluster evaluation, more expense is added due to the cost of evaluating each of the individual projects in the cluster. The additional lessons garnered and the human capital that is leveraged, however, usually amply justify the additional investment required.

External Networking

Through its ongoing work, every foundation becomes a member of many networks and is acquainted with or has access to others. You can introduce grantees to these networks in order to magnify program outcomes. An obvious way to do this is to introduce the grantees to other funders. Another example: if a foundation has funded a museum to preserve the history of community development efforts in a particular city, it can network the museum with its community development grantees so that the museum can get access to sources of artifacts and information. You can play the role of matchmaker in external networking, and usually with excellent results.

Strategic Communications

Strategic communications can multiply impact by sharing lessons with influential audiences. If, for example, a project is demonstrating that the use of nurse practitioners can ease physician shortages in rural communities, a strategic communications program can be crafted to share this message with health professions educators, rural community leaders, and federal health policymakers. The communications program may not, in itself, result in more nurse practitioners being placed in rural areas, but it lays the groundwork for social marketing programs that can have this outcome.

Increasing Impact After the Project Is Closed

After a project is closed, there are still opportunities to expand and extend its impact. One set of opportunities centers on getting the word out, while the other set centers on planting the seeds of the program in other locations.

Dissemination and Social Marketing

As mentioned previously, dissemination and social marketing are different approaches to moving impact beyond local effects. Dissemination is akin to broadcasting; it spreads information widely, without a clear connection to change and behavior. Social marketing is analogous to the newer concept of narrowcasting; it targets specific audiences and attempts to change their behavior in demonstrable ways.

Dissemination is most appropriate when it is important to share the lessons learned from a project with a widely dispersed audience. For example, if the foundation has funded a project that it feels has demonstrated an important new approach to organizing and promoting the arts, then it would be useful to share what has been learned with all local arts councils across the nation. This can be done through the traditional means of holding an invitational conference, producing a book, or publishing in a journal. The advent of desktop publishing has driven down costs; and technologies such as blast faxing, the Internet, and website postings have made dissemination cheaper and more effective still. Yet dissemination has a weakness that cannot be overlooked: it merely informs. Unless the person being informed has a predisposition to act, the information will be received, but behavior probably will not appreciably change. As the old foundation adage goes, "The book will just sit on the shelf."

This is where social marketing comes in. Just as marketing in a for-profit context seeks to motivate consumers to *do* something, so does marketing in a social context. And just as marketing in the for-profit world targets specific audiences using a variety of media, so does marketing in the foundation world. For example, if the foundation has funded a project that has discovered a better way to recruit and retain adult mentors for young people, it may wish to launch a social marketing program aimed at youth-serving organizations that rely on mentors, with a goal of persuading them to emulate the project's methods for recruitment and retention of mentors. Different media might be used to approach different organizations. A combined Internet-based and print campaign, coupled with video presentations and meetings, might be designed for larger organizations such as Big Brothers and Big Sisters, while a simpler video-based campaign might be directed at smaller organizations. In any case, social marketing requires the foundation to follow up with the targeted audiences to monitor progress, determine if behavioral change is actually occurring, and to gauge whether additional efforts are needed. The follow-up is needed so that marketing materials do not just sit on the shelf and, most important, so that behavior is changed.

Traditionally, the success of a dissemination campaign has been measured by volume: number of people exposed to the message, number of brochures distributed, and so on. The success of the social marketing campaign should be measured by changes: number of people who are doing things differently as a result of the campaign. Some program officers balk at the idea of social marketing, for to them it smacks of commercialism, perhaps even hucksterism. There is certainly a danger that, if carried to extremes, social marketing can become a manipulative tool that does more harm than good. No one wants to see program officers become the charitable version of Madison Avenue pitchmeisters. If used judiciously, however, social marketing is a powerful tool that not merely informs but also persuades, not merely tells of how practice could be improved but actually inspires improvement.

Bringing the Project to Scale

In the early history of foundations, the notion of dramatically expanding the number of program sites was referred to as replication, a concept that has since largely fallen out of favor. The underlying assumption of replication was that, if it worked in Pawtucket, it would work in Punxsutawney. Replication was an Industrial Age concept savoring of interchangeable parts and the assembly line; all one had to do was to take the same formula and the same funding that made a project thrive in Pawtucket, apply it to Punxsutawney, and an equally successful project would grow in the shadow of the famed groundhog, Phil. Except, of course, that replication usually did not work. Would-be replicators discovered that different cities in different states have different histories and different cultures; an approach that thrived among New England Yankees might experience indifferent success in the Quaker State and bog down completely in Dixie. Cost structures varied as well, so that what was an adequate amount of support in the Midwest might well be far too little on either coast. All in all, the old concept of replication is by now quite thoroughly out of vogue in the foundation world.

Bringing a project to scale, in contrast, is very much in vogue, at least for certain projects. The cost of doing so is very high, which will always limit its application. But bringing a project to scale is the ultimate in magnifying impact, so it will always be highly desirable. Defining *bringing to scale*, however, poses some real challenges. First, the "scale" is not absolute. For some projects, bringing to scale means establishing a national network of projects reaching millions of people with their services. For other projects, it may mean establishing two or three similar efforts so that other neighborhoods in a small town have access to the needed services.

Second, the process of expansion is distinctive for each project that is brought to scale; there is no formula that works in the same way for different projects. Unlike the notion of replication, which could be symbolized by a photocopier, the notion of bringing to scale could be symbolized by a buffet line. The pilot project is but a starting point. Each of the new projects to be established can pick and choose what they need from this model. It is possible that they will want to copy it completely "as is." It is far more likely, however, that they will want to take some elements, leave others, modify still others, and invent a few of their own.

Third, outcomes are likely to be mixed. Almost inevitably, in a large group of projects, the individual projects will resolve themselves into a sort of bell curve, with a few stellar ones, a few duds, and all shades of quality in between. No matter how outstanding the model, this mixed bag of outcomes is all but inevitable once effort is made to bring the model to scale.

There are many other considerations for you to keep in mind when seeking to take projects beyond the model stage. Many a program officer has lived to regret ignoring these considerations when launching a take-to-scale effort.

1. *Make sure the model project is* really *that good and that the evaluation results are compelling.* The great weight of taking an idea to scale cannot be supported by a thin reed of a model project, for any weaknesses will be exacerbated under stress. If there are any

questions, it is better to pass on scaling up until a stronger model becomes available.

2. *Be certain that the foundation is committed for the long haul.* Bringing programs to scale is an undertaking best measured in years, not months, and ideally in many years, not just a few. If the foundation is likely to tire halfway through such a process, it will do a grave disservice to everyone trying to build the effort. Moreover, there are bound to be delays and discouragements along the way. The foundation will need staying power if it wants to remain in this business. It is far better not to start at all than to abandon the ship halfway into the voyage.

3. *Be sure that the foundation is willing to find the "long green" necessary to complete this "long march."* In truth, few foundations have the financial resources needed to be the exclusive funder of a take-to-scale venture of any size. Most will need to recruit funding partners. Here, too, there are questions: Is the foundation ready and willing to have partners? Will the loss of sole ownership be a problem? Are you (and are the officers of the foundation) able and willing to build a funders' collaborative to support this effort? In any case, you should never underestimate the substantial ongoing resources, as measured in both money and time, that must be invested to bring about the desired effects.

4. *Be aware that taking a project to scale will exponentially increase the demand for technical assistance.* Common sense would seem to suggest that two projects would require twice as much technical assistance (TA) as one. It does not work that way in practice; because the two are new and the one is mature, the TA needs for the new one will be on the order of four times as great. Therefore, while the number of projects in a take-to-scale effort may grow in an arithmetic progression, the TA needs are likely to grow in a geometric progression. If the take-to-scale effort is a large one, the TA demands will rapidly grow beyond the capacity of any one program officer—often beyond the capacity of a single foundation—to provide them.

In such cases, it is sensible to consider making a grant to an intermediary organization to provide the TA. You work with the intermediary and provide general oversight, but the employees of the intermediary are the ones who provide the actual hands-on TA. In fact, it may sometimes be desirable to employ an intermediary as the grantmaker. In such arrangements, the foundation makes a large grant to the intermediary organization, which then makes subgrants to start new organizations as the program is brought toward scale. Subgrant arrangements have the disadvantage of placing the foundation at one remove from the grantee, but they offer the huge advantage of preventing the foundation from being buried under an impossible workload. Of course, you must take great care to choose the right intermediary, and you must work closely with the intermediary once it is chosen to ensure that the relationship unfolds as the foundation hopes. In some cases, no ideal intermediary exists, and the foundation may need to help develop one before it can begin to fund the projects that it wants the intermediary to manage.

Intermediaries are typically chosen early on, so that they can help the foundation plan the grantmaking program. As Heidrich (1999) states in her excellent primer on the subject, the intermediary organization can support individual projects within a grantmaking program by, for example, conducting site visits, offering TA, and providing general grant management. The intermediary organization can also offer services to every project in the program, including planning and implementing networking conferences, developing and maintaining a website and e-mail listservs, and facilitating data collection for the evaluators. Intermediary organizations are often better positioned than the foundation itself to give management attention to a program, and they sometimes have the ability to raise the level of visibility as well. If chosen judiciously and managed well, an intermediary organization can make it possible for the foundation's reach to considerably exceed its grasp.

5. *Before getting into any take-to-scale effort, formulate a way to get out.* No foundation, no matter how large, has the wherewithal to fund large networks of grantees forever. Sooner or later, no matter how successful a take-to-scale effort is, the foundation will need to stop supporting it and go on to other opportunities. This is best done with an exit plan, and the plan is best made early on—with the participation and consent of all stakeholders, including grantees—even before the take-to-scale effort is launched. Attempting to improvise an escape strategy once in the middle of the momentum and excitement of bringing a project to scale is like starting to think about how to land when blasting off atop a rocket.

Conclusion

The impact of grants can be compared to the effect of throwing rocks into a pond. Every rock, no matter what its size, will make ripples across the pond's surface. Although it is easier to make big ripples by throwing big rocks, you can find, if you are diligent, denser rocks that make bigger ripples than less dense rocks of a similar size. Searching for ways to multiply impact is very much like searching for the denser rocks. Find one, and you can make bigger ripples than someone else who throws a rock of exactly the same size. Why do it? A simple reason is that grants with greater impact help more people at a lower cost per person. There is also the moral imperative to do as much good as you can with the resources at your command. Increasing the impact of grants provides a happy marriage of efficiency and compassion, or as Jeremy Bentham might have said, it yields the greatest good for the greatest number at the least cost.

Chapter Thirteen

Influencing Policy

Perhaps the most profound way for a foundation to leverage additional impact is through active participation in public and organizational policy activities. Public policy can be defined as the legal and regulatory actions taken by the executive, legislative, and judicial branches of the government at the federal, state, and local levels. Organizational policy can be defined as formal rules and regulations that govern behavior and practice within publicly chartered organizations. Creating and applying public or organizational policy is the province of elected and appointed governmental officials or leaders of publicly chartered institutions, but influencing the formation of such policy is the right—and responsibility—of every citizen, and certainly of every organization with a mission to serve the common good. Public policy impinges directly on every issue or program area in which foundations have interest.

Laws and regulations can be of immense assistance in magnifying impact and in bringing projects to scale, or they can derail projects altogether. For example, if a foundation funds a pilot project that demonstrates that service-learning is an effective K–12 educational strategy, it can be quickly brought to scale if state boards of education can be persuaded to add service-learning to their approved curricula or if the federal Department of Education can be convinced to provide funding for wide-scale start-up of such programs. Conversely, should a promising social services pilot project funded by a foundation be passed over for support by a governmental agency in favor of another approach, it can effectively pull the plug on bringing the foundation's approach to scale.

Foundations can also take a very active role in the development of sound public policy by funding models that policymakers can observe as a prototype before making policy decisions. For example, a foundation may fund a cluster of school-based health clinics, evaluate their effectiveness, then disseminate the lessons learned to policymakers, who will then have the benefit of real-world models before making decisions about policy. Foundations can thus fund "policy prototypes" in a deliberate effort to shape the formation of policy that will promote the common good.

There is another, more threatening, aspect to public policy with which all foundations must be concerned. Foundations, and the nonprofit sector of which they are a part, exist and operate within a legal and regulatory framework that has evolved for hundreds of years; the antecedents of this framework are lodged in the Common Law of Great Britain. This body of law, regulation, and custom is highly dynamic and continues constantly to evolve. New laws and regulations may smile or frown on foundations and on the nonprofit organizations to which foundations make grants. Legislation to lower the excise tax paid by private foundations, for example, has allowed these entities to increase their grantmaking accordingly. Other legislation has dramatically increased the formation of new foundations by allowing gifts of highly appreciated publicly traded stock that are used to establish foundations to be fully tax-deductible. On the downside, during the 1990s alone, bills were introduced into Congress to eliminate the charitable deduction, to cap the amount of gifts a donor could deduct, and to abolish the advocacy rights of any nonprofit that accepts funding from the federal government. These bills were all defeated, thanks in large part to the efforts of foundations and nonprofits mobilized by INDEPENDENT SECTOR and the Council on Foundations. Public policy has an effect on much more than individual projects: it can dramatically enhance—or disastrously limit—the power and effectiveness of foundations and nonprofit organizations as social institutions. Policy considerations, therefore, should be a key factor in planning any initiative or grantmaking program.

Foundation Phobias Regarding Public Policy

Given the make-or-break potential of public policy to leverage or deflate project impact and to advance or harm the field, one might assume that foundations are generally eager to enter the policy fray. Such an assumption would be incorrect. Although a number of foundations do participate effectively in the policy process (among the exemplars are the Robert Wood Johnson Foundation and the Kaiser Family Foundation in health care; the Annie E. Casey Foundation in youth development; and the Kettering and Johnson Foundations in multiple areas of interest), the vast majority of U.S. foundations participate sporadically, if at all. There are a number of reasons for this: some based on conscious choices, others predicated on misunderstandings.

Conscious Choices

Many foundations simply disdain political processes. The powerful reaction during the last quarter of the twentieth century against the perceived excesses of "big government" affected foundations just as it did the grassroots voter. If one believes that "government is the problem" or feels with Mark Twain that "there is no distinctly native American criminal class except Congress," then spending time and resources on public policy seems to be a waste of both.

Another conscious choice is to avoid controversy. Policy debates are usually contentious, and there is always the risk of alienating people on either side of an issue. A number of foundations simply shy away from this sort of conflict. Then too, there are internal concerns. Foundations are not monolithic entities; their boards and staffs consist of people, usually people of divergent viewpoints. It may be easy to get all these diverse ideologies to come together in support of nonpartisan concepts like volunteerism or the fine arts, but as soon as political considerations are injected into the mix, these differences can flare into the open. It is often easier to keep "peace in the family" by avoiding the policy arena altogether.

Misunderstandings

As widespread as such conscious choices may be, however, the leading reasons for foundation reluctance to become involved with policy efforts revolve around simple misunderstandings. A grantmaker's typical response to a request to get involved in policy activities might be, "The Tax Reform Act of 1969 prohibits foundations from lobbying, so we cannot get involved in policy matters." This misconception is of the most insidious variety: one that has enough accuracy mixed with error to thoroughly convince people of the rightness of their mistaken ideas. The Tax Reform Act of 1969 did in fact prohibit foundations from conducting or supporting certain types of lobbying and partisan political activities. On the whole, however, it left foundations with great flexibility to legally participate in the public policy process. It is important for every program officer to know what foundations can and cannot do, and what nonprofits to whom foundations make grants can and cannot do, within the broad arena of public policy.

What Foundations Cannot Do

The Tax Reform Act of 1969, its accompanying regulations, and subsequent laws and regulations enacted during the next three decades have explicitly prohibited four activities by foundations in the policy arena.

1. Foundations may not make grants for or against the passage of *specific legislation*, which includes acts, bills, resolutions, ballot initiatives, and referenda. Foundations may not expend money directly to support or defeat specific pieces of legislation, nor are they allowed to make grants to nonprofit organizations to support or defeat specific pieces of legislation.

2. Foundations may not engage in *direct lobbying*. This includes meeting with legislators or their staffs to discuss the following things: specific pieces of legislation, drafting a bill, the merits of a presidential or gubernatorial veto, or the contents of a vetoed bill when it is ready for review. The key word here is *direct;* there is no problem with discussing general principles with a legislator. For example, whereas it would be inappropriate for you to meet with a member of Congress to urge passage of a specific House bill to extend the charitable deduction to those who do not itemize on their income taxes, it is perfectly legitimate to meet with a congressperson to generally discuss the importance of the charitable deduction in sustaining projects that the foundation funds.

3. Foundations may not make a *call to action*. Calls to action include foundation communications to the public that take a stand on a specific piece of legislation or a defined issue. Foundations are also prohibited from providing to the public any petition advocating action on a specific issue; furnishing a legislator's address, telephone number, or e-mail address; and identifying a legislator as

being for, against, or undecided on a particular issue. All such calls to action are clearly grassroots lobbying activities and are off-limits.

4. Foundations may not violate the *mass media rule*. This rule prohibits foundations from paying for mass media advertisements that take a position on highly publicized pieces of legislation and that air within two weeks of a legislative vote on such bills.

What Foundations Can Do

The aforementioned areas of proscription are narrow and specific, which means that the field of things that foundations *can* do in the public policy arena is broad and flexible. Generally speaking, of course, foundations can do anything that is not specifically prohibited. This means that foundations can work on behalf of anything that is not a specific piece of legislation; can advocate, so long as they do not engage in direct lobbying; can educate broadly on policy issues, so long as they avoid a call to action; and can take out ads, so long as they do not violate the mass media rule. It is always wise to keep in mind, however, the elementary school rule that one should not define by negation, so the following paragraphs describe four allowed activities that positively define the wide latitude that Congress has given foundations to be players in the policy arena.

1. Foundations may engage in *nonpartisan analysis and research*. A foundation can actually take a position on a specific piece of legislation *if* it does so in the context of a paper that presents a sufficiently full and fair exposition of public policy issues so that the reader can form his or her own conclusions. The key words here are *full* and *fair*. The paper must not leave out important points, nor can it be heavily biased for or against one point of view. This exception allows a foundation to take a definite position on any specific piece of legislation, so long as it is taken after presenting a complete and even-handed consideration of the situation.

2. Foundations may give *technical assistance* to units of government. This allows a foundation to respond to written requests for technical information from a legislative committee, subcommittee, or other governmental body. Foundations, by virtue of the lessons they have learned from their programming, are potential sources

of valuable information to units of government. When directly asked for assistance by a legislative committee or a school board, for example, the foundation can include specific positions in its answer without fear of crossing the line into prohibited lobbying. It should be emphasized, however, that this exception holds only if foundations are asked by the governmental body to provide such information; it does not allow them to volunteer the information.

3. Foundations may act in *self-defense*. Should Congress or a state legislature introduce legislation that would, if passed, affect a foundation's powers, duties, tax-exempt status, right to receive tax-deductible contributions, or its very existence, the foundation has the right to communicate directly with governmental officials and to take specific stands on the threatening issues.

Sometimes foundations face clear-cut self-defense issues. Legislation that would double the excise tax rate for private foundations, for example, would clearly fall under the self-defense exception. Legislation that would place limits on the ability of nonprofits to raise funds, in contrast, is not so clear-cut. Because nonprofits are foundations' delivery system, a self-defense argument could plausibly be made, but the self-defense issues would not be unassailable. It would be best to consult with an attorney who practices in this area before proceeding with advocacy or grantmaking on all but the most unambiguous of the self-defense issues.

4. Foundations may seek *safe harbor*. This exception provides considerable flexibility in grantmaking: foundations can, under certain circumstances, make grants for a project that includes a lobbying component. For example, if there was an effort afoot in Congress to limit the advocacy rights of nonprofit organizations, a foundation could make a grant to an organization that was advocating against such legislation, so long as the requirements of the safe harbor exception were met. Because the requirements are somewhat involved, it would be wise to seek competent legal assistance before making such grants.

These exceptions provide foundations with great opportunities to participate in the policy process with perfect safety and legality. True, they do not allow foundations to do everything, but they do permit foundations to do much more than is proscribed. It is important to note that this discussion is a highly simplified distillation of the regulations. Much fuller explanations, along with detailed guides to grantmaking around policy issues, can be found in such guidebooks as *Foundations and Lobbying* (Edie, 1991) and *The Nonprofit Lobbying Guide* (Smucker, 1999). You should consult one or both of these guides before venturing into policy work in earnest. The Council on Foundations is also an excellent resource in general; its Committee on Legislation and Regulations (affectionately known as Legs and Regs) keeps close tabs on congressional and executive branch policy developments. The council's government relations unit is always helpful to foundations with questions about policy-related activity. The Association of Small Foundations is also a useful source of assistance on policy work.

What Nonprofits Cannot Do

It is not enough for you to know only the definition and limits of the foundation's rights in policy work. Because foundations make grants to nonprofit organizations, it is essential to know the definition and limits of nonprofit rights in the policy arena.

The 1976 lobbying law, explicated by a set of regulations issued by the Internal Revenue Service in 1990, is very kind to nonprofits that wish to engage in public policy activities. However, the law is written in such a way that no nonprofit need exercise these rights if it does not wish to do so. Charities may "elect" to come under the law; if they do so elect, they are given broad latitude to lobby. If they do not elect to come under the law, they exist in a murky limbo in which they are required to limit expenditures for lobbying to an "insubstantial" percentage of their total expenditures. Just what "insubstantial" might mean on a balance sheet has never been defined, so any foundation making an advocacy grant to a nonelecting nonprofit should be very conservative in terms of the amount granted. There is no sense in tempting fate by making a large grant that could be deemed "substantial" by the Internal Revenue Service.

What Nonprofits Can Do

Once a nonprofit elects to come under the 1976 law, it is allowed to spend 20 percent of its first $500,000 of annual expenditures on lobbying ($100,000); 15 percent of the next $500,000, and so on, up to $1 million per year. This is obviously quite ample, but it is even more generous than it appears, for there are seven legislation-related activities that nonprofits may conduct that are not considered lobbying by the Internal Revenue Service and thus can be done without counting against the $1 million limit. The first three of these are similar to those that private foundations enjoy: nonpartisan analysis and research, technical assistance to committees, and self-defense. The other allowed activities are making contact with executive branch employees or legislators in support of or opposition to proposed regulations; lobbying by the organization's volunteers; communications with the nonprofit organization's members (so long as the organization does not explicitly encourage its members to lobby); and verbal discussions of broad issues with members of the legislative or executive branches, so long as specific legislation is not discussed. Clearly, once a nonprofit organization has elected, its options for participation in the policy arena are many and varied. Again, this is a very condensed version of the rules. INDEPENDENT SECTOR has created an extremely helpful handbook, *The Nonprofit Lobbying Guide* (Smucker, 1999), and it would be wise to read this for a fuller understanding of the subject before making grants in this area.

Types of Policy Impacts

Whenever a foundation supports a grantee's public policy work, the outcome should be some impact on the way policy is made or administered. There are four major types of policy impacts, three corresponding with levels of government, the fourth pertaining to organizations.

1. *Federal-level impact.* When most program officers think of policy, this is probably what comes to mind: a bill pending in Congress or a regulatory ruling from the Internal Revenue Service. Bills and rulings certainly are examples of federal-level policy, but the federal level has more dimensions than the legislative and the regulatory. Federal-level policy is also made and interpreted by the executive and judiciary branches of government, for some policies can be made or undone by executive order and others can be created or overturned by judicial fiat. Policy work at the federal level

offers potentially enormous payoffs, for decisions made there truly affect all Americans, as well as millions in other nations. The potential costs, too, are high, in terms of travel, lodging, educational activities, and especially time spent on these tasks.

2. *Statewide impact.* Each of the fifty states presents a smaller version of the federal level, with executive, legislative, and judicial branches, along with regulatory agencies. The payoff for work at the state level is not as high, for a legislative victory in Washington affects all fifty states, whereas a legislative victory in Montpelier, for example, affects only one state, and a small one at that. Nonetheless, statewide policy is important for many reasons. It serves as a laboratory for approaches that may be copied by other states or possibly adopted at the federal level. Indeed, if it "plays in Peoria"— and the rest of Illinois—it may well be ready to play at the federal level. Then, too, because foundations live in states just as do corporations, they will frequently attempt to be "good corporate citizens" by supporting initiatives that affect their home state. It is sometimes possible to take lessons learned statewide and move them down to the local level. Fortunately, as compared to those of working with Washington, costs at the state level are generally modest, so the foundation can almost always make its policy dollars go farther. Finally, the process of devolution has increased the power and authority of state-level leaders and thus elevated the significance of statewide policy efforts.

3. *Local impact.* Once again, at this level the foundation must deal with an executive (mayor), a legislature (city council), and a judiciary (district and circuit courts). In addition, the local level contains various other layers of government (county, city, township), plus quasi-governmental entities, such as school boards and library districts. Policy work at the local level is generally low cost, but it can be very time intensive and is, of course, localized in its impact. That localized impact, it is true, may be only the starting point, for it is possible for policy to percolate up through networks (such as from a local school district to a regional school district up to the state board of education). Some issues, moreover, must be addressed locally, because the final arbiters of the issues are locally based. Educational issues are a good example; they can be influenced at the federal and state levels but must be decided by local school boards. On the one hand, because of the lower costs and

because foundations generally have more clout closer to home than farther away, the local level is where foundations can get lots of policy bang for their buck. On the other hand, dealing with multiple jurisdictions often makes this the most time-intensive of all kinds of policy work.

4. *Organizational impact.* Large institutions, such as universities and federated nonprofits, offer a chance to create enormous local, regional, or even national impact through changes in their internal policies. For example, if a project can succeed in persuading a university to alter the way in which it trains teachers, the resulting impact will be felt across the nation in every school where those students go to teach after they have graduated. Similarly, securing a change in policy at one of the larger federations of nonprofits— for example, the YMCA—can have a real impact on the way in which people throughout the country are served locally. Cost, measured in both dollars and time, as well as impact achieved, will vary with the many different types of policy projects possible in this arena. In any case, foundations should not overlook institutional efforts in the mistaken belief that policy work can be done only in a governmental setting.

In all four of these arenas, foundations can help initiate policy (propose ideas never before considered); formulate policy (work with officials to shape the evolution of laws and regulations); assist in the implementation of policy (by monitoring, testing, and reporting on the impact of policies); and revise policy (by suggesting alternatives or improvements to policies already in place). In short, foundations can be effective at any point in the policy process.

Overt Ideology Versus Ideological Neutrality

There are essentially only two ways to do policy work. One way is to take an ideological position and pursue it with gusto. The other is to strive to be perceived as a nonideological, neutral source of information and advice. If you are working for a peremptory foundation, chances are that it will stake out an ideological position and defend it pugnaciously. Very few passive foundations bother themselves with policy work. It is the prescriptive and the proactive foundations, then, that are faced with the tough question of whether to be overtly ideological or to strive for neutrality. Both stances offer advantages and disadvantages to the foundation choosing them.

The ideological stance offers an unambiguous mission. For example, if a foundation is convinced that access to primary health care is a basic human right and that all Americans are entitled to it at no cost to themselves, then its task is clear. Focused on this target, the foundation can ignore any evidence or people not supportive of its views, and zero in on only those data and people likely to move its cause forward. Its focus and discipline allow the foundation to gain and wield a power that is often disproportionately high in relation to the number of dollars that it spends. For example, conservative foundations such as Scaife and Bradley, although outnumbered and outspent by liberal foundations, were consistently more effective in the public policy arena in the 1980s and 1990s because of their focused strategy and zealous adherence to their ideological beliefs.

Although it can undeniably be effective, the ideological stance also presents very real costs. If a foundation makes no pretense of being ideologically balanced, it immediately loses credibility with those of the opposite ideological persuasion and risks losing its credibility with a relatively small but strategically important "non-aligned bloc" between the two camps. If it is too strident, the foundation may find itself only preaching to the choir and could well stir up a counterreaction on the other side of the ideological divide. If so, any gains achieved might be ephemeral, and the counterreaction could even cause the position favored by the foundation to lose ground in the long run.

The ideologically neutral stance is based on the belief that foundations should engage in nonpartisan, nonideological research and testing to promote the common good in society. If a foundation consistently produces work that is fair, even-handed, and unbiased, then its work will be respected and used by people of goodwill from both sides of the ideological divide in order to find ways to improve society. There is also a very practical reason to keep to the middle: in a democracy, political parties come and go from power. Becoming too closely identified with one side or the other will mean that when "your" side is out of power, the foundation will be ostracized. By staying in the middle, the foundation will have influence no matter which party is in power at the moment.

The nonideological stance seems to be a strategy for all seasons, but it is also problematic. At the national level, there is no question that during the 1990s, the post–World War II political consensus largely collapsed. In the late 1990s, partisanship became the order of the day, and critics of the nonideological approach maintain that in such an atmosphere there are limits to the effectiveness of high-minded neutrality. "If you ain't with us, you're agin' us" is the new motto of both parties, so fair, even-handed research can fall into a narrow demilitarized zone between the warring ideologies, lacking champions on either side to put it to good social use. In an ideological war zone, a reputation for neutrality may be hard to hold. Ultimately, the stance of the foundation will be judged by its body of grantmaking, which is likely, over time, to veer one way or another away from dead center. And there is always the chance that critics will judge the foundation's work by taking one or two grants out of context. A single award to Promise Keepers or to Sojourners may brand the foundation as right or left on the spectrum. This is particularly the case in the popular press, when critics are wont to cite only one or two grants to "prove" that the foundation is a haven for either babbling Birchers or malignant Marxists. In short, a foundation striving for neutrality may find itself to be everyone's enemy and largely ineffective in the policy sphere.

No clear winner emerges from this debate. Although ideologically motivated foundations have gained better results lately, it is still an open question as to whether this winning streak will last. Should Americans tire of the bare-knuckles partisanship in the nation's capital, the backlash could swamp the ideological foundations along with the political ideologues. In the end, a foundation must choose a policy stance that is most congenial to its values and sense of ethics. It is likely that both ideological and nonideological foundations will coexist, however uneasily, for some time to come.

Creating a Policy Framework

One framework for conducting policy work is that developed by the W. K. Kellogg Foundation. This is only one method, and others can be equally valid, but it does provide a useful way of conceptualizing policy activities.

Program policy focus: a complex issue that is selected for policy work. Foci may be as broad as tax policy or as narrow as a single regulation. Foci are measurable, have the potential for movement, and could involve any number of possible positions, some of which may be controversial. An example of a focus is health care access for uninsured children. The number of uninsured children is measurable and may increase or decrease, and a foundation could take many different positions on the subject.

Policy change objective: a clear direction of movement in the program policy focus that the foundation supports. For example, a foundation may choose as its policy change objective a dramatic decrease in the number of uninsured children.

Approach: the array of options that grantees and their partners choose to address in order to accomplish the policy change objective. The approach identifies the strategies that the grantees will embrace, including identification and analysis of relevant policies. In the case of health care for uninsured children, approaches might include operation of a demonstration project, educational efforts, or policy initiatives.

Leverage points: the strategic actions taken by the foundation to support a policy change objective. These may include developing models, giving technical assistance, and convening meetings. An example would be support for a model demonstrating a better method of providing health care for uninsured children.

Resources: the tools that the foundation applies to support the grantee's approaches, in order to achieve the change objectives. In the case of health care access for uninsured children, this might include making specific grants and contracts, or using strategic communications or social marketing to inform policy development.

In creating a policy framework, the easiest things to do generally are the selection of a program policy focus and the identification of a policy change objective. If the foundation is interested in health care, selecting a focus of access to health care for uninsured children is easy enough, as is identifying a policy change objective of dramatically decreasing the number of uninsured children. It is a bigger challenge to discern the best approaches that grantees may take and the most powerful leverage points that the foundation may employ. Most challenging of all is to choose and employ the specific resources that the foundation can mobilize to achieve the policy change objective. Gathering all of these steps into a single framework assures that policy work will be done systematically and not haphazardly.

Developing a Public Policy Message

Whether a foundation chooses to be partisan or neutral, and whatever the framework it chooses, it still must design the policy message it wishes to convey. A recent survey by Susan Rees (1998) asked lawmakers in Washington which organizations they consider to be the most successful at affecting public policy. Twelve organizations, ranging in ideology from the Brookings Institution to the Heritage Foundation, rose to the top, and Rees then studied the methods of these organizations. She discovered that for the most part they tended to reach out to both Democrats and Republicans, worked in coalitions, and focused resources on one or two top policy priorities. They also approached policy as a two-way street and involved policymakers on their own advisory commissions.

Rees discovered that all twelve organizations use similar methods when developing a public policy message. Not all of the twelve use exactly the same methods, but there was enough overlap for Rees to identify ten that they all used from time to time. Although these methods were created specifically by nonprofits, no foundation could go wrong by following the "top ten" methods listed here:

1. Eliminate inflammatory or empty rhetoric and loaded words.
2. Define the problem or situation in terms that make it appear manageable.
3. Give lawmakers data on the issue that you compiled in their state or district.
4. Take account of public attitudes through polling or focus groups in framing the message.
5. Comb through official data to make the case.
6. State facts and arguments in brief bulleted points.
7. Use economic arguments, such as increased efficiency and job and revenue growth.
8. Call on government to establish fairness and level the playing field.

9. Appeal to democratic, constitutional, and historic principles, as well as to congressional precedent.
10. When sending a message that is controversial, target known supporters first.

It might be objected that these top ten methods simply describe commonsense ideas. This is true, but it is surprising how often attempts to influence policy violate such commonsense approaches. It is very easy, for example, to provide such an exhaustive analysis of the problems connected with an initiative that the problems appear completely insurmountable. If a foundation carefully follows the methods given here, it should be able to craft highly effective public policy messages.

The Relational Nature of Policy Work

Much has been written about the revolution in electronic communications and its effect of "annihilating distance." Supposedly e-mail will shortly replace letters, and teleconferencing will make travel superfluous. This may be true in some contexts, but it is not the case in policy work. Tip O'Neill rightly remarked that "all politics is local," and by the same token, all policy work is personal. It is necessary to form a relationship with a policymaker before one can realistically hope to garner his or her support. Such relationships must be built face-to-face; the policymaker will not return e-mails. In fact, on Capitol Hill, e-mails are the lowest-valued form of communication, on the theory that they are easy to write and cheap to send. The much-reviled "snail mail," in contrast, is highly valued, on the theory that if someone goes to the expense and trouble of writing a letter, he or she must care deeply about an issue.

Some facets of relational policy work can be counterintuitive. For example, it is sometimes sensible to call upon your representative and ask for nothing. It might be useful to consider some rules to follow while actually engaged in these activities. Although these rules are specifically tailored toward working with members of Congress, they can be easily modified for meetings with other types of policymakers.

1. *Use the power of constituency.* Although you can visit with any of the 535 members of Congress, it makes sense to concentrate on the member of the House in whose district the foundation resides

and on the senators from the foundation's home state. Members of Congress always pay most attention to people who can vote for (or against) them. A secondary priority is to meet with congresspeople from districts and states where the foundation does significant programming. Although the foundation is not a constituent of these individuals, it does make grants to their constituents and thus has some clout.

2. *Visit* before *asking for something*. The best time to ask for support is not two minutes after first having met someone. Yet that is exactly what will be necessary if you wait until there is a crisis to go and meet members of Congress. It is far better to start building a relationship with a congressperson *before* you have anything in particular to support or oppose. You can use these initial visits to educate the congressperson about the good that philanthropy in general and that your foundation in particular has done for his or her constituents. Then, when you must request support, you will be doing so in the context of a relationship rather than that of a cold call.

3. *Try to meet the congressperson's key staffers.* Meeting with the congressperson is important, but not enough. Members of Congress are extremely busy, and it is usually their key staffers who do the research that will largely determine the way they vote. Even if you have secured a meeting with a congressperson, therefore, it is sensible to try to meet with his or her chief of staff or with other key aides. If, as frequently happens, the congressperson cannot be seen or needs to cancel, all is not lost. In fact, it is often just as valuable to meet with the staffer as with the congressperson, as the staffer has fewer distractions and will probably be able to devote more time and attention to the subject of the meeting.

4. *Take no more than five minutes.* Members of Congress must often attend literally a dozen meetings or more daily, some of them rather lengthy. They can probably spare you about fifteen minutes at the most. Therefore, presentations, complete with any action to be requested, should be completed within no more than five minutes. If the congressperson has questions, this allows time for him or her to ask them. If not, you score points by concluding the meeting ahead of schedule.

5. *Bring along "leave behind" materials.* It is a mistake to have a meeting with a member of Congress without leaving behind something on paper to remind him or her of the meeting and of the

concerns discussed in it. It is also a mistake, however, to leave too many tree carcasses in your wake. Ideally, you should prepare, for every major subject you will discuss, a one-page summary to be left with the congressperson or his or her staffers. One-pagers often are read, whereas tomes almost never are. If, however, the foundation has published a lengthy but well-illustrated annual report or "coffee table" book about its grantmaking, you should offer a copy, for it makes excellent display material in the reception areas of the congressperson's office and educates visitors about your foundation.

6. *Follow up the visit with a letter.* The visit is not complete until you send a follow-up letter thanking the congressperson and staffers for their hospitality and reiterating the points covered during the meeting. As previously mentioned, this should be an honest-to-goodness letter, not an e-mail, and it should be personalized, not a form letter.

7. *Write and visit often.* The best advice for continuing contact is to make sure that contact continues. Write and visit often; whenever possible, you should be in contact without a favor to ask of a congressperson. These contacts build the relationship and make it easier to ask for help on those occasions when it is really needed.

8. *Be* for *something.* Some program officers make the error of visiting the congresspeople who represent them only when they are attempting to head off ill-conceived ideas. After a while, such a program officer begins to look negative, a veritable Dr. No of the foundation world. Whenever you *must* oppose pending ideas, it is good to be able to offer a positive alternative. To the congressperson, it is always more congenial to work with people who are for good things than with those who are against bad things.

9. *Be a resource.* Program officers are often expert on a number of subjects of interest to the congressperson. Instead of asking for something, you can actually offer something: access to your expertise. Congressional staffs frequently have "knowledge gaps," just as do foundation staffs, and you can appropriately serve in the place of a consultant. You must take care, of course, to avoid becoming an unpaid staffer for the congressperson on a full-time basis, but helping out on occasion is beneficial both to the congressperson and to the foundation. Such assistance is also handy in fending off inappropriate requests the congressperson might make. You must recognize that it is likely that the congressperson, sooner or later

in the relationship, will ask the foundation for something. As sages have noted, "When you get into bed with the government, you've got to expect more than a good night's sleep." Providing expertise to a member of Congress from time to time is certainly a more acceptable quid pro quo than to make grants to his or her pet charities. And, of course, it helps build and maintain the relationship so that it will be strong when really needed.

Using Policy to Leverage Impact

One of the primary uses of policy in the foundation world is to extend the impact of funded projects. Willie Sutton robbed banks because "that is where the money is"; likewise, one of the most compelling reasons for foundations to become involved in policy is for the cash needed to bring projects to scale. Despite much talk over the past decades of government cutbacks, federal and state government resources continue to overshadow those of the nonprofit sector. The combined payout of the five largest private foundations in 1998 would have been insufficient to pay for one B-2 bomber—and the Department of Defense during that year was engaged in building twenty B-2 bombers. Securing a stream of governmental support for a project can quickly bring it to scale.

An excellent example of this phenomenon is the youth service movement in the United States. The idea of young people serving their nation as civilians as well as in the military is an old one, stretching back to the writing of William James in the nineteenth century and the experience of the Civilian Conservation Corps during the Great Depression. When World War II put an end to FDR's youth service experiments, the idea went dormant. In the early 1980s, Franklin Thomas, president of the Ford Foundation, began to advocate a return to youth service. Ford supported several pilot projects, along with providing start-up funds for an umbrella policy organization called Youth Service America. Soon Ford was joined by other funders, such as Kellogg, Mott, and Rockefeller Brothers Fund. These foundations funded exemplary projects like City Year and the Youth Volunteer Corps of America, which defined principles of best practice in the field. The movement received a tremendous boost in 1989, when George Bush came to the White House and established the Points of Light

Foundation to promote volunteerism. Working closely with the Points of Light Foundation and the new White House Office of National Service, a number of foundation and corporate funders advocated for increased government support of youth service programs. The result was the Community and National Service Act of 1990, which created the Commission for National Service. The commission served as the vehicle for distribution of $62 million per year to existing and new youth service programs. Then, in 1993, newly elected president Bill Clinton made it a priority to support the National and Community Service Act of 1993, which subsumed the Commission for National Service and existing federal organizations like ACTION and VISTA into the Corporation for National Service. The corporation, working through commissions appointed by governors in all fifty states, dispenses, as of this writing, $515 million annually to operate AmeriCorps (youth service) and Learn and Serve America (service-learning) programs across the nation. As a result of this bringing to scale, foundations have now mainly ceased funding pilot projects in youth service. Many, however, remain as funders of the Corporation for National Service, and some continue to do national service-related policy work.

It took more than a decade for the pioneering work done by the Ford Foundation to come completely to scale. This was achieved by the cooperative (and occasionally collaborative) work of more than twenty major funders, both foundations and corporations. It began with model project development. The creation of Youth Service America as a policy advocate, best practices arbiter, networker, and communications clearinghouse was an important step. Helping bellwether projects like City Year develop into major exemplars of practice was another strategic development. The most essential policy work was done in conjunction with the executive branch, first in the Bush administration through the Points of Light Foundation, then in the Clinton administration through the Corporation for National Service. Good policy work was also done in both houses of Congress, which set the stage for the passage of federal legislation in 1990 and again in 1993.

This story underlines several instructive lessons about using policy to bring projects to scale:

1. It is a time-consuming process that will take many years.
2. It is best done by a coalition of funders, not just one.

3. Many different models need to be created and tested, and the lessons learned from them must be shared.
4. It makes sense to create an umbrella organization to take the lead on policy work for the field.
5. It is important to develop allies in both the executive and legislative branches of government.
6. More than just dollars are required; the funder must be directly involved and provide personal leadership.

One other thing must be kept in mind: that which the government appropriateth, the government can cutteth. From 1994 until the end of the decade, Congress threatened at various times to reduce or eliminate altogether funding for the Corporation for National Service and the Points of Light Foundation. In response, the funders that had led the charge in model development formed the Grantmaker Forum on Community and National Service, an advocacy organization dedicated to building public support for the concept of service and the national and community service movement itself. This experience illustrates that even when funders are successful in bringing a project to scale, there is rarely a time when they can afford to follow Sen. George Aiken's advice about Vietnam, which was to "declare victory then go home." They need instead to protect their past investments, occasionally by making grants but especially by being perpetually vigilant.

Public Policy and Public Will

Whenever foundations work with government officials, there is a danger that the result could be an elitist project remote from the needs and desires of the general public. Indeed, one can point to examples, such as certain programs in President Lyndon Johnson's "War on Poverty," where this has happened. To guard against this tendency, foundations should make sure that public will is taken into account in all of their policy activities. Thanks to the pioneering work of the Union Institute (Jones and Siegal, 1993), we have a working definition of public will: "The collective recognition of the need for change in a societal condition that leads to making choices, setting goals, and acting to achieve those goals. It is generated when individuals come together, out of concern for the public good, to influence the policy process and demand accountability from those with influence and authority over the lives of citizens."

Public will is important, not just as a vaguely democratic concept but in the very practical sense that foundations and government ignore it at their own peril. As Jones and Siegal (1993) note, "Some initiatives fail because policymakers set goals and establish programs without popular support or even popular understanding of the need for them. This lack of connection to public will allows initiatives to be undertaken in a vacuum. Without the public's recognition of their importance . . . such attempts are doomed." One way to determine public expectations and understanding is to conduct stakeholder analyses and to carefully evaluate outcomes of funded projects. The lessons learned from these activities can help foundations to gauge the current state of public will but also can suggest methods of building public will to support needed social changes.

Foundations are perfectly placed to ensure that public will is represented in the formation of public policy. As discussed elsewhere in this book, in all grantmaking, whether or not that grantmaking has a policy dimension, principles of best practice demand that the needs and desires of the people affected by the project be taken into account and that these stakeholders have a real say in how the project is conceived, planned, executed, and managed. You should bring these people together on advisory or management boards, listen carefully to them, and heed their wishes. Foundations should also share project outcomes with key audiences by means of strategic communications and social marketing in a conscious effort to build public will. In short, consideration of public will should be an integral part of every project funded by a foundation.

If it is, then the inclusion of public will in the policy process will be well-nigh automatic. All stakeholders of the project should be involved in policy-related activities and be included in meetings with and communications to policymakers. The result will be a policy initiative that is connected to popular understanding and that has the chance to gain popular support.

Conclusion

A possibly apocryphal story tells of Benjamin Franklin, at the close of the Constitutional Convention, being asked by a lady, "Dr.

Franklin, what sort of government have you given us?" "A republic, Ma'am," replied the good doctor, "if you can keep it." Indeed, the framers gave us a republic because they distrusted direct democracy. All three branches of that republican government—executive, legislative, judicial—plus the large institutions (such as universities and federated nonprofits) that have grown up outside of the government, have tremendous power to influence the lives of citizens. Foundations, through their policy work, can do much to ensure that this power is used to promote the common good. By bringing forward tested projects that can be brought to scale, and by reflecting and promoting the public will, foundations can help serve as an effective counterbalance to the unchecked power of the government and large institutions. Through their policy work, foundations can go a long way toward helping us keep the republic that the framers gave us.

Chapter Fourteen

Initiative-Based Grantmaking

One of the traits of organized philanthropy that is endearing or infuriating (depending on one's point of view) is its tendency to live focused on the future and in ignorance of the past. This tendency is good, of course, in that philanthropy should be confronting the human ills that loom ahead. It is bad, however, in that grantmakers are often clueless—or at least poorly informed—about their own history. A perfect example of this situation is found in the way in which each succeeding generation of program officers "invents" initiative-based grantmaking. And they do invent it, in the same way in which Columbus "discovered" America—and the twenty million people who were already living there.

Initiative-based grantmaking can be defined as a prescriptive, integrated blend of planning; grantmaking; formative, cluster, and summative evaluation; extensive strategic communications; and social marketing—all with an explicit systems change objective or policy change objective (or both) and a defined exit strategy. Its successive waves of "inventors" continually advance it as a more sophisticated, higher-impact method of grantmaking than "traditional" cluster or passive grantmaking styles. In contrast to individual grants that can dry up and blow away for want of follow-up support, the initiative "stays longer and funds stronger." It stakes out its territory, funds intensively within that territory, provides TA and other supports, and keeps at it until demonstrable impact occurs. This "novel" approach, its advocates believe, will transform philanthropy into a more significant social force.

With all due respect to generations of earnest reformers, anyone who has ever read Robert H. Bremner's classic history, *Ameri-*

can Philanthropy ([1960] 1987), knows that initiative-based grant-making is fine old wine in spiffy new bottles. As Bremner points out, after the Civil War the old religious underpinnings of charity and benevolence were overthrown in favor of "the development of a more scientific spirit and method in philanthropy." As time went by, the "charity organization" movement sought to enhance impact by increasing the efficiency and cooperation of various philanthropic institutions. Andrew Carnegie, as previously mentioned, concentrated his giving on libraries, museums, and educational institutions such as the Cooper Union and the Pratt Institute, which he collectively called "ladders upon which the aspiring can rise" (Carnegie, [1889] 1992b); John D. Rockefeller supported the establishment of the University of Chicago for much the same reason. Rockefeller's General Education Board, as previously discussed, launched an initiative in 1902 to improve agricultural production and secondary education in the American South, with a special focus on improving the lives of African Americans and on improving and reforming higher education and medical education throughout the nation. The General Education Board was a model of longevity (it was not liquidated until the early 1960s) and impact. Initiative-based grantmaking, in short, has been with us since even before the modern foundation appeared in the United States.

Initiatives: Pros and Cons

Although the approach is by no means new, it is undeniable that initiative-based grantmaking can be a very powerful way for a foundation to pursue its mission. As with any approach to philanthropy, however, trade-offs are inescapable. Any foundation choosing to employ initiatives should therefore be aware of both the advantages and the opportunity costs involved in this type of programming.

Advantages

There are at least six major advantages of initiative-based grant-making. Some of these advantages are powerful indeed.

1. *Focus.* It is all too easy for foundations to suffer from the sin that Frederick Gates, John D. Rockefeller Sr.'s philanthropic adviser,

called scatteration. Potentially high-impact opportunities beckon on a regular basis, and the temptation is to put a little bit of money into each one. Soon, of course, the foundation has diluted its grantmaking to the point that it is achieving no significant impacts whatsoever. Initiative-based grantmaking imposes a discipline on foundations, forcing them to define a certain problem or set of interconnected problems and to focus a significant portion of their grantmaking within this set of activities. The results of such focusing can often be dramatic. In 1934, for example, the Daniel and Florence Guggenheim Foundation launched a nine-year initiative to support fundamental research on rocketry. Their grantee, Robert Goddard, conducted the basic and practical science that led, twenty-five years after the initiative ended, to the launching into orbit of the first U.S. satellite. To use a metaphor that returns the discussion to earth, one might say that passive grantmaking broadcasts seeds, some of which will grow. Initiative-based grantmaking carefully chooses a field in which to plant seeds, and cultivates them faithfully so that as many germinate as possible.

2. *Patience.* Individual grants typically have a life span of less than five years; most last three years or fewer. This is simply too short a time for significant social changes to evolve. Although foundations often do make follow-up grants, there are rarely any assurances of follow-up given at the outset, so grantees must live with insecurity and often focus energy on renewing grant support that could be better spent on developing the project. Because initiative-based grantmaking is generally a long-term proposition, more security is built in for the grantee. Everyone can focus on doing a better job instead of on chasing grants, and the outcomes can be much stronger because of it.

3. *Integration.* Cluster-based grantmaking can fall into a series of discrete steps that seem to be sequential rather than holistic: plan, consider, pilot, evaluate, disseminate, seek policy impact, try to bring to scale. Initiative-based grantmaking, in contrast, aims to do everything in a coordinated fashion. From the very beginning of the initiative, policy impact (to take one example) is one of the goals and is carefully planned. Pilot projects are considered explicitly with the intention of bringing them to scale later. Evaluation and strategic communications are planned from the start to facilitate the transition from pilot to scale. In short, all the elements of

the grantmaking cycle are mobilized and integrated so as to multiply the potential of the initiative.

4. *Partnership with grantees.* It simply is not possible to conduct an initiative in a fire-and-forget fashion. Foundations become closely involved with their initiative grantees and thus cannot avoid a share of the credit when things go well or a share of the blame when they do not. By pooling the abilities of both foundation and grantee, the initiative can create a powerful force for change.

5. *"Return on investment."* By focusing on a delimited area, having the patience to continue supporting work on this area for a long time period, and integrating all the resources at its command, the foundation can potentially magnify many times over the impacts it is likely to achieve through cluster-based grantmaking. This is especially true if the foundation can realize its intentional efforts at policy change, for then the much greater resources of government or large institutions can support the advances piloted with foundation support. For example, the Carnegie Corporation provided the American Foundation for the Blind with resources to develop recorded books for the blind, the majority of whom cannot use Braille. After the "talking books" pilot had proven its worth, Congress began appropriating money to the Library of Congress to bring the program to scale nationwide.

6. *Convening power of the foundation.* An initiative can bring to the table many key players to work as a team, players that would never have teamed up on their own. An initiative, therefore, can serve as a rallying point around which people and organizations can coalesce for the common good.

Costs

Although its advantages are many and formidable, initiative-based grantmaking also has its costs for any foundation interested in practicing it.

1. *Opportunities lost.* This cost is essentially the mirror image of the advantages of focusing. If the focusing is faithfully adhered to, the foundation will not be able to pursue other opportunities. Generally, this does not cause much pain at first, because the foundation presumably looked at all of its options before deciding to

launch a particular initiative. Later, however, as unforeseen opportunities come along, the foundation will find it necessary to decline interest in many good things—probably, in fact, in a few potentially *wonderful* things—in order to retain focus on the initiative. These opportunities might come in the form of over-the-transom grant requests, invitations to join consortia of funders, or other potential new initiatives. If Frederick Gates's scatteration is a sin, so too must be excessive concentration: being so inflexibly invested in initiatives that no leeway is left to respond to unforeseen opportunities. Initiatives should not, as a rule, consume all of a foundation's allocated spending in any given year. Setting some upward limit—perhaps one-half or at most two-thirds of that year's payout—will ensure that the foundation is maintaining flexibility to respond to individual opportunities. Meanwhile, the foundation should phase out older initiatives on a rolling basis so that there is always room at the inn for starting up new initiatives. It would be melancholy, indeed, if a foundation had to decline a proposal that might have had enormous impact or to forego starting a new initiative that might literally have changed the world, merely because it was committed to funding a series of initiatives of only middling impact.

2. *Potential obsolescence.* Initiatives take time to plan and pilot. It may be many months—even years—before the grantmaking phase begins in earnest. If all goes according to plan, the grants will be poised to leverage exciting outcomes within six or seven years of the start date. But in a world in which the half-life of just about everything is shrinking, all may not be going according to plan. In fact, events may have moved in a very different direction from that predicted at the start of an initiative. For example, funders interested in welfare reform were in the middle of a number of initiatives when the Republicans captured Congress from the Democrats in 1994. The policy shifts that followed in 1995 rendered a number of these initiatives immediately obsolete. Any foundation doing initiative work must be prepared to risk being mugged by unplanned (and unpredictable) obsolescence.

3. *Inescapable hubris.* Any time a foundation decides exactly how it wants to have society changed and then consciously delimits the range and scope of organizations it will fund toward that end, it is saying, in effect, to the rest of the world, "We know the answers."

It is also saying, in effect, to the excluded organizations, "Your ideas do not count."

A foundation can mitigate these messages by carefully seeking input from the field while planning the initiative, getting feedback about the initiative while it is in process, and getting reactions once it is completed, but the fact remains that it is the foundation that ultimately is making the calls. Some foundations have been justly criticized for their blunderbuss style in conducting initiative-based grantmaking: parachuting in without consultation, selecting grantees using dubious or secret criteria, and frankly not caring a fig about how stakeholders reacted to it all. Those who would do initiatives have an extra obligation to include stakeholders as substantive partners in the process and to form as much of a partnership as is possible. Foundations can ill afford to become perceived as a sort of renegade Colonel Kurtz or as a pompous and unresponsive Colonel Blimp. If carelessly done, initiative-based grantmaking can promote these perceptions.

4. *Sheer complexity.* Trying to integrate strategic planning, grantmaking, evaluation, networking conferences, social marketing, and policy activities—all with strong stakeholder involvement—is a huge task, involving many different people and multiple activities. Anything with such a large number of moving parts is prone to breakdowns, and they do happen. These make it difficult to meet the targeted timetable and, especially in the early months of the initiative, difficult to show that anything is being accomplished. Henry David Thoreau's advice in *Walden* rings very much true for the management of initiatives: "Our life is frittered away by detail. . . . Simplify, simplify" ([1854] 1973). By their nature, initiatives are complex things, difficult to manage well. Adding additional layers of complexity to them is sheer madness. All who conduct initiatives should resolve to do no more than is necessary to achieve the desired outcomes. This "bare minimum" will prove to be more than enough work for any staff.

The sharp-eyed reader will notice that "expense" is not included as a "cost" of initiative-based grantmaking. This is simply because the foundation would have to spend 5 percent of its net asset value on grantmaking in any event. If not expended on an initiative, it would have to be spent on cluster grantmaking, individual grants, or operated programs. Thus, the expense of initiatives, though considerable, is not listed as a cost to consider.

Starting the Initiative

All initiatives, in a very literal sense, start at the end. That is, they begin when a program officer visualizes a positive outcome in society that could be effected by a well-planned and well-executed initiative. It then becomes necessary to work backwards, as it were: to plan all the operations needed to achieve the desired outcome. *Plan* is the operative word: in order to make the many and complicated pieces of the initiative work together, planning is utterly essential. In many ways, the planning process is like that described for cluster grantmaking in Chapter One. You need to identify a niche, review the literature, scan the field, consult those most affected, and possibly make a few learning grants. You should also go beyond merely consulting with those who will be affected by the initiative and include their representatives on the management team for the initiative.

The need for a management team also differentiates initiative-based grantmaking from cluster grantmaking. Whereas a single program officer is sufficient to take the lead on a cluster of eight to twelve projects, the more intensive management demands of an initiative require that a team of program officers manage its activities. Ideally, the team should include a program officer with expertise in each of the major subject areas covered by the initiative; at least one representative of the stakeholders; and professionals skilled in evaluation, strategic communications, social marketing, and policy issues. A single person may cover more than one area, of course, and not all team members need be foundation employees; consultants are frequently required to provide expertise not available on the foundation staff. In smaller foundations, nearly everyone on the initiative team may be a consultant. It is important to designate a clear leader or coleaders for the team, and the leader or leaders must make it a priority to manage the team for harmonious working relationships and high productivity. Many a conceptually sound initiative has foundered on the rocks of management team discord.

The entire team must avoid the temptation to begin programming too fast. It is not unusual for the preliminary research, stakeholder work, and planning to take a year or even longer. Initiatives have a lot of "ducks," and it is simply not possible to get them all in a row in a matter of weeks. In the meantime, opportunities to make grants beckon on the outside, while pressure to show results can build on the inside. The temptation to prematurely start grantmaking, therefore, is very strong, but it must be resisted. The motto of program officers running initiatives should be, "We will make no grant before its time."

The Integrated Action Plan

With so many threads making it up, the initiative tapestry is all but guaranteed to unravel unless there is a careful plan to keep all the stitches in place. In fact, the simple word *plan* is somewhat inadequate; because so many elements need to work in unison, a better term is *integrated action plan* (IAP). The IAP is integrated because it brings together, in one document, all the plans for grantmaking, evaluation, strategic communications, social marketing, bringing to scale, and policy work. The IAP is an action plan because it lays out what is slated to happen, when it is scheduled to happen, and whose responsibility it is to make it happen. And, for all these activities, the IAP includes a timeline and a budget.

One of the prime early responsibilities of the initiative's management team is to create the IAP. One method for doing this is to have each person on the team draw up his or her own "wish list" to cover the parts of the initiative for which he or she is responsible, then to come together as a team to negotiate the reductions needed to fit within time and budgetary constraints. An alternative (and probably preferable) method is to craft the IAP from scratch as a team, building up to the resources available, rather than reducing down to them. Variations on these basic approaches are also possible, but no matter how the IAP is constructed, it is critically important that team members feel that the process is fair and that their values have been understood and respected. If there is dissension on the management team, the initiative will never achieve its full potential.

One of the basic tenets of initiative management is that all activities must be coordinated and that most should begin at the same time. Formative evaluation should begin as close to the start of the initiative as possible. One element of the formative evaluation, a baseline evaluation survey, must be done *before* any grants are made, so as to set a meaningful fixed mark against which summative evaluation can be conducted later. Strategic communications and possibly social marketing should begin contemporaneously with the project as well, so as to prepare the way for bringing models to scale. Policy groundwork should commence at the very beginning, for usually much preliminary work needs to be done before policy can be affected.

The most difficult thing about writing an IAP is the need to follow single pieces of the initiative chronologically from beginning to end while *simultaneously* writing about how other pieces of the initiative fit with it. For example, it is necessary to plan the trajectory of projects within the initiative from the request for proposals to the desired policy outcome, while at the same time writing about how evaluation, strategic communications, policy work, and other pieces interact with the projects. One method of doing this is to write about each component separately, then to unify them with a timeline. Another method is to write about time blocks within the project, including inside each block an explanation of how different factors interact within that time period. For this method, too, you will probably use a timeline to provide a visual means of understanding how an initiative unfolds. Naturally, you must include a budget that illustrates the projected cost for every element of the initiative.

The Integrated Action Plan: One Model

There is no best model for working on an IAP. You can work with a variety of formats, and different initiatives will require different formats. The following model is presented as one illustration of how you can organize an IAP.

1. *Program or executive summary.* Because IAPs tend to be long documents, it is helpful to start them with a brief (one- to three-page) summary of the initiative. It should concisely explain the goals

of the initiative, the actions that will be taken to achieve the goals, and the expected outcomes. It is usually easier to write this section later, after you have written the other sections in greater detail.

2. *Background or context.* Every initiative exists in a context. This section should share, in five to seven pages, the key elements of that context, including history, how the initiative meets societal needs (or seizes societal opportunities), and what impacts it may be expected to have on future events.

3. *Strategic or operational plan.* This is the heart of the IAP, and it must, in ten to fifteen pages, tell exactly how the initiative will work. What jobs need to be done, and according to what timeline? What outcomes are projected to occur, and by what time? Are there contingency plans in case the stated plan goes awry? The strategic plan must inform its readers of how the initiative will work, so it should be detailed and specific.

4. *Timeline.* Although the timeline is described verbally in the strategic or operational plan, it should be presented visually in this section. You may need to create more than one line or to use intersecting lines in order to convey the complexity of an initiative's operations. This timeline should clearly identify all the benchmarks by which progress will be judged. It is ideal to place this on a single page so that the readers can see the whole timeline at a glance. If you decide to include a logic model (about which more later), you could put it in this section.

5. *Procedures.* In two to four pages, this section specifies the policies by which the initiative will operate and identifies the major tasks and the people responsible for discharging them. The roles of any consultants and intermediary employees who will be working with foundation employees on the initiative must also be spelled out in this section.

6. *Stakeholder analysis.* Stakeholders are those people and organizations that have a vital and direct interest in the outcomes of a project or an initiative. These can be divided into two groups: those inside the foundation and those outside. There will always be at least three internal stakeholders: the board, the executive officers, and the program officers and ancillary staff who are actually working on the initiative. There may be others, especially in larger foundations, such as members of the evaluation and communications staffs. There will likely be a larger number of external stakeholders, such

as the people directly affected by the initiative, the grantee organization and its collaborators, policymakers, regulators, and so on.

For each of the internal and external stakeholder groups, it is necessary to identify not only their interest in the initiative but also the desired changes that each will experience as a result of the initiative's programming. The stakeholder analysis should be four to eight pages in length.

7. *Strategic communications.* This section, which should be three to five pages long, identifies the basic themes and the important messages that should be used in all communications regarding the initiative. Although these messages will undoubtedly change as the initiative unfolds, it is useful to agree on the basic themes before the initiative is launched.

8. *Dissemination and social marketing.* Although these activities are necessarily rudimentary at the IAP-writing stage, it is good to plan for them in the IAP itself. This one- to three-page section should identify target audiences and techniques that will be used to communicate the basic themes and important messages of the projects within the initiative.

9. *Evaluation.* This section of three to five pages needs to identify the context in which the initiative will be evaluated, the process by which programming will be assessed, and how outcomes will be judged. It must list the important questions that the evaluation will be designed to answer, delineate the roles and responsibilities of all stakeholders, and make explicit the roles and responsibilities of the external evaluator or evaluation firm.

10. *Public policy education.* This section will vary in length according to the policy content of the initiative itself. For those initiatives that contain significant policy content, it would be advisable to create a policy framework. At minimum, this framework should contain the elements explained in Chapter Thirteen: program policy focus, policy change objectives, approaches, leverage points, and resources. If any of the policy foci chosen are likely to be controversial, this section should include a brief analysis of risks and benefits.

11. *Budget.* This section obviously needs to detail the costs for each section of the initiative. Ideally, it should be compressed into a single page so that readers can compare all of the costs without having to flip pages back and forth. If the initiative is complex

enough, it may be necessary to create a single-page simplified budget and a multipage detailed budget. Alternatively, you might use a simplified budget with explanatory annotations on the following pages. In any case, the budget is presented in line-item form and details expenditures made over time.

The Logic Model

The more complex the initiative, the more useful it is for the IAP to employ visual elements in order to depict how all the parts will unfold. It is difficult to keep track of many simultaneously occurring elements when they are presented in a purely descriptive format, but if they are all charted out graphically, the reader can understand—literally at a glance—many complex concepts and their interactions. Timelines, as mentioned, are one means of illustration. They offer the great virtue of depicting chronology, so that the reader can understand change over time. However, the timeline alone is rarely sufficient. It is one-dimensional, which forces everything to fit onto a single line; it is also linear, whereas certain components of an initiative, such as evaluation and strategic communications, tend to cut across different parts of the initiative. It is therefore usually handy to borrow a tool from the evaluation literature—the logic model—to illustrate the IAP.

The logic model can be constructed in a number of ways, but in its most basic form, it is a variation on the classic flow chart so beloved of manufacturing engineers. A simple logic model can be conceptualized as having five columns:

Column one is headed Context. Under this rubric fall all the factors influencing the initiative. These would include the problems that the initiative is trying to solve (or the opportunities it is attempting to seize) and everything that will be done during the initiative to understand them: needs assessment, literature search, stakeholder studies, advisory panels, and baseline studies.

The second column is headed Inputs. Under this rubric are listed all the resources that the initiative brings to the table, such as funds, local leadership, volunteerism, institutional partnerships, TA, strategic communications, and policy activities.

Column three is headed Processes. Under this rubric are listed all the major activities that will be undertaken during the life span of the initiative, including grants, formative and summative evaluation, a strategic communications program, plans to bring the project to scale, and policy work. This column will usually include more sheer activity than any of the others.

Column four is headed Outcomes. Under this rubric are listed the most important achievements that the initiative is expected to produce. The outcomes will be a direct result of the inputs and processes. For example, an institutional partner (input) and a grant for $100,000 to combat teen smoking (process) should lead to fewer teens smoking cigarettes (outcome).

The fifth column is headed Impacts. Under this rubric fall all the changes in society caused by the outcomes of the initiative. If fewer teens smoking cigarettes is the outcome, then the impact would be improved health among teenagers, fewer health problems among babies born to teen mothers, and so on. The impacts are changes in the problems the initiative is addressing, and they thus loop back to the Context column. Put another way, the impacts are the societal changes that the initiative is expected to achieve.

A simplified logic model using an initiative to reduce teen smoking as an example is illustrated in Figure 14.1. You can find more sophisticated models in the evaluation literature cited in the Bibliography of this book.

The logic model allows for both a linear understanding of how an initiative will unfold and more complex interpretations. Although some elements relate to each other in a neat, linear fashion across the columns (funds ⇒ grantmaking ⇒ lower teen smoking and mortality rates ⇒ improved teen health), other elements connect in more complex ways to multiple items in different columns or rows. (For example, the antismoking strategic communications campaign listed in the Processes column, by communicating directly with teens, leads to lower teen and infant sickness and mortality rates, listed under Outcomes; that campaign also communicates directly with policymakers, thus leading to more legal restrictions on teen smoking.) Ultimately, the logic model illustrates how all the pieces come together to form the mosaic of an initiative and, more important, allows one to understand the interrelationships of its many different pieces to each other.

Figure 14.1. Logic Model.

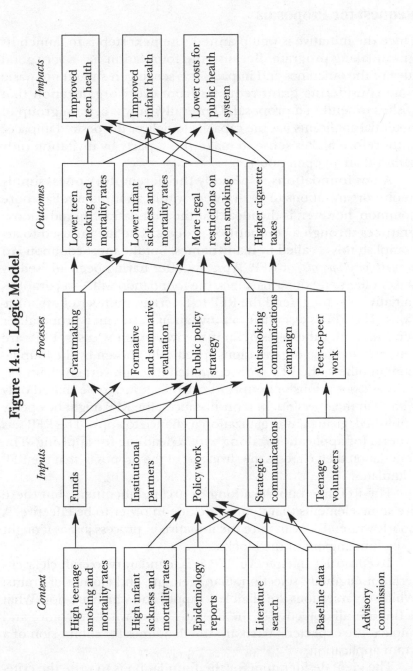

Context	Inputs	Processes	Outcomes	Impacts
High teenage smoking and mortality rates	Funds	Grantmaking	Lower teen smoking and mortality rates	Improved teen health
High infant sickness and mortality rates	Institutional partners	Formative and summative evaluation	Lower infant sickness and mortality rates	Improved infant health
Epidemiology reports	Policy work	Public policy strategy	More legal restrictions on teen smoking	Lower costs for public health system
Literature search	Strategic communications	Antismoking communications campaign	Higher cigarette taxes	
Baseline data	Teenage volunteers	Peer-to-peer work		
Advisory commission				

Request for Proposals

Once the initiative is well planned, the next step is to launch its grantmaking program. Because the foundation has a very good idea of the outcomes and impacts it is seeking, it should not waste time considering grant requests from every organization that wishes to send in a proposal. Generally, only a certain group of potential applicants has the capacity to deliver the desired impacts. It therefore makes sense to make this a party by invitation only rather than an open house.

A few foundations, especially the peremptory ones, simply anoint organizations to be grantees within an initiative. Far more common, however, is the idea that the foundation should choose grantees through a competitive process. The means used to accomplish this is called by many names, but the most common is a *request for proposals,* or RFP. Typically, after having been advised by stakeholders and other partners, the foundation will, as a part of its initiative planning, send the RFP to a certain number of organizations. The RFP is essentially an invitation to submit a proposal for funding under the aegis of an initiative. In many cases, RFPs are sent only to those organizations specifically chosen by the foundation; in others, the RFP is disseminated through certain channels, such as associations of nonprofit organizations, to be shared only with their membership. In rarer instances, the RFP might be openly published, giving any organization a chance to apply. The RFP sets criteria for applications, along with a deadline for applying. The foundation then chooses the strongest of the proposals that the RFP stimulates.

The RFP need not be a long or arcane document, but there are some elements that it must include in order to be effective. A poorly written RFP can mire the initiative in process just as it ought to be bursting out of the blocks.

To construct an effective RFP, it is mandatory to craft clear criteria for eligibility, selection, management, and closure of grants: Which organizations are eligible to apply, and which are not? What is the overall objective of the initiative, and what outcomes and impacts are expected? What are the deadlines for submission of a grant application?

The great desideratum for the foundation is to write the criteria so that unsuitable organizations do not apply and so that suitable organizations that do apply will submit relatively uniform applications. Uniformity makes it easier for the foundation to directly compare proposals and choose the strongest. Therefore, the criteria should include the exact format in which the foundation wants to see its proposals; the minimum and maximum acceptable page length; any dollar or time limits; whether attachments are acceptable, and if so, what kind; and any other foundation-imposed expectation, such as requirements that the grantees invest some of their own money in the project or that they must cooperate with the cluster evaluator.

The RFP should openly share the criteria for project selection. What elements must the proposal address? What will be the minimally acceptable outcomes? What budgetary amount and line-item distribution will be allowed? Are there any line items that must be included in or excluded from the budget? The document should share the basic method by which the proposals will be ranked; for example, if continuation and evaluation plans are important, this should be disclosed. The RFP should also inform applicants about when the funding decisions will be made and how applicants will be informed of the verdict.

The RFP should carefully define the criteria for grant management. What are the foundation's expectations regarding reporting on progress? Will there be networking meetings? What are the rules regarding budget management? The document should take particular care in discussing the expectations surrounding evaluation. At the project level, it should cover the importance of both formative and summative evaluation; at the initiative level, it should discuss cluster evaluation activities. And the RFP should explain the foundation's expectations with regard to strategic communications.

Perhaps counterintuitively for a document that is mainly *prospective* in nature, the RFP needs to share clear criteria regarding project closure. What are the predicted timelines for the initiative? Are grants renewable? If so, by what procedure? If not, what are the exit procedures? What obligations might there be to share lessons learned? Even after the formal grant period ends, foundations often expect that the grantees will remain networked with still-active portions of the initiative, perhaps as part of an effort to bring the projects to scale or possibly in terms of strategic communications efforts. If the foundation has such a requirement, the RFP must spell it out.

Although no foundation hopes to issue a four-hundred-page RFP (and none would be forgiven for doing so), the RFP is one document that should not be mindlessly foreshortened. Many a foundation has issued short documents in haste and then repented at leisure when the lack of clarity or completeness caused problems later. It is far better to write a long RFP that spells out all the rules than a short one that omits key points or explains them insufficiently. The general rule for RFP writers should be "When in doubt, spell it out."

Strategic Communications

Many of the concepts surrounding initiative management, such as evaluation, social marketing, cluster evaluation, and bringing projects to scale, have already been discussed. The concept of strategic communications, however, requires more explanation. As previously mentioned, foundations vary widely in their approach to communications. Some prefer to toil in anonymity; a few seek the klieg lights. Most staffed foundations have some sort of communications capacity, although often the professionals assigned to do the work are pretty much limited to writing an annual report and responding to criticisms appearing from time to time in the press. Many foundation leaders fear that communicating more aggressively than this could lead to either a flood of unwanted proposals or unwelcome scrutiny on the part of regulators or both. The concept of strategic communications takes just the opposite tack: that educating the public about a foundation's interests will result in fewer out-of-scope proposals and make it less likely to be scrutinized, for foundations that communicate strategically will appear to be less secretive.

At the heart of strategic communications is the belief that the lessons being learned by the foundation and its grantees should be shared—and shared vigorously—so as to magnify their impact. This requires more than an episodic or opportunistic effort every now and then; it requires an ongoing program strategically aimed at achieving the foundation's ends. Proponents also stress that it is far better for the foundation to proactively define itself to the public than to let others define the foundation to suit their agenda.

When the foundation is planning an initiative, strategic communications and social marketing are closely related but not synonymous. There must be a message before one can market anything, and a program of strategic communications helps craft that message. Policy efforts, too, can and should be preceded by solid communications programs. These efforts need not be managed on a day-to-day basis by a communications professional, but they do take time to do right, so they should be assigned as a *primary* responsibility to whomever takes the lead on them.

Like traditional dissemination efforts, traditional communications relied on broadcasting: news briefings, press releases, and general publications. Although each of these approaches has its uses in strategic communications, more recent narrowcasting approaches have been added to the mix, just as they have in social marketing. Targeting certain audiences through e-mail listservs, specialized publications, and other carefully selected media, and developing ongoing relationships with certain members of the media and policymakers, ensure that key people receive important messages at the right times.

The Communications Network, originally an affinity group of the Council on Foundations but now a freestanding 501(c)(3) organization, defines strategic communications as having four essential attributes: (1) informing potential grantseekers about foundation application and review processes and procedures, including what the foundation does and does not fund, and how and when to apply; (2) making foundation and grantee experiences widely accessible; (3) supporting community actions vital to furthering the missions of the foundation and its grantees; (4) making sure the foundation is appropriately accountable (Karel, 1999).

As conceptualized by the Communications Network, strategic communications become an essential part of the programming of the initiative. The third attribute, for example, helps build community capacity to successfully support the programmatic actions of the initiative. All four attributes cost money, of course, and you must remember to properly budget for strategic communications at the beginning of the initiative. Retrofitting the communications after an initiative has been planned is never as effective as planning for it from the outset.

Special Management Challenges of Initiatives

Many of the tasks of managing an initiative are the same as those of managing an individual grant or a cluster of grants. There are, however, a few challenges that distinguish initiative management from other forms.

1. *"Intensivity" versus "extensivity."* When you are managing an initiative you work with fewer grantees than you do when you are managing clusters of grants, but the initiative requires much more intensive work per grantee. In managing initiatives, you do less project development and more project oversight; you have less hands-on contact with grantees and do more work with intermediary organizations.

2. *Coordination versus individual management.* Whether you are managing an initiative or clusters, there are bound to be several "balls in the air." There are more if you are an initiative manager, however, and they need to be closely coordinated in order to prevent their falling to earth. Integrating grantmaking with evaluation, strategic communications, social marketing, and policy work is a full-time task in itself. You truly must learn to be a master juggler to keep all these balls in the air.

3. *Narrowing versus broadening.* Managing an initiative can be so time-intensive that it leaves little time for you to interact with other colleagues, whether they be colleagues in the foundation or those working for other foundations. There are many benefits to be gained by focusing on a single initiative, but inevitably there are costs in terms of loss of flexibility and ability to work broadly across different areas.

4. *Planned versus organic development.* Initiatives have a targeted outcome in mind from the start, whereas clusters have a less defined goal. Any veteran program officer will affirm that projects, whether they are part of an initiative or part of a cluster, will often develop very unpredictably. Sometimes, in fact, the serendipitous outcomes of a project are far more impressive and important than the expected outcomes. In a cluster, with its more developmental sensibility, it is often possible to abandon the original plan and improvise to move in the new direction that is working well. Within the tighter, more strategic sensibility of the initiative, it is difficult

to abandon—or even to extensively modify—the original plan. You must find ways to keep initiative projects on track, avoiding temptations to go off on intriguing but strategy-busting tangents. And you must keep the projects moving at approximately the same pace—no mean feat in a world in which just about everything, and projects most of all, tend to develop at their own rates.

5. *Losing one aircraft carrier versus losing many frigates.* In cluster grantmaking, there are a large number of grantees per cluster, and the cluster itself is somewhat loosely connected, so that if a couple of grants "slip beneath the waves," the cluster itself can survive. If a couple of grants in a tightly coordinated initiative should sink, they could pull the entire initiative down to the depths with them. Therefore, instead of losing just a couple of grants (which is bad enough), the foundation could lose a lot of money and the years of work that it took to develop the initiative (which is very much akin to the Navy losing an aircraft carrier). If you are managing an initiative, you will want to avoid that scenario, lest you discover *why* the captain of an aircraft carrier would choose to go down with the ship.

Conclusion

"In the long run," Henry David Thoreau wrote in *Walden*, "men hit only what they aim at" ([1854] 1973). Initiative-based grantmaking allows foundations to take deliberate aim at significant targets and, through very careful application, to hit them. Initiatives are a very powerful medicine in the foundation pharmacopoeia, but like many drugs, the effective dose is uncomfortably close to the lethal dose. That is to say, initiatives are effective only when they are exhaustive, and they are exhaustive only when they are intensive, comprehensive, and expensive. Foundations should never try to undertake initiatives if they cannot spare program officers to *concentrate* on them; never attempt them if they cannot marshal all the elements needed to *complete* them; never launch them if they cannot *afford* them. If, however, the foundation has the resources and the determination, initiatives can make remarkable impacts. In fact, they can actually achieve the outcome described in that trite expression often loosely used to summarize foundation work: they can change the world.

Chapter Fifteen

The Ethics of Grantmaking

Henry David Thoreau no doubt would be amused by the irony of seeing his words hanging in full calligraphic glory on the walls of many grantmakers: "Philanthropy is almost the only virtue which is sufficiently appreciated by mankind" ([1854] 1973). Program officers frame the words and bask in Thoreau's approval, but a closer reading suggests that the sage of Walden was offering a tart criticism to the do-good tribe. Other virtues are *underappreciated;* they are better than they are generally understood to be. Philanthropy is almost the only one that is no better than it is perceived to be.

If Thoreau was right, there are many reasons for it. First of all, there is the simple fact that philanthropy does not have the same level of accountability as do other callings. Program officers are accountable to their officers and boards, of course, but they do not have constituents who can vote them out of office, or shareholders who can fire them for failing to turn an adequate profit. This freedom from accountability can give courage to be bold—but it can also give license to fall short of excellence.

There can be no denying that some program officers have taken that license. Whether unwittingly or uncaringly, these grantmakers do harm, surrender to arrogance, tell lies, become involved in conflicts of interest, lose touch with their spirit, miss big opportunities, and lapse into formulaic behavior.

Avoiding the Seven Deadly Sins of Philanthropy

Habitually failing in the aforementioned ways is a charge that can be laid at the door of only the tiniest fraction of grantmakers. But most program officers, from time to time, are guilty of one or more of the lapses. People who make their living practicing philanthropy probably, as a class, have ethics no worse than those of other professions. However, given the high ideals of philanthropy and the enormous potential it offers to society, the public has a right to expect that the ethical behavior of program officers should be *higher* than that of the average professional. That belief has infused the foregoing chapters, in which I have implicitly addressed ethical issues without labeling them as such. The ethical sensibility being so essential to grantmaking, however, it seems appropriate to dedicate this chapter to a distillation of important ethical issues, moral imperatives you will find important to follow.

First, Do No Harm

This idea comes, of course, directly from the oath of Hippocrates, but it is just as appropriate to the world of twenty-first-century philanthropy as it was to the world of Greek medicine in the fourth century B.C. The focus of this book has been on making *positive* change, and that is as it should be. As a grantmaker, you should concentrate on maximizing the enormous potential inherent in philanthropy to change the world for the better.

It is good to remember, however, that the best of intentions can render the worst of results. Helping hands can also inadvertently do harm. To be sure, there are probably no program officers whose first thought on rising in the morning is, "I cannot wait to do some social damage today!" But harm done unwittingly is still harm. And the types of unwitting destructiveness that grantmakers can wreak are many and varied. How can you unwittingly do damage? By turning away risky but high-potential ideas. By funding them but ending support too soon. By funding too long, thus fostering dependence. By giving a project too much money too soon. By taking too long to make up your mind. By requiring an applicant to jump endlessly through hoops. By funding an organization that has no credibility in its own community (and refusing to fund organizations that have local credibility).

The really insidious thing about the types of unwitting harm described here is that the grantmaker can cite so many seemingly good reasons for making the decisions that cause the problems. The high-potential grant is too risky. The foundation needs a high turnover rate in its grant commitments so as to retain flexibility in grantmaking. Some projects are "old friends" and deserve support indefinitely. This project is so promising, it needs to brought to scale *quickly*. Quality decisions cannot be rushed. The foundation needs a lot of information before it can be expected to make a decision. It is important to fund stable and respectable organizations, not shaky fringe groups. Good rationalizations all, but the road to programming hell is cobbled with good rationalizations, and those listed here make excellent paving stones. The ethical program officer must focus on doing good and resist the blandishments of the many "good" reasons for doing harm.

Brook No Arrogance

Abraham Flexner, much-respected former program officer with the Carnegie Corporation and the Rockefeller Foundation and author of the eponymously titled report that transformed medical education in the United States, repeatedly admonished his fellow program officers, "Remember: the grantseeker always comes to you, psychologically, on his knees" (1952). The power dynamic is clear, and it is clearly unequal: foundations have the money, and grantseekers need the money. Although it is true that enlightened program officers realize that foundations need good grantseekers too, the fact remains that you can act as imperiously as a Roman Emperor and still experience no shortage of people willing to tolerate the abuse in order to get the grants. True, the absence of any semblance of a partnership in such situations renders it unlikely that the grants will have a positive impact, but imperious grantmakers can generally be as arrogant as they wish to be, so long as they continue to meet the minimum 5 percent payout requirement.

It is difficult to overstate the damage that program officers with ravenous egos can do. They can crush creativity, stifle initiative, and wreck partnerships. A "do it my way or hit the highway" grantmaker sometimes inspires grantees to say what they must in order to get the grant, then, after getting it, to surreptitiously do what they wanted to do anyway. But whether grantees abjectly do as the program officer dictates or rebelliously violate the terms of the grant, in either case the power of partnership is squandered.

Like a persistent current, the flow of foundation work pushes grantmakers toward arrogance. They are flattered and feted, charmed and cheered. It is all too easy to progress from being surprised by this royal treatment, to enjoying it, to expecting it, to demanding it. As a program officer, you cannot proclaim innocence simply because you are not deliberately swimming with the current. If you merely float, it will sweep you away. The ethical grantmaker must constantly swim *against* that current of arrogance. You must treat all proposals and all people with respect. An open attitude is essential, and as we discussed in Chapter Two, you should discount much of the praise you receive. Self-criticism and humility are just as important to your work as are creativity and intelligence. You must always be a steward of resources, a servant as well as a leader.

Tell No Lies

Work in foundations is particularly rife with opportunities to spare yourself unpleasantness by telling the proverbial little white lies. An applicant may be hurt if you were to candidly critique his or her proposal; how much more pleasant it would be to blame a negative decision on a cut in the grantmaking program's budget rather than on the inferiority of the idea described in the proposal. A trustee at a board meeting asks a question that you cannot answer; you could admit to ignorance before God and everyone, but how much less embarrassing to concoct a plausible answer. The director of a funded project is alienating a potential funding partner by her behavior; how much simpler it would be to pretend not to notice and to advise her to keep to the same course.

Little white lies have the seductive attribute of feeling good at the moment they are uttered. They promote pleasantness, avoid embarrassment, save work. Like so many other quick fixes, however, they usually turn sour as time goes by. The negative effects are sometimes subtle, but they intrude on the near, middle, and long terms. In the near term, opportunities to learn and grow—for all involved—are lost when you take the easy way out. In the middle term, you will, if you fib often enough, at some point be caught in a lie. In the long term, if you are caught often enough, your credibility will sink to the level of that late, unlamented daily, *Pravda.*

How much better it is in the long run, then, simply to tell the truth. Mark Twain once sardonically wrote: "Truth is the most valuable thing we have. Let us economize it." Shorn of their cynicism, his words hold good advice. It is unnecessary to be tactless about truth telling, nor do you need to disclose every bit of information in your possession. If, however, you take care to ensure that everything you say and write is true, the result will be the happy conjunction of the morally right and the pragmatically sensible. The ethical program officer will regard truth telling as a beacon and focus on it, no matter how high the seas. To ignore this beacon is to chart a sure course for the rocks.

Tolerate No Conflicts of Interest

An old lament goes like this: "When I became a grantmaker, I found that I had eaten my last bad meal and lost my last true friend." Although that may overstate the case, it is true that program officers are constantly being courted by people who want money. Frequently, these grantseekers come bearing gifts. You soon discover that you rarely need to pay for a lunch and frequently are offered enticing gifts: books, fountain pens, even high-tech gizmos. It may be more blessed to give than to receive, but in philanthropy you seemingly get to do both.

The ethical question this raises is easy to frame: When does a gift cross the line and become a bribe? Some foundations have a simple answer: accept no gifts, no matter how modest. If you accept *nothing*, not so much as an after-dinner mint, you cannot have worries about the ethics of accepting *something*. Although effective, this policy is also pretty crude. In some cultures, such as in Japan and in Latin America, gift giving is an important part of any relationship, and refusing a small gift creates a large insult. Such a "zero tolerance" policy can also give rise to absurdities. If, while you are on a site visit, an applicant offers you a one-mile ride across campus in a university vehicle, should you refuse and opt to walk or, perhaps, accept the ride and then requisition a few dimes from the foundation's petty cash drawer to reimburse the university for its transportation cost? To avoid such ludicrous situations, most foundation allow program officers to accept a single gift of less than $25 in value. This allows the foundation to respect the customs of others and avoid absurdities, while proscribing transactions big enough to influence a program officer's judgment.

This is a sensible compromise, but it is not a panacea. For one thing, it requires you to become an appraiser, constantly gauging whether the proffered gift has a market value of $25 or more. If there is any question in your mind, you should follow the old rule: "When in doubt, your wallet should come out." Certainly, you should pay for all meals, lodging, and significant transportation expenses. Anything that is close to the $25 line should be declined: accept an imprinted ball-point pen, for example, but decline the gift of a gold-filled fountain pen.

Apply a similar logic to board memberships: it is acceptable to be on the board of an organization applying for assistance from the foundation that employs you, so long as you make the conflict known and excuse yourself from reviewing the request or managing the project should it be funded. The ethical program officer gains no undue benefit from the position, whether in terms of monetary gain or intangible influence. The standard need not be the same as that for Caesar's wife, who had to be "above suspicion," but should meet what might be called the *Daily News* standard. You should behave in such a way that no embarrassment would come to you or to the foundation should your actions become the subject of the banner headlines in the *Daily News*.

Another conflict of interest that you should avoid is to serve as the lead program officer on a request from an organization to which you have connections. Examples would include an organization whose CEO or board chair is a friend of yours; an organization that until recently employed you; an organization that employs or has as a board member a close relative of yours; or your alma mater. Such situations, at the very least, would call into question your objectivity, and could raise issues of favoritism or even nepotism. It is always best to ask a colleague to handle such requests, for no matter how meritorious they might be, your handling them would not satisfy the *Daily News* standard.

Accept No Exclusive Diet of Materialism

To paraphrase Calvin Coolidge, the currency of philanthropy is mainly currency. Moreover, the staffs of many foundations are dominated by businesspeople or academics. Small wonder, then, that philanthropy tends to focus on the material and the intellectual, to the exclusion of the spiritual and the affective. Much that is good can be accomplished by focusing on lucre and learning, but not *all* good things can be achieved with only these two ingredients.

Many, if not most, program officers were drawn to philanthropy in the first place by their passion and by their sense of connection to a larger good. Once the grantmakers are working in a foundation, however, these spiritual motives tend to be overshadowed, if not overwhelmed, by the daily demands of budgets, strategic planning, and policy work. After the material world has crowded out every other consideration, program officers may be efficient, intelligent, and financially savvy, but probably not as compassionate, empathic, or able to perceive deeper meanings as they should be to properly give away money. Cut loose from its spiritual moorings, philanthropy becomes indistinguishable from any other calling: it merely recycles money made in the private sector quite efficiently into the nonprofit sector, instead of making grants that go to the heart of human needs and longings. This is philanthropy as it might have been practiced by Mussolini; the trains run on time, but in the larger human sense, they have nowhere to go.

Keeping a connection to the spiritual in foundation work does not happen automatically or serendipitously; it must be a conscious act of will. Just as you must set aside time for strategic planning and budgeting, so you must reserve time for reflection and connections to deeper meanings. If you do not, the material quickly crowds out the spiritual, and you lose a crucial dimension of your work. The ethical program officer is moved by the spiritual as well as by the material, by what cannot be measured as well as by what can. You must always remember that "not everything that counts can be counted."

Lose No Opportunities

The required 5 percent payout measures only the flow of dollars; it does nothing to ensure that those dollars are spent wisely and effectively. On a dollar-for-dollar basis, the dullest, safest, and most unimaginative grants count for just as much in terms of meeting payout as the sharpest, riskiest, most imaginative ones. It is up to you to take the extra step of seizing opportunity—that is, getting the most out of every dollar spent.

In some foundations, the dichotomy between ossification and opportunity in grantmaking comes into sharp focus when one examines the types of organizations that get supported. The old, established, wealthy, and large—in short, "safe"—organizations get the grants, while the new, struggling, poor, and small—in short, "risky"—ones get the rejection letters. It is far easier to give grants to the "old guard," for it requires less pregrant due diligence and less postgrant management and TA. But in nearly every case, it is also true that more of the grant funds are consumed by the higher overhead of these larger organizations, so that, on a dollar-for-dollar basis, the impact they can deliver is sometimes less than that of their "new" counterparts.

It requires an act of will for you to see that opportunities are not lost in the face of "business as usual." This is not to say that some grants to old-guard organizations are not justified or useful, or that they should be cut out of the foundation's agenda altogether. It is to say, however, that you must make room so that the "new" organizations have a realistic chance to be funded. What you need is openness to both the great ideas and the extra risk and work, so that philanthropy can do the most for those who have the least. Foundations should not run an exclusive club of grantees. The ethical program officer ensures that opportunities remain viable for those organizations that can produce societal change, whatever their past record or current balance sheet may be.

Allow No Formulaic Responses

Some anonymous grantseeking sage once remarked that the number one killer among foundations is a dread disease called "hardening of the categories." Once the foundation has contracted this illness, it begins to lose its flexibility. Not only does it tend to fund members of the old guard exclusively, but it goes beyond that to demand only tried-and-true ideas from these organizations. Funding hardens into a set formula, and the formula becomes sacrosanct. No matter how potentially significant a proposal might be, and even if it issues from the oldest of the old guard, if it is out of the formula, it is out of luck.

Individual program officers, just as much as foundations in general, are susceptible to hardening of the categories, particularly if they have been in philanthropy for a long time. Funding by formula is an occupational hazard, caused by a witch's brew consisting of too much work, too little time for reflection, and too little attention to the requirements of the spirit. The formulaic program officer is a negative force, given to ignoring most good ideas and jamming the rest into preconceived pigeonholes so tightly that they lose their potential for doing good in the world.

Formulaic funding can be counteracted. Some larger foundations offer senior program officers sabbaticals so that they can refresh and renew themselves. The subjects of these sabbaticals can take many forms, from quiet study to strident activism, from private journal work to public commentary. Some program officers are "loaned" to other organizations, to work in entirely different environments. Smaller foundations sometimes support more modest efforts, such as allowing program officers to attend multiday workshops. Even a brief change of pace can work wonders in breaking the back of formulaic grantmaking. Any foundation, no matter what its size, can schedule time for reflection and nurturing of the spirit. Whatever the arrangement, the hope is that the grantmaker will return to work refreshed, with intellectual curiosity revived, openness to new ideas restored, and a willingness to take risks revivified.

The ethical program officer will constantly strive for the flexibility and the creativity that are the antithesis of funding by formula. If you feel yourself slipping, seek an opportunity for renewal. Should that not prove efficacious, step aside and let others with a fresh perspective take on the challenges of grantmaking.

Conclusion

In 1991, INDEPENDENT SECTOR published a report on ethics in the nonprofit sector titled "Obedience to the Unenforceable" (1991). This is a superb one-phrase summary of how you must approach the ethics of grantmaking. None of the seven issues discussed in this chapter, with the possible exception of conflict of interest, can be effectively addressed by written rules or books of statutes. You must observe most ethical commandments as an act of obedience to the unenforceable. Ironically, although there is no external reward for compliance, there are many punishments, both great and small, for transgressions. The punishments range from the inner pangs of an outraged conscience to the public humiliation of banner headlines in the *Chronicle of Philanthropy*. There is, however, one powerful intangible reward for ethical behavior. It comes from the knowledge that, as a program officer, you have been a faithful steward of the trust placed in your hands to distribute private funds for the promotion of the common good. On balance, that should be reward enough.

The Future of Formal Philanthropy

Of all of the major societal institutions in the United States, formalized philanthropy—and private foundations in particular—are among the newest. Harvard University had celebrated a quarter-millennium of existence before the first U.S. private foundation opened its doors for business. Although invented in the late nineteenth century, the private foundation did not hit its stride until the twentieth. And the twentieth has been a century of considerable achievement for private foundations. With their support, diseases have been conquered, educational opportunities at all levels have been increased, human services have been enhanced, the arts have been enriched, the environment has been improved, and economic development has been boosted.

As solid as this twentieth-century record has been, the prospect for the twenty-first century and beyond looms even larger. The nearly twenty-year bull market in equities that closed the twentieth century has led to the creation of many new foundations, among them some of the largest, which will vastly increase the sheer heft of philanthropy. Foundations are thus likely to become much more significant actors on the social stage. It seems sensible, therefore, to close this book with a look at some of the changes—for good or for ill—that may shape the world of formal philanthropy during the first decades of the twenty-first century.

Big Bull Market Boosts Foundations

When the 1980s dawned, the Dow Jones Industrial Index stood at less than one thousand. By March 1999, that same index had crossed the ten thousand mark. There were 13 billionaires in the United States in 1982; by 1997, that number had jumped to 170 ("Philanthropy in America," 1998). The wealth generated by this twenty-year bull market was unprecedented in U.S. history.

Foundations, of course, bobbed along on this rising tide of money. In 1980, the Foundation Center's *Foundation Directory* counted approximately twenty-two thousand foundations of all types, with the largest in asset value being the Ford Foundation at $2.76 billion. Only the Robert Wood Johnson Foundation joined Ford above the charmed $1 billion mark. The 1998 edition of the *Foundation Directory* told a very different story: no fewer than thirty-one foundations topped $1 billion in assets. In February 1999, the *Chronicle of Philanthropy* published a survey of U.S. foundations, which showed the Lilly Endowment in the first slot with more than $15 billion in assets (Blum and Dundjerski, 1999). The tenth largest was the Andrew W. Mellon Foundation at $3.3 billion— meaning that the largest foundation of 1980 could not crack the top ten of 1999. Although the size of the larger foundations is impressive, the vast majority of foundations in the United States remain smaller: almost three-quarters of them as of 1997 had assets of $10 million or less. Many of these are locally based family foundations. Even after the bull market ends, it is likely that new foundations will continue to form at a brisk pace for several years as owners of successful enterprises reap the benefits of their commercial ventures.

The sheer growth in the number and size of foundations has resulted in a corresponding increase in the number of foundations interested in policy work. Prior to the 1990s, most foundations did very little policy work, or, at most, they responded to threats. Few had an ongoing interest in magnifying impact by interacting with governments or large institutions. This began to change, for a number of reasons, during the 1990s. Throughout the decade, the number of regional associations of grantmakers began to grow, and these "trade associations" included policy work in their agendas. The president of the Council on Foundations, Dorothy S. Ridings, made it her mission, as soon as she took office in 1996, to increase the capacity of foundations to tell their stories and to enhance communications with policymakers in particular. The Association of Small Foundations, formerly an affinity group of the Council on Foundations, became a freestanding nonprofit organization in 1996 and began encouraging its members to participate more actively in the policy process. A measurement of the growth of foundation participation in policy activities is the rising number of grantmakers taking part in the annual RAGs on the Hill Day, sponsored by the Forum of Regional Associations of Grantmakers (RAGs). The first such day, in 1993, attracted fewer than twenty participants from around the nation to visit with members of Congress in Washington. The seventh, in 1999, drew more than one hundred. As philanthropy grows in size and importance during the years to come, it seems likely that its involvement in the policy arena will continue to expand and intensify.

Diversity and Foundations

When the big bull market began in the early 1980s, the overwhelming majority of people employed by foundations were white. Although women were fairly well represented (especially in smaller foundations), the officers and trustees of foundations, especially those foundations with over $10 million in assets, tended to be white males. The demographics of foundation employment and board membership began to change slowly during the 1980s, and the rate of that change accelerated slightly in the 1990s. Women and African Americans made the greatest gains, both on the staff rolls and in the boardroom. Latino participation grew more slowly; Asian Americans and Native Americans experienced the smallest increases. The hard truth, unfortunately, is that foundations have not been the leaders in diversifying their staffs and boards. In fact, many foundations have been badly retrograde on this issue. The progress of the 1990s has been a positive sign, but it is proceeding very slowly. Still, all trend lines were moving up by the decade's end.

During the 1990s, however, a new and more profound approach to diversifying philanthropy gained favor: funds endowed by and managed by women and people of color. These funds take many forms, from private foundations to donor-advised funds in community foundations. One popular approach for organizing such entities is that of the public charity, which is a grantmaking corporation possessing a 501(c)(3) designation from the Internal Revenue Service. As such, it must meet the public support test. (In highly simplified terms, it must prove that, over a period of four years, at least a third of its income is derived from public sources.) Perhaps the lion's share of grantmaking entities by and for people of color are component funds of community foundations, but others are freestanding nonprofits. These funds are changing the philanthropic dynamic. Being in charge of funding decisions that most affect them has given these formerly excluded populations real philanthropic influence. It has also proved a boon to philanthropy, for these populations have brought new ideas and new donors to the table.

In the 1990s, women and people of color began to change the face of philanthropy. That change is likely to accelerate in the years to come, as access to greater economic opportunity allows these populations to amass more capital. This trend will go far toward correcting the long-standing racial and gender imbalance between the people governing and managing foundations and the people whom foundations seek to serve.

Intergenerational Transfer of Wealth

Cornell University economists Michael Rendall and Robert Avery (1993) caught everyone's attention in the early 1990s when they published research indicating that, during the first four decades of the twenty-first century, America's World War II and baby-boom generations will bequeath estates amounting to the staggering sum of $10.4 trillion, with $4.8 trillion of this passing by the year 2020. This enormous amount was nearly twice the U.S. gross national product in 1996 and more than fifty times the total of private savings in the United States for that year.

Rendall and Avery, however, conducted their research before the unprecedented economic growth of the 1990s both created vast new wealth and dramatically multiplied the value of previously existing wealth. Researchers John J. Havens and Paul G. Schervish (1999), using more recent data, have revised the estimated value of the intergenerational transfer of wealth dramatically upward. According to their calculations, during the fifty-five-year period from 1998 to 2052, the total wealth transfer will amount to a figure in the range of $41 trillion to $136 trillion. Havens and Schervish also estimate that $6 trillion to $25 trillion in charitable bequests will take place during that period. This would include bequests to charities of all types, of course, and not just foundations, but it could still fuel the establishment of thousands of new foundations. Because the number of foundations more than doubled (from 22,000 to over 58,000) during the twenty years from 1980 to 2000, it does not seem unreasonable to assume, in light of Havens and Schervish's research, that the intergenerational transfers will accelerate the rate of growth. It seems safe to predict, therefore, that the number of foundations will exceed 250,000 by the year 2050.

This prospect of greatly increased numbers and magnitude of foundations bodes well for strapped nonprofits and innovators hoping to start new social ventures. There is no reason to suspect that the overall asset profile of foundations will change (the great majority of new foundations will probably be smaller than $10 million in assets, as is the case today), but the types may well be different. Community foundations, once a mainly midwestern phenomenon, are becoming more popular around the nation. Women's funds and foundations created by communities of color are likely to increase rapidly. Corporate giving programs, too, are likely to see significant growth in numbers.

All of these new foundations will require more workers, so there will no doubt be an increased demand for program officers and other types of foundation employees. The magnitude of the increased demand remains to be seen. As the 1990s came to an end, U.S. foundations of all types employed about six thousand employees of all sorts. If the new foundations tend to choose lean grantmaking models of operation, that number will increase relatively slowly. If they choose to operate programs or choose other staff-intensive grantmaking styles, the number will rise rapidly.

Many of these positions will be open to people who have been traditionally underrepresented on foundation staffs and boards. These new foundations will control vast new resources and give rein to new and creative approaches to philanthropy. But, on the principle that every silver lining surrounds a dark cloud, it is also likely that an influx of new foundations, new employees to serve them, and new trustees to govern them will bring a small percentage who, whether from naïveté or mendacity, will do things to show disrespect for applicants, cross ethical boundaries, or even violate the law. Foundations will need to do a far better job than they have in the past of identifying best practices in grantmaking, training new professionals in these best practices, and insisting on "obedience to the unenforceable" in ethical standards. If they are content with the status quo in these areas, foundations undoubtedly will come to remember the intergenerational transfer of wealth with all the affection of Carthaginians remembering the Romans sowing their fields with salt.

Threats on the Horizon

The possible influx of untrained staff and trustees is far from the only threat facing foundation philanthropy. Foundations exist by the grace of God, Congress, and the Internal Revenue Code, and as some jaded foundation executives remark, not necessarily in that order. Congress can, at any given moment, create a threat to foundations by means of legislation; and federal agencies, such as the Internal Revenue Service, can do the same by issuing regulations. Only rarely in history have regulatory agencies or Congress deliberately drawn a bead on foundations, but in the course of aiming "silver bullets" at unrelated problems, members of Congress and regulators often discover that the bullet passes through its target and maims innocent bystanders. It is in fact these unintended consequences that often pose the greatest danger to foundations.

An example of such an unintended consequence springs from the desire to repeal the estate tax. Critics of the tax say that it is so confiscatory that upon the death of a senior member of a family, the survivors often find that the only way to pay "death duties" is to sell the family farm or family business. To prevent such hardships, many members of Congress wish to abolish the estate tax altogether. This would solve the problem of forced sales, but an unintended consequence would be a severe drop in the number of new foundations established, because substantial estate taxes encourage people to use charitable vehicles to escape the consequences of those taxes. For example, a study on tax-restructuring proposals, authored jointly by the accounting firm of Price Waterhouse and the Washington law firm of Caplin & Drysdale (1997), concluded that abolishing the estate tax would have reduced charitable bequests in 1996 from about $7 billion to about $4 billion. The challenge for foundations is to find some way to relieve the distress of family farmers and family business owners without destroying an important incentive to be charitable that has done so much lasting good for society.

There is no shortage of ominous ideas that occasionally make their way down from Capitol Hill. From time to time, someone on that eminence concludes that the 5 percent payout rate is too modest, and launches an effort to raise it. In fact, as previously mentioned, after the Tax Reform Act of 1969, the payout rate was higher, set first at 6 percent, then at 6.75 percent of the foundation's net asset value or all of the foundation's income, whichever was higher. And because the act imposed a 4 percent excise tax, the actual annual cost of running a foundation exceeded the returns of conservatively invested foundation portfolios. If the 6.75 percent of net asset value or all of net income rule had stood, most foundations would have been simply shrunken out of existence. The reduction to the minimum payout rate of 5 percent of net asset value (and the reduction of the excise tax to a maximum of 2 percent) allowed foundations to invest their portfolios in such a way as to meet total expenses (in most years) through income, reinvest excess income in their corpus (in good years), and only resort to invading the principal in bad years. This formula in turn allowed foundations to grow in order to offset inflation and meet future needs.

The big bull market of the 1980s and 1990s, however, brought some fabulous years in which foundation portfolios approached a 20 percent increase in assets. Critics complained that the 5 percent rule, which was meant to be a minimum, was being treated by foundations as a maximum. It was obscene, they said, for foundations to make 20 percent and pay out much less. Foundation leaders replied that overhead expenses and the excise tax caused the total demand on the portfolio to considerably exceed the nominal payout rate. Moreover, when they chose to reinvest any surplus in the corpus rather than pay it out in that year, they *were* increasing future payout, because 5 percent of the reinvestment would have to be paid out next year. It was a matter, they said, of investing in the future by planting the seed corn rather than eating it.

This view was backed empirically by a study conducted by DeMarche Associates for the Council on Foundations, which found that, over time, a 5 percent payout rate resulted in *more* payout than a 6 or 7 percent payout rate. This seemingly paradoxical outcome occurs because, over the years, a 5 percent rate results in greater portfolio growth than that yielded by either the 6 or 7 percent rates, and a larger portfolio makes possible a higher long-term payout (Trotter, [1992] 1995). Specifically, the study followed three hypothetical foundations, each beginning in 1950 with a corpus of $1 million, and each investing it in identical ways. One foundation paid out consistently at a 5 percent rate, another at 6 percent, and the last at 7 percent. Initially, of course, the higher-payout foundations paid out more, but the 5 percent foundation, due to its faster corpus growth, soon began to close the gap. By 1967, it was paying out more annually than the 7 percent foundation; by 1968, more than the 6 percent foundation. By 1994, the *total* payout of the 5 percent foundation stood at 27.4 percent more than that of the 6 percent foundation, and 67.2 percent more than that of the foundation paying out 7 percent.

These facts notwithstanding, as foundations grow in the future there are likely to be continuing efforts to raise the 5 percent payout rate. Most efforts will be motivated by an honest belief that foundations can afford to give more. A few will be veiled attempts to make foundations spend themselves out of existence. All would result, in the long run, in fewer dollars being available for philanthropic purposes—precisely the opposite of the result that well-meaning folks are trying to achieve.

A few foundation critics immodestly eschew the veil and bluntly call for the passage of laws to limit the life span of foundations. Over time, they say, foundation staffs stray from the intent of the donor, who would be horrified, could she or he come back to earth, to see what causes the foundation is now supporting. As a case in point, such critics often cite the Ford Foundation, whose generally left-of-center funding (so they say) would scandalize the famously far-right-wing Henry Ford. Most of these critics would like to see foundations established for a maximum life span of twenty-five to fifty years, paying out a combination of corpus and income during that time period to spend themselves into oblivion. This is a responsible act, they say, because the U.S. economy will always generate new wealth to replace the old.

Defenders of the foundation ideal argue that donors tend to be successful entrepreneurs who recognize the need to change with the marketplace. This was certainly the case with Andrew Carnegie and John D. Rockefeller Sr., who understood that inflexibility in philanthropy would be just as ruinous as inflexibility in business. Spending foundations out of existence, assert their defenders, has less to do with sound social policy than it does with dubious political ideology. It violates the first law of prudent asset management, which is to preserve the principal. It is also historically reckless; spending assets on the theory that they will be replaced in the near future would have been a dreadful mistake in the 1920s and the 1960s, and may be so again today. Similar reasoning has rendered the Social Security and Medicare trust funds insolvent. Properly managed, foundations can be a perpetual asset, and forever is a long time—long enough to allow society to repent at leisure a death sentence for foundations passed in haste.

The "limited life" advocates can point to some distinguished foundations that chose to spend themselves into the history books. Among them were the Rosenwald Foundation of Chicago, which partnered with the Rockefeller-funded General Education Board in its early years to bring educational benefits to African Americans in the South, and more recently the Aaron Diamond Foundation, which distinguished itself by supporting intensive research on the cause and cure of HIV infection. These foundations made a greater impact, say the critics, by spending more in a shorter time frame. Defenders respond that there was still no cure for HIV when the Aaron Diamond Foundation lapsed, and when the next dread epidemic is visited upon us, that foundation will not be there to take the lead on funding research to combat it.

It can be safely predicted that legislation aimed at limiting foundation life spans will be introduced on more than one occasion in the future. Such efforts are laden with political meaning and are usually introduced by those who disagree with the ideological direction in which foundations seem to be heading. The Council on Foundations takes a judicious middle view, holding that choice is important. A donor should have the right to choose to create a traditional perpetual foundation vehicle *or* a time-limited one. There is room for both under philanthropy's tent; however, it is unwise to arbitrarily force every foundation to do things in the same way. It is a safe prediction that foundation leaders of the future will be confronting this issue again and again as the field grows.

Daunting as such threats (and others as yet unanticipated) may be, foundation employees can take comfort in the fact that they are better organized and have more clout with which to do battle than ever before. When the hearings that led to the Tax Reform Act of 1969 began in the mid-1960s, philanthropy was ill prepared to defend itself. INDEPENDENT SECTOR did not exist, and few foundations belonged to a regional association of grantmakers. The Council on Foundations was in existence, but it did not have a government relations department. As the new century begins, INDEPENDENT SECTOR mobilizes an alliance between foundations and their nonprofit grantees; many foundations belong to a regional association; and the regional associations are united under the umbrella of the Forum of RAGs. The Council on Foundations has a strong and seasoned government relations team, and all three of these organizations work in tandem on Capitol Hill and in state capitals to represent the concerns and defend the prerogatives of philanthropic and voluntary organizations. The growth of the foundation world in the years ahead should increase the clout of foundations at the policy table. Although no one should discount the threats that the future may hold, none should feel that foundations are powerless to defend themselves.

Philanthropy as Social Venture Capital

An article that appeared in the *Harvard Business Review* (Letts, Ryan, and Grossman, 1997) has sparked a great deal of discussion about a distinctive way of understanding foundation philanthropy. "Virtuous Capital: What Foundations Can Learn from Venture Capitalists" advances the thesis that philanthropy should be perceived as social venture capital, somewhat analogous to commercial venture capital. Under the traditional philanthropic model, say the authors, a foundation makes a grant based on the efficacy of a program, in the hope of making that program a model that can be eventually brought to scale. The "venture philanthropy" approach, by contrast, operates on principles borrowed from the marketplace. The foundation regards itself as an investor. It invests not in a program but in the organizational capacity of the entity operating the program. This involves securing multiple investors and developing the organization toward self-sufficiency, so that its program innovation can be rapidly brought to scale. In order to protect the investment, the investor must be personally involved. Just as a venture capitalist will demand a seat on the board of a business start-up that he or she is financing, so should the grantmaker-investor demand a seat on the board of the nonprofit organization being funded.

Proponents of venture philanthropy offer it as a much better model for achieving impact than that presented by traditional philanthropy. Foundations, they say, focus on ideas rather than on organizations. No matter how good the ideas may be, they often wither when the organization itself cannot survive after the foundation stops funding it. Foundations therefore are great at the "research and development" of ideas but lousy at bringing these ideas "to market" (that is, to scale). Foundations not only prematurely pull the plug on support but also do too little to be helpful while they are supporting the ideas. The grantee organizations need guidance, TA, even "tough love." Grantmakers who do not get deeply involved in the success of their grantees are squandering their foundation's investment.

In sum, then, traditional philanthropy focuses on ideas instead of organizations, takes a hand-off approach when it should take a hands-on approach, terminates its support too soon, and does not do enough to secure other investors for the organization. The result is too many good ideas going to waste instead of going to market.

Critics of the venture philanthropy approach counter that placing the focus on the organization rather than the idea is hardly guaranteed to succeed. Just as venture capitalists have failures as well as successes, venture philanthropists will also spend much time and money developing organizations that will ultimately go out of business. This may be particularly true of those venture philanthropists who pride themselves on avoiding the "bureaucratic" decision making of foundations. For example, one such grantmaker, the chairman of a high-tech company foundation, was quoted in the *New York Times* as saying, "Some of the checks I have written have been after one-and-a-half minute conversations" (Myerson, 1999). Just because foundations focus on sustainability does not guarantee that they will actually achieve it.

Deep involvement can be problematic in two ways. First, it is not possible for program officers to make such a major investment of time in more than a small handful of projects. If the foundation is to meet the 5 percent payout requirement, it follows that these few projects would have to be very big-ticket items. This means that venture philanthropy could inadvertently shut the door on foundation support for smaller, riskier, community-based organizations. The second problem with intense involvement lies in its dictatorial potential. Having the major funder on the board—or having a board with several major funders sitting on it—would put control of the project not in the hands of the organization doing the work but rather in the hands of the funders. Critics say that this would be an example of the "golden rule" in action: those who have the gold make the rules. Some nonprofit organizations will openly resist this level of donor control, most will at least passively resist, and the project will be caught in this cross fire over who is in charge. Such a level of control by investors is a part of the culture of the commercial sector, but it most decidedly is not part of the culture of the nonprofit sector, in which organizations prize their independence. One might also question whether every program officer is qualified to manage in such a way as to be helpful to their grantees.

Finally, critics also raise the "kicking a dead horse" scenario: that foundations, having heavily invested both time and money in an organization that is not making the grade, will continue to throw good money after bad while hoping for a miraculous turnaround. Venture philanthropy, say the detractors, would take too much time, and spend too much money, on organizational development that may or may not deliver programmatic dividends. It would crowd out smaller projects, make the funders unnecessarily intrusive in project management, and offer some disincentives for the foundation to cut its losses in a timely way. The result will be too many good ideas going to waste instead of going to market (that is, to scale).

The truth probably lies somewhere between the extremes of these two arguments. Venture philanthropy will probably fail to bring as many great ideas to scale as its proponents predict, but it will probably not do nearly as much damage as its critics fear. It is good to remember that venture philanthropy is, in many ways, a refinement of a style of charitable operation that has been with us for quite some time, a style that has proved to be neither a panacea nor a problem. Nonprofits like Goodwill Industries and the Girl Scouts have a long history of selling products to sustain their activities. Grantmakers have experimented with loan funds and program-related investments, and have supported microenterprise efforts such as the Grameen Bank. Although it is hardly new, venture philanthropy is in some ways distinctive, especially in its unabashed embrace of the methods and mores of the market.

Both the proponents and the opponents of venture philanthropy have strong arguments to offer. Detractors are right to point out the danger of foundation employees acting in a high-handed fashion while on the board of a funded project, but most of the rest of their criticisms can be neutralized with careful management. Venture philanthropists' assertions that program officers often do too little to help a funded project and then pull out too early are regrettably sometimes accurate. The determination of venture philanthropists to provide hands-on help over the long term is laudable, so long as appropriate limits are set and respected in order to avoid inappropriate levels of foundation control and also to prevent the grantee organization from becoming too dependent on the foundation. Although it is true that venture philanthropy can lead to a focusing on larger grantees at the expense of the smaller ones, there is no reason why some foundations should not dedicate themselves to the venture philanthropy approach, while others follow more common styles. Just as the Council on Foundations feels that there should be room in philanthropy for both time-limited and perpetual foundations, so too should there be room for both venture philanthropy and traditional philanthropy.

The Future of Philanthropy

Society has traditionally been divided into sectors, the main three being the private (business), the public (government), and the nonprofit (charitable) sectors. The mission of the private sector is to create wealth and jobs; the mission of the public sector is to create law and order; the mission of the nonprofit sector is to relieve suffering and enhance the quality of life. There is much overlap in these missions, of course; for example, corporate foundations and government agencies frequently provide funds to nonprofit organizations. Most of the overlaps, however, have been strictly monetary in nature. Overlaps involving exchanges of intellectual capital have been much rarer.

During the 1980s, however, that long-standing conception began to change. Many factors drove this transformation. The Reagan-era cuts in federal support forced nonprofits to become more entrepreneurial. According to figures compiled by Salamon (1992), fully half of the revenue of nonprofits is now derived from earned income, as compared to a mere 18 percent provided by philanthropy. Some nonprofits have even formed for-profit, tax-paying subsidiaries. Companies became concerned about the quality of entry workers' job skills and grew increasingly involved in educational systems and job training programs. For-profit companies have even taken on the administration of certain social welfare programs. Governments have increasingly looked to privatize institutions they historically operated, such as schools, transportation systems, and prisons. Companies also saw profit opportunities in realms once exclusively the province of the nonprofit sector, such as hospitals. In fact, during the 1990s, one of the highest growth areas in the foundation world came from endowments created by the conversion of nonprofit hospitals to for-profits. And the fastest-growing grantmaking institution of the 1990s was not a foundation but the Fidelity Investments Charitable Gift Fund, a charitable entity created by the Wall Street investment giant.

As the lines between the sectors began to blur, nimble nonprofits began to take on a hybrid appearance. City Year, the Boston-based youth service program, is a classic example. City Year was launched by a grant from the nonprofit Boston Foundation. It expanded with support from the corporate giving program of the for-profit Bank of Boston. It doubled in size with a major grant from the nonprofit W. K. Kellogg Foundation. Then federal funding, first from the Commission on National and Community Service, then from the AmeriCorps program of the Corporation for National Service, helped City Year expand to more than ten additional cities. Simultaneously, City Year entered into an agreement with the for-profit Timberland Company, which allowed Timberland to use City Year in a marketing campaign in exchange for cash grants, gear for corps members, and the positive exposure created by Timberland's marketing.

The City Year example provides a glimpse of the future for philanthropy. Foundations will remain funders, of course, but are less likely to be sole funders, and even less likely to have *only* other foundations as funding partners. Grantees are likely to get support from across sectoral lines—private, public, and nonprofit. Support will come in the form of traditional grants but will also come in other guises, such as the $60 million marketing contract consummated in 1998 between the Boys and Girls Clubs of America and Coca-Cola. Foundations will undoubtedly be called on to give away more than money, for the time and expertise of their employees will be in high demand. In giving that time, the foundation employees are likely to rub shoulders with people based in for-profits, in nonprofits, and in units of government at every level. Rather than the traditional grantor-grantee relationship, there is likely to be a primary partnership between the foundation and the grantee organization, which will be woven into overlapping webs of partnerships among the organization and its various funders and partners.

Projects that cross the traditional lines have come to be called examples of intersectoral activity. The future will constitute a brave new intersectoral world, unquestionably different from the one that foundations inhabited during much of the twentieth century, but will it be better? Certainly, risks abound. The nonprofit sector is much smaller in terms of income and power than either of the other two sectors. There is a real concern that so-called intersectoral partnerships might really amount to nonprofits being pushed around by bigger and richer government and business players. Some fear that nonprofits, having inhabited a more genteel world, will be overwhelmed by the political machinations of government or the hardball tactics of business. Other critics warn that the corrupting influence of big money will sully the idealism and values of the nonprofits. More succinctly put, these critics are afraid that the lure of $60 million marketing deals will cause nonprofits to sell their souls.

The dangers are undeniably real, but so are the potential gains. The social problems with which the nonprofit sector is grappling have grown large, complex, interconnected, and deep rooted. It has become increasingly clear that no single sector of American life, especially not the smallest of the three, can hope to successfully take on these problems by itself. There is ample precedent in

U.S. history for embracing the intersectoral model to tackle problems of daunting complexity. During World War II, for example, all sectors of society united to direct the nation's total resources toward the common goal of waging all-out war. The social problems of the early twenty-first century will undoubtedly prove to be the greatest threat to the republic since the military problem posed by the Axis powers in the 1940s. An intersectoral solution is thus just as imperative to promote the common good in the twenty-first century as it was to save democracy in the twentieth.

Foundations that view the current situation of society as the moral equivalent of war, to borrow the words of William James, have little choice but to join with all willing and honorable partners in common cause against the social villains of the times. The private and public sectors bring vast resources in their train: money, human ingenuity, and logistical support most particularly. As organizations form alliances across the old sectoral boundaries, they will unleash a formidable new force for the common good. The problems of making these partnerships work will be pervasive. The dangers will be real. But the enormous potential payoff makes these risks well worth taking.

Conclusion

Foundation philanthropy at the dawn of the new century and new millennium can look back on a proud heritage, but it should instead concentrate on a future that is quickening with power and potential. The big bull market has made foundation philanthropy strong. The intergenerational transfer of wealth will make it large. Venture philanthropy will make it more significant. And intersectoral alliances will make it resourceful beyond the wildest dreams of only a few years ago.

For all of this glory and promise, foundations sometimes fall short of the ideal. Some are too slow to make decisions, some too quick to move on to other things. A few have staffs that are too amateurish, others have no staff at all. Some are too passive, others too meddlesome. Some boards are rubber stamps, others too prescriptive. Some foundations lack imagination, whereas others have grandiose and impractical ideas. An argument could be made that, for all of their wealth and power, and for all of the freedom given them by society, foundations have returned too little value to the nation and the world.

The same critique, of course, could be leveled at pharmaceutical researchers, who often experiment with dozens of ineffective compounds before finding one that can cure a disease. And, just as critics can point to a number of underperforming foundations, so can admirers point to overachieving foundations that have found innovative ways to invest relatively small amounts of money strategically to make significant changes for the better. Echoing Archimedes, foundation professionals might truly say, "Give me where to stand, and I will move the earth."

It is no accident that the modern form of both the private and the community foundations is an American invention. Befitting a paradoxical nation that fiercely holds to simultaneous beliefs in egalitarianism and unlimited accumulation of wealth, foundations have provided an ingenious way to begin to reconcile these contradictory tenets. Foundations allow private individuals to convert private fortunes into entities that, whether public (community foundations) or private (private foundations and corporate giving programs), explicitly serve the public and strive to promote the common good.

Foundations also serve as the vehicle for "giving back" to society. All living people owe debts to previous generations, debts that they cannot repay in any conventional sense. We all live in houses we did not build, travel on roads we did not construct, visit museums we did not establish, and take cures in hospitals we did not create. All of these are fruits of investments made by others for our benefit, often long before we were born. How can today's citizens discharge these obligations? Abigail Scott Duniway's answer is simple: "The debt that each generation owes to the past, it must pay to the future." This concept has been formalized by scholar Kenneth Boulding (1973) as "serial reciprocity": repaying our obligations to past generations by placing future generations in *our* debt. A foundation is perhaps the highest form of serial reciprocity, for, properly managed, it will repay those debts owed to earlier generations, not just to the next generation, but to endless generations into the infinite future.

What, then, could be a higher calling than to serve that process of repayment? And what could be more important than ensuring that this work is done thoughtfully, spiritually, creatively, and ethically? So much depends on it that it behooves anyone wishing to work in foundations to remember the words of Aristotle, and strive always to serve posterity by today doing work that is rare, praiseworthy, and noble.

References

Andrews, F. E. *Philanthropic Foundations.* New York: Russell Sage Foundation, 1956.

Aristotle. *Nicomachean Ethics* (M. Ostwald, trans.) New York: Bobbs-Merrill, 1962.

Billiteri, T. J. "Top Ten Public Charities Gave $677 Million." *Chronicle of Philanthropy,* June 18, 1998, p. 22.

Blum, D. E., and Dundjerski, M. "Foundations' Giving Surges." *Chronicle of Philanthropy,* Feb. 25, 1999. Available at [http://philanthropy.com/premium/articles/vll/i09/09000101.htm]. Accessed Nov. 20, 1999.

Boulding, K. *The Economy of Love and Fear.* Belmont, Calif.: Wadsworth, 1973.

Bremner, R. H. *American Philanthropy.* Chicago: University of Chicago Press, 1987. (Originally published 1960.)

Carnegie, A. "The Best Fields for Philanthropy." In D. Burlingame (ed.), *The Responsibilities of Wealth.* Bloomington: Indiana University Press, 1992a. (Originally published 1889.)

Carnegie, A. "Wealth." In D. Burlingame (ed.), *The Responsibilities of Wealth.* Bloomington: Indiana University Press, 1992b. (Originally published 1889.)

Covey, S. R. *The Seven Habits of Highly Effective People: Restoring the Character Ethic.* New York: Simon & Schuster, 1989.

Edie, J. A. *Foundations and Lobbying: Safe Ways to Affect Public Policy.* Washington, D.C.: Council on Foundations, 1991.

Fine, A. H., Thayer, C. E., and Coghlan, A. *Program Evaluation Practice in the Nonprofit Sector.* Washington, D.C.: Innovation Network, 1998.

Flexner, A. *Funds and Foundations: Their Policies, Past and Present.* New York: HarperCollins, 1952.

Fosdick, R. B. *The Story of the Rockefeller Foundation.* New York: HarperCollins, 1952.

Gladden, W. "Tainted Money." *Outlook,* 1895, *52,* 886–887.

Greenleaf, R. K. *Servant Leadership: A Journey into the Nature of Legitimate Power and Greatness.* New York: Paulist Press, 1977

Havens, J. J., and Schervish, P. G. "Millionaires and the Millennium: New Estimates of the Forthcoming Wealth Transfer and the Prospects for a Golden Age of Philanthropy." Social Welfare Research Institute, Boston College. [http://www.bc.edu/bc_org/avp/gsas/swri/m&m .html]. Accessed Nov. 1999.

Heidrich, K. W. *Foundation-Intermediary Partnerships: One Model.* New Lenox, Ill. CenterPoint Institute, 1999.

Hendrick, B. J. *The Life of Andrew Carnegie.* (2 vols.) New York: Doubleday, 1932.

INDEPENDENT SECTOR. *Ethics and the Nation's Voluntary and Philanthropic Community: Obedience to the Unenforceable.* Washington, D.C.: INDEPENDENT SECTOR, 1991.

Institute for Global Ethics. "Cornerstones for Ethical Foundations." (CD-ROM version.) Camden, Maine: Institute for Global Ethics, 1999.

Jones, S. E., and Siegal, M. A. *Public Will: Its Connection to Public Policy and Philanthropy.* Washington, D.C.: Union Institute, 1993.

Kaplan, A. E. (ed.). *Giving USA: 1999. The Annual Report on Philanthropy for the Year 1998.* New York: American Association of Fund-Raising Counsel Trust for Philanthropy, 1999.

Karel, F. "Now Is the Time for All Good Foundations to . . . Communicate." *Foundation News and Commentary,* Jan./Feb. 1999, pp. 32–35.

Lehman, R. "The Heart of Philanthropy." Keynote address given at the twelfth annual Family Foundations conference of the Council on Foundations, Feb. 23, 1998.

Letts, C., Ryan, W. P., and Grossman, A. "Virtuous Capital: What Foundations Can Learn from Venture Capitalists." *Harvard Business Review,* Mar./Apr. 1997, pp. 36–44.

Macdonald, D. *The Ford Foundation: The Men and the Millions.* New York: Reynal & Company, 1956.

Millett, R. A. *W. K. Kellogg Foundation Evaluation Handbook.* Battle Creek, Mich.: W. K. Kellogg Foundation, 1998.

Myerson, A. R. "Techies Discover the Joy of Giving." *New York Times,* Jan. 31, 1999, section 3, p. 1.

Patton, M. Q. *Practical Evaluation.* Thousand Oaks, Calif.: Sage, 1982.

"Philanthropy in America." *Economist,* May 30–June 5, 1998, pp. 19–21.

Pifer, A. "President's Message." *Annual Report of the Carnegie Corporation of New York.* New York: Carnegie Corporation, 1973.

Pifer, A. *Speaking Out: Reflections on Thirty Years of Foundation Work.* Washington, D.C.: Council on Foundations, 1984.

Plimpton, G. *Paper Lion.* New York: HarperCollins, 1966.

Price Waterhouse LLP and Caplin & Drysdale, Chartered. *Impact of Tax Restructuring on Tax-Exempt Organizations.* Washington, D.C.: Council on Foundations and INDEPENDENT SECTOR, 1997.

Rees, S. *Effective Nonprofit Advocacy.* Washington, D.C.: Aspen Institute Nonprofit Sector Research Fund, 1998.

Rendall, M., and Avery, R. "Estimating the Size and Distribution of Baby Boomers' Prospective Inheritances." Ithaca, N.Y.: Department of Economics, Cornell University, 1993.

Salamon, L. M. *America's Nonprofit Sector: A Primer.* New York: Foundation Center, 1992.

Sarnoff, P. *The Money King.* New York: Obolensky, 1965.

Seltzer, M. *Securing Your Organization's Future: A Complete Guide to Fundraising Strategies.* New York: Foundation Center, 1987.

Shakely, J. "Characters in Search of a Title." *California Community Foundations Forum,* 1988, 7(4), 4.

Shore, B. *Revolution of the Heart: A New Strategy for Creating Wealth and Meaningful Change.* New York: Riverhead Books, 1995.

Simons, R., Lengsfelder, P., and Miller, L. F. *Nonprofit Piggy Goes to Market: How the Denver Children's Museum Earns $600,000 Annually.* Denver, Colo.: Children's Museum of Denver, 1984.

Smucker, B. *The Nonprofit Lobbying Guide.* (2nd ed.) Washington, D.C.: INDEPENDENT SECTOR, 1999.

Thoreau, H. D. *The Illustrated Walden.* Princeton, N.J.: Princeton University Press, 1973. (Originally published 1854.)

Trotter, D. W. *Payout Policies and Investment Planning for Foundations: A Structure for Determining a Foundation's Asset Mix.* Report by DeMarche Associates. Washington, D.C.: Council on Foundations, 1995. (Originally published 1992).

Troyer, T. A. "The Cataclysm of Sixty-Nine." *Foundation News and Commentary,* Mar./Apr. 1999, pp. 40–47.

Union of Experimenting Colleges and Universities. *Part of the Solution: Innovative Approaches to Nonprofit Funding.* Washington, D.C.: Union of Experimenting Colleges and Universities, 1988.

U.S. Treasury. *Treasury Department Report on Private Foundations.* Washington, D.C.: U.S. Treasury, 1965.

Weaver, W. *U.S. Philanthropic Foundations: Their History, Structure, Management, and Record.* New York: HarperCollins, 1967.

White, D. "Report Cards on Program Officers." *Foundation News and Commentary,* Sept./Oct. 1998, 10–11.

Bibliography

Abramson, A. J. (ed.). *Foundations: Exploring Their Unique Roles and Impacts on Society*. Washington, D.C.: Aspen Institute Nonprofit Sector Research Fund, 1998.

Advocacy Institute. *The Elements of a Successful Public Interest Advocacy Campaign*. Washington, D.C.: Advocacy Institute, 1990.

Alie, R. E., and Seita, J. R. "Who's Using Evaluation and How?" *Nonprofit World*, Sept./Oct. 1997, pp. 40–49.

Allen, Y. "How Foundations Evaluate Requests." In F. Emerson Andrews (ed.), *Foundations: Twenty Viewpoints*. New York: Russell Sage Foundation, 1965.

Anderson, A. "Aristotle and the Ethics of Philanthropy." In D. Burlingame (ed.), *The Responsibilities of Wealth*. Bloomington: Indiana University Press, 1992.

Backer, T. E., and Koon, S. L. "Demonstrate, Evaluate, Disseminate. Repeat." *Foundation News and Commentary*, Mar./Apr. 1995, pp. 28–34.

Boris, E., and Odendahl, T. *America's Wealthy and the Future of Foundations*. New York: Foundation Center, 1987.

Boris, E., and Odendahl, T. "Ethical Issues in Fund Raising and Philanthropy." In J. Van Til and Associates (eds.), *Critical Issues in American Philanthropy: Strengthening Theory and Practice*. San Francisco: Jossey-Bass, 1990.

Brim, O. "Do We Know What We Are Doing?" In F. Heimann (ed.), *The Future of Foundations*. Englewood Cliffs, N.J.: Prentice Hall, 1973.

Brown, D. "Ford and Other Foundations in Public Affairs." In F. E. Andrews (ed.), *Foundations: Twenty Viewpoints*. New York: Russell Sage Foundation, 1965.

Calkins, R. D. *The Role of the Philanthropic Foundation*. Washington, D.C.: Cosmos Club, 1969.

Castle, A. L. *Evaluation Essentials for Small Private Foundations*. Washington, D.C.: Council on Foundations, 1991.

Ciba Foundation. *The Future of Philanthropic Foundations*. Ciba Foundation Symposium 30. Amsterdam: Elsevier, 1975.

Clotfelter, C. T., and Erlich, T. (eds.). *Philanthropy and the Nonprofit Sector in a Changing America.* Bloomington: Indiana University Press, 1999.

Colwell, M.A.C. *Private Foundations and Public Policy: The Political Role of Philanthropy.* New York: Garland, 1993.

Couch, J. "Focus for the Sake of Focus." *Foundation News and Commentary,* Mar./Apr. 1997, pp. 23–24.

Council on Foundations. *Principles and Practices for Effective Grantmaking.* (Rev. ed.) Washington, D.C.: Council on Foundations, 1986.

Council on Foundations. *Patterns of Cooperation Among Grantmakers.* Washington, D.C.: Council on Foundations, 1991.

Council on Foundations. *Enhancing Philanthropy Through Inclusiveness in Governance, Staffing and Grantmaking.* Washington, D.C.: Council on Foundations, 1993.

Council on Foundations. *Evaluation for Foundations: Concepts, Cases, Guidelines, and Resources.* San Francisco: Jossey-Bass, 1993.

Craig, J. E., Jr. "In Favor of Five Percent." *Foundation News and Commentary,* May/June 1999, pp. 23–25.

Cuninggim, M. *Private Money and Public Service: The Role of Foundations in American Society.* New York: McGraw-Hill, 1972.

Curtis, J. "Forever Is a Long Time." *Foundation News and Commentary,* Mar./Apr. 1998, pp. 38–41.

Daca, D. "How Foundations Undergo the Grantmaking Process." *Fund Raising Management,* Aug. 1981, p. 51.

Dillon, D. *The Role of Private Philanthropy in Modern American Society.* New York: Rockefeller Foundation, 1971.

Edie, J. A. *Congress and Private Foundations: An Historical Analysis.* Washington, D.C.: Council on Foundations, 1987.

Edie, J. A. "Prudent Payout Pays Off." *Foundation News,* Mar./Apr. 1994, pp. 30–31.

Eisenberg, P. "Philanthropic Ethics from a Donee Perspective." *Foundation News,* Sept./Oct. 1983, p. 50.

Fosdick, R. B. *A Philosophy for a Foundation, on the Fiftieth Anniversary of the Rockefeller Foundation, 1913–1963.* New York: Rockefeller Foundation, 1963.

Foundation Center. *Foundations and the Tax Reform Act of 1969.* New York: Foundation Center, 1970.

Freeman, D. F. *The Handbook on Private Foundations.* New York: Foundation Center, 1991.

Friedman, R. E. "Private Foundation–Government Relationships." In F. Heimann (ed.), *The Future of Foundations.* Englewood Cliffs, N.J.: Prentice Hall, 1973.

Frumkin, P. "Candor Comes First: Let's Start by Improving the Honesty of Foundation-Nonprofit Relations." *Foundation News and Commentary*, July/Aug. 1998, pp. 34–35.

Frumkin, P. "Private Foundations in an Era of Shrinking Public Resources: Three Obstacles to Effective Philanthropy." [http://www.ncpcr.org/report/frumkin.html]. Accessed May 1999.

Furano, K., Jucovy, L. Z., Racine, D. P., and Smith, T. J. *The Essential Connection: Using Evaluation to Identify Programs Worth Replicating.* Philadelphia: Replication and Program Strategies, Inc., 1995.

Gates, F. T. *Chapters in My Life.* New York: Free Press, 1977.

Goodwin, W. M. "Thirty Questions to Cut Funding Risks." *Foundation News*, Mar./Apr. 1976, p. 32.

Gorman, J. "Adding the Human Dimension." *Foundation News*, May/June 1987, pp. 32–37. [On the topic of site visits.]

Gorman, M. "A Strategic Approach to NPO Financial Statements: Opportunities and Pitfalls in NPO Financial Reporting." *Philanthropy Monthly*, Sept. 1997, pp. 33–39.

Goulden, J. C. *The Money Givers: An Examination of the Myths and Realities of Foundation Philanthropy in America.* New York: Random House, 1971.

Greene, J. D. *A Memorandum on Principles and Policies of Giving.* New York: Rockefeller Foundation, 1913.

Greene, S. G. "Should More Grants Fail?" *Chronicle of Philanthropy*, Aug. 7, 1990, pp. 2, 10–11.

Greenleaf, W. *From These Beginnings: The Early Philanthropies of Henry and Edsel Ford, 1911–1936.* Detroit: Wayne State University Press, 1964.

Grobman, G. M., Grant, G. B., and Roller, S. *Fundraising on the Internet: How to Use the Internet to Raise Funds and Sharpen Your Fundraising Skills.* Nonprofit Field Guide Series. Danbury, Conn.: Amherst H. Wilder Foundation, 1998.

Hall, H. "The Great Game of Grantsmanship." *Chronicle of Philanthropy*, June 13, 1989, p. 18.

Harrison, S. M., and Andrews, F. E. *American Foundations for Social Welfare.* New York: Russell Sage Foundation, 1946.

Hart, J. "Foundations and Social Activism: A Critical View." In F. Heimann (ed.), *The Future of Foundations.* Englewood Cliffs, N.J.: Prentice Hall, 1973.

Havens, J. J., and Schervish, P. G. "Wealth and Commonwealth: New Findings on the Trends in Wealth and Philanthropy." Paper presented at the annual meeting of the Association for Research on Nonprofit Organizations and Voluntary Action, Nov. 1997.

Healey, J. K. "Not Yet a Profession." *Foundation News*, July/Aug. 1987, pp. 26–27.

Heimann, F. (ed.). *The Future of Foundations.* Englewood Cliffs, N.J.: Prentice Hall, 1973.

Himmelfarb, G. "The Age of Philanthropy." *Wilson Quarterly,* Spring 1997, pp. 48–55.

INDEPENDENT SECTOR. *Evaluation with Power.* Washington, D.C.: INDEPENDENT SECTOR, 1986.

Jacquette, F. L., and Jacquette, B. "What Makes a Good Proposal?" *Foundation News,* Jan./Feb. 1973, pp. 18, 20.

James, H. T. "Perspectives on the Internal Functioning of Foundations." In F. Heimann (ed.), *The Future of Foundations.* Englewood Cliffs, N.J.: Prentice Hall, 1973.

Jenkins, C. J. "Nonprofit Organizations and Policy Advocacy." In W. W. Powell (ed.), *The Nonprofit Sector: A Research Handbook.* New Haven, Conn.: Yale University Press, 1987.

Jenkins, C. J. "Social Movement Philanthropy and American Democracy." In R. Magat (ed.), *Philanthropic Giving: Studies in Varieties and Goals.* New York: Oxford University Press, 1989.

Johnston, D. "Looking for an Honest Answer." *Foundation News,* Jan./Feb. 1988, p. 55.

Joseph, J. A. *Private Philanthropy and the Making of Public Policy.* Washington, D.C.: Council on Foundations, 1985.

Joseph, J. A. "The Other Side of Professionalism." *Foundation News,* May/June 1986, p. 51.

Josephson, M. *Ethics in Grantmaking and Grantseeking: Making Philanthropy Better.* Marina Del Rey, Calif.: Joseph & Edna Josephson Institute of Ethics, 1992.

Karl, B. D. "The Moral Basis of Capitalist Philanthropy." In INDEPENDENT SECTOR (ed.), *Working Papers for the Spring Research Forum: Philanthropy, Voluntary Action, and the Public Good.* Washington, D.C.: INDEPENDENT SECTOR, 1986.

Karl, B. D., and Katz, S. "The American Private Philanthropic Foundation and the Public Sphere, 1890–1930." *Minerva,* 1981, *19,* 236–270.

Katz, M. *The Modern Foundation: Its Dual Character, Public and Private.* New York: Foundation Library Center, 1968.

Kearney, A. T. *Relationship Marketing: A White Paper on Leveraging Consumer Information to Build Customer Equity.* Chicago: Kearney, 1997.

Keener, D., and others. *Evaluation from the Start.* Columbia: Institute for Families in Society, University of South Carolina, 1998.

W. K. Kellogg Foundation. *Leaders Against Family Violence: A Fictionalized Account of a W. K. Kellogg Foundation–Sponsored Cluster Evaluation.* Battle Creek, Mich.: W. K. Kellogg Foundation, 1998.

Kibbe, B. D., Setterberg, F., and Wilbur, C. S. *Grantmaking Basics: A Field Guide for Funders*. Washington, D. C.: The David and Lucile Packard Foundation and the Council on Foundations, 1999.

Kimball, L. F. "Guidelines on Grantmaking." *Foundation News,* Mar./Apr. 1974, pp. 43–44.

Lagemann, E. C. *Philanthropic Foundations: New Scholarship, New Possibilities*. Bloomington: Indiana University Press, 1999.

Layton, D. N. *Philanthropy and Voluntarism: An Annotated Bibliography*. New York: The Foundation Center, 1987.

Lukas, C. A. *Consulting with Nonprofits: A Practitioner's Guide*. Nonprofit Field Guide Series. Danbury, Conn.: Amherst H. Wilder Foundation, 1999.

Magat, R. "Introduction." In R. Magat (ed.), *Philanthropic Giving: Studies in Varieties and Goals*. New York: Oxford University Press, 1989.

Magat, R. *Prospective Views of Research on Philanthropy and the Voluntary Sector.* New York: Foundation Center, 1990.

Magat, R. *Publishing About Philanthropy: Essays on Philanthropy*. Indianapolis: Indiana University Center on Philanthropy, 1990.

Mathews, D. "The Civil Opportunities of Foundations." *Foundation News,* Mar./Apr. 1991, pp. 30–33.

Mayer, S. E. *Building Community Capacity: The Potential of Community Foundations*. Minneapolis, Minn.: Rainbow Research, 1994.

McIlnay, D. "Four Moments in Time." *Foundation News and Commentary,* Sept./Oct. 1998, pp. 30–36.

McIlnay, D. *How Foundations Work: What Grantseekers Need to Know About the Many Faces of Foundations*. San Francisco: Jossey-Bass, 1998.

McNamara, C. *Grantmakers Communications Manual*. Washington, D.C.: Council on Foundations and Forum of Regional Associations of Grantmakers, 1998.

Millett, R. A. "The Kellogg Approach to Evaluation." *Leadership,* Jan./Mar. 1996, p. 12.

Netting, F. E., and Williams, F. G. "Is There an Afterlife? How Nonprofits Move to Self-Sufficiency as Foundation Dollars End." *Nonprofit Management and Leadership,* 1997, 7(3), 291–304.

Nielsen, W. A. *The Big Foundations*. New York: Columbia University Press, 1972.

Nielsen, W. A. *The Golden Donors*. New York: NAL/Dutton, 1985.

Nielsen, W. A. *Inside American Philanthropy: The Dramas of Donorship*. Norman: University of Oklahoma Press, 1996.

O'Connell, B. *America's Voluntary Spirit: A Book of Readings*. New York: Foundation Center, 1983.

Odendahl, T., and Boris, E. "The Grantmaking Process." *Foundation News*, Sept.–Oct. 1983, pp. 22–31.

Odendahl, T., Boris, E., and Daniels, A. *Working in Foundations: Career Patterns of Women and Men*. New York: Foundation Center, 1985.

O'Keefe, M. "Rules to Give By." *Foundation News and Commentary*, Nov./Dec. 1997, pp. 16–19. [On the topic of ethics.]

O'Neill, M. *The Third America: The Emergence of the Nonprofit Sector in the United States*. San Francisco: Jossey-Bass, 1989.

Orosz, J. J., and Ellis, P. R. "Smoothing the Process Between Grant Seeking and Grant Making." In M. K. Murphy (ed.), *Cultivating Foundation Support for Education*. Washington, D.C.: Council for Advancement and Support of Education, 1989.

Ostrander, S. A., and Schervish, P. G. "Giving and Getting: Philanthropy as a Social Relation." In J. V. Til and Associates (eds.), *Critical Issues in American Philanthropy: Strengthening Theory and Practice*. San Francisco: Jossey-Bass, 1990.

Patrizi, P., and McMullan, B. *Evaluation in Foundations: The Unrealized Potential*. Battle Creek, Mich.: W. K. Kellogg Foundation, 1998.

Patrizi, P., and McMullan, B. "Realizing the Potential of Program Evaluation." *Foundation News and Commentary*, May/June 1999, pp. 30–35.

Payton, R. *Major Challenges to Philanthropy: A Discussion Paper for INDEPENDENT SECTOR*. Washington, D.C.: INDEPENDENT SECTOR, 1984.

Payton, R. *Philanthropy: Voluntary Action for the Public Good*. Old Tappan, N.J.: Macmillan, 1988.

Payton, R. "Philanthropy as Moral Discourse." In L. Berkowitz and Associates (eds.), *America in Theory: Theory in America*. New York: Oxford University Press, 1989.

Peterson, P. G. *Foundations, Private Giving and Public Policy: Report and Recommendations of the Commission on Foundations and Private Philanthropy*. Chicago: University of Chicago Press, 1970.

Pifer, A. "Foundations and Public Policy Formation." In A. Pifer (ed.), *Philanthropy in an Age of Transition*. New York: Foundation Center, 1984.

Pifer, A. "Foundations at the Service of the Public." In A. Pifer (ed.), *Philanthropy in an Age of Transition*. New York: Foundation Center, 1984.

Pifer, A. "Twenty Years in Retrospect: A Personal View." In A. Pifer (ed.), *Philanthropy in an Age of Transition*. New York: Foundation Center, 1984.

Porter, M. E., and Kramer, M. R. "Philanthropy's New Agenda: Creating Value." *Harvard Business Review*, Nov.–Dec. 1999, pp. 121–130.

Prince, R. A., File, K. M., and Gillespie, J. E. "Philanthropic Styles." *Nonprofit Management and Leadership*, 1993, *3*(3), 255–268.

Racine, D. P. *Replicating Programs and Social Markets.* Philadelphia: Replication and Program Strategies, 1998.

Radtke, J. M. *Strategic Communications for Nonprofit Organizations.* New York: Wiley, 1998.

Reeves, T. C. *Foundations Under Fire.* Ithaca, N.Y.: Cornell University Press, 1970.

Reis, T., and Clohesy, S. *Unleashing New Resources and Entrepreneurship for the Common Good: A Scan, Synthesis, and Scenario for Action.* Battle Creek, Mich.: W. K. Kellogg Foundation, 1999.

Rusk, D. *The Role of the Foundation in American Life.* Claremont, Calif.: Claremont University Press, 1961.

Russell, J. M. *Giving and Taking: Across the Foundation Desk.* New York: Columbia University Press, 1977.

Russell Sage Foundation. *Report of the Princeton Conference on the History of Philanthropy in the United States.* New York: Russell Sage Foundation, 1956.

Scully, P. L., and Harwood, R. C. "A Word from Our Grantees: Some Advice on What Grantmakers Are Doing Right and Suggestions for Six Acts That They Could Improve On." *Foundation News and Commentary,* July/Aug. 1996, pp. 22–25.

Seeley, J. A. "Five Steps to Effective Evaluation." *Leadership,* Jan./Mar. 1996, p. 11.

Shaplen, R. *Toward the Well-Being of Mankind: Fifty Years of the Rockefeller Foundation.* New York: Doubleday, 1964.

Sievers, B. "If Pigs Had Wings." *Foundations News and Commentary,* Nov./Dec. 1997, pp. 44–45. [Critique of venture philanthropy.]

Sievers, B., and Wilson, K. "Our Half Century." *Foundations News and Commentary,* Mar./Apr. 1999, pp. 32–39. [A history of the Council on Foundations.]

Simon, J. S. *Conducting Successful Focus Groups.* Nonprofit Field Guide Series. Danbury, Conn.: Amherst H. Wilder Foundation, 1999.

Siska, D. "Looking for Satisfaction." *Foundation News and Commentary,* Sept./Oct. 1998, pp. 44–45.

Smith, J. A. "The Philanthropic Revolution." *Foundation News and Commentary,* Mar./Apr. 1999, p. 39.

Stern, G. J. *Marketing Workbook for Nonprofit Organizations.* Vol. 1: *Develop the Plan.* Nonprofit Field Guide Series. Danbury, Conn.: Amherst H. Wilder Foundation, 1995.

Stern, G. J. *Marketing Workbook for Nonprofit Organizations.* Vol. 11: *Mobilize People for Marketing Success.* Nonprofit Field Guide Series. Danbury, Conn.: Amherst H. Wilder Foundation, 1997.

Taft, J. R. *Understanding Foundations.* New York: McGraw-Hill, 1967.

Tarbell, I. *History of the Standard Oil Company*. New York: McClure, Phillips, 1904.

Townsend, T. H. "Criteria Grantors Use in Assessing Proposals." *Foundations News*, Mar./Apr. 1974, pp. 31–36.

Tuckman, H. P., and Chang, C. F. "A Methodology for Measuring the Financial Vulnerability of Charitable Nonprofit Organizations." *Nonprofit and Voluntary Sector Quarterly*, 1991, *20*(4), 445–460.

Walker, G., and Grossman, J. B. *Philanthropy and Outcomes: Dilemmas in the Quest for Accountability*. Philadelphia: Public/Private Ventures, 1999.

Walker, K. E., Watson, B. H., and Jucovy, L. Z. *Resident Involvement in Community Change: The Experiences of Two Initiatives*. Philadelphia: Public/Private Ventures, 1999.

Wall, J. F. *Andrew Carnegie*. New York: Oxford University Press, 1970.

Whitaker, B. *The Philanthropoids: Foundation and Society. An Unsubsidized Anatomy of the Burden of Benevolence*. New York: Morrow, 1974.

Winer, M., and Ray, K. *Collaboration Handbook: Creating, Sustaining and Enjoying the Journey*. Nonprofit Field Guide Series. Danbury, Conn.: Amherst H. Wilder Foundation, 1995.

Wisely, D. S., and Lynn, E. M. *A Foundation's Relationship to Its Public: Legacies and Lessons for the Lilly Endowment*. Indianapolis: Indiana University Center on Philanthropy, 1995.

Ylvisaker, P. N. "Ethics and Philanthropy." Keynote address presented to the annual meeting of the Associated Grantmakers of Massachusetts, Mar. 18, 1982.

Ylvisaker, P. N. "Foundations and Nonprofit Organizations." In W. W. Powell (ed.), *The Nonprofit Sector: A Research Handbook*. New Haven, Conn.: Yale University Press, 1987.

Ylvisaker, P. N. "Is Philanthropy Losing Its Soul?" *Foundation News*, May/June 1987, p. 63.

Ylvisaker, P. N. *Small Can Be Effective*. Washington, D.C.: Council on Foundations, 1989.

Ylvisaker, P. N. "Foundations and Faith-Keeping." *Foundation News and Commentary*, Jan./Feb. 1996, pp. 22–24.

Zehr, M. A. "Occupational Hazard: Ossification. What to Be Wary of If You Choose to Make a Career out of Giving Away Money." *Foundation News and Commentary*, July/Aug. 1996, pp. 12–17.

Zurcher, A., and Dustan, J. *The Foundation Administrator: A Study of Those Who Manage American Foundations*. New York: Russell Sage Foundation, 1972.

Index

A

Abbreviations, in funding documents, 148
Accountability, of program officers, 46, 252
Acronyms, in funding documents, 148
African Americans, early foundation efforts targeting, 8, 11, 233, 270. *See also* Diversity
Agnew, S., 75
Aiken, G., 229
American Association of Fund-Raising Counsel Trust for Philanthropy, 18, 71
American Foundation for the Blind, 235
AmeriCorps, 228, 275
Andrews, F. E., 16
Anthropological evaluation, 88
Applicants. *See* Grantseekers
Approving proposals: as group decision, 59, 68–69, 102; notifying grantees after, 174–177; steward role when, 75, 76
Archimedes, 278
Aristotle, 1
Arrogance, 40–41, 254–255
Association of Small Foundations, 216, 263–264
Atticus, H., 1–2
Avery, R., 265

B

Bank of Boston, 275
Bentham, J., 209
Bill of rights, grantseeker, 46–48

Billiteri, T. J., 84
Blum, D. E., 263
Board of trustees: program officers on, 257; relationships between program officers and, 164–165
Boston Foundation, 275
Boulding, K., 278
Boys and Girls Clubs of America, 276
Bradley Foundation, 220
Bremner, R. H., 9, 232–233
Bringing projects to scale, 206–208; using government funds, 235; using intermediary organizations, 207–208; using public policies, 210, 227–229, 231
Brookings Institution, 223
Bryan, W. J., 165
Budgets: assessing, when reviewing proposals, 92–93; grant agreement provisions on, 175–176; in integrated action plans, 242–243; to leverage impact of grant, 199–201
Bundy, M., 14
Burnham, D. H., 8
Bush, G., 227–228

C

Calls to action, 213–214
Capital proposals, 70
Caplin & Drysdale, 267
Capote, T., 138
Carnegie, A., 9, 82, 233, 270; "The Gospel of Wealth," 6; as prototypical philanthropist, 5–8

Carnegie Corporation of New York, 7, 235
Carnegie Endowment for International Peace, 7
Carnegie Foundation for the Advancement of Teaching, 7, 8
Carnegie Hero Fund, 7
Carnegie Institution of Washington, 7
Annie E. Casey Foundation, 212
Change, orientation toward, 25–28
Churchill, W., 24, 165
City Year (youth service program), 227, 228, 275–276
Claudius (Roman emperor), 41
Cleese, J., 125
Cleveland Foundation, 11
Clinton, B., 228
Closing projects, 183–195; exit strategies for, 181–182, 184–185, 208; grantee reports aiding decisions on, 186–190; leveraging impact after, 203–208; making decisions about, 183–190; program officer's closing summary statement on, 190–192; using lessons learned after, 192–195
Closing summary statements, 190–192
Cluster evaluation, 202, 203
Coaching applicants: on evaluation plans, 87–92; on initial writing of proposal, 56; in Q&C letter, 119–121
Coca-Cola, 276
Coghlan, A., 85, 92
Collaborative funding, 198–199
Commission for National Service, 228
Commission on National and Community Service, 275
Communication: avoiding misinterpretation in, 58–62, 103; explaining foundation to grantseekers, 47, 55–56, 58; nonverbal, 60–61,

136–137, 160, 161–162. *See also* Letters; Meetings; Oral presentations; Strategic communications; Telephone calls
Communications Network, 249
Community and National Service Acts, 228
Community foundations, 22, 278; diversity in, 265; increasing number of, 266; prototype for, 11; Tax Reform Act of 1969 on, 16, 17
Compassion, 51–52
Concept papers, for initial proposal submission, 67–68
Conflicts of interest, 256–257
Congress, suggestions for working with members of, 224–227
Constantine I (Roman emperor), 2
Consultants: to conduct site visits, 141; for technical assistance when managing projects, 178–180. *See also* Contract grantwriters
Continuation: plans for, in proposals, 81–82, 83–85; sources of information on, 84
Contract grantwriters, 74–75
Coolidge, C., 257
Cooper Union, 233
Cooperative funding, 198
Corporate foundations, 278; increasing number of, 266; pass-through or endowed, 11, 17
Corporation for National Service, 228, 229, 275
Cost: of evaluation, 48, 88, 89; as reason for declining proposals, 98; of site visits, 131
Council on Foundations, 46; government relations efforts of, 211, 271; on limiting life span of foundations, 270; as source of information on public policy, 216; study on effect of change in payout rate, 268–269; on Tax Reform Act of 1969, 14, 15

Covey, S. R., 171
Creighton, M., 32
Cromwell, O., 191
Cy pres doctrine, 4
Cynicism, 42, 50

D

Dayton Hudson, 84
Deadlines, for receiving and reviewing proposals, 67
Declining proposals, 68–69, 96–109;
 avoiding impersonality when,
 103–105; character needed in,
 102; clarity as essential in, 103;
 compassion needed in, 49,
 51–52; explicit mention of possibility of, 60; grantseekers' criticisms of manner and method of,
 96–97, 99, 103–107; after having
 sent Q&C, 128–129; openness
 about reasons for, 101–102,
 105–106; from persistent proposers, 101–102, 108; after presenting funding document, 164;
 reasons for, 98–100; referrals to
 other foundations when,
 106–107; sentry role when,
 75–76; after site visits, 139–141;
 timing of, 97, 99, 107
Aaron Diamond Foundation, 270
Dillon, D., 13
Disraeli, B., 149
Dissemination, 193, 194, 204, 205;
 defined, 200; funding for, 200,
 201; in integrated action plan,
 242
Diversity, foundations and, 264–265.
 See also African Americans
Documentation: as aid when complaint filed by grantseeker, 108;
 of meetings and telephone calls,
 62; in program officer's closing
 summary statement, 190–192; in
 project file, 63–64; of site visit,
 138–139, 186. *See also* Reports

Dundjerski, M., 263
Duniway, A. S., 278

E

Edie, J. A., 216
Edison, T., 50
Edward VI (king of England), 2
Ellis, P., rules for conducting meetings, 58–62
Employment, in foundations of the
 future, 266–267
Estate taxes, 267–268
Ethical principles, 252–261; avoiding
 arrogance and egotism, 254–255;
 avoiding conflicts of interest,
 256–257; avoiding formulaic
 responses, 259–260; doing no
 harm, 253–254; remaining open
 to new opportunities, 258–259;
 retaining spiritual connection,
 257–258; telling no lies, 255–256;
 unenforceability of, 260–261
Evaluation, 193, 194; approaches to,
 85–86; budgeting adequate funding for, 199–200; cluster, 202, 203;
 cost of, 88, 89; evaluators to conduct, 88, 90–91; final report on,
 188–190; formative versus summative, 90, 189–190; foundations'
 requiring but not paying for, 48;
 in integrated action plan, 242;
 methodologies for, 88; principles
 of participatory approach to,
 86–87; in proposals, 81, 85–92;
 sources of information on, 92
Excise tax: reductions in, 15, 211;
 Tax Reform Act of 1969 provisions on, 14, 15
Exit strategies, 181–182, 184–185,
 208
Expectations, 110–111; in coaching
 sessions, 120–121; in meetings
 and telephone calls, 58–62; with
 site visits, 131–132
Experimental evaluation, 88

F

Family foundations, 17, 263
Federal government: initiatives made obsolescent by policies of, 236; intersectoral activity by, 274–277; legislative and regulatory threats from, 211, 267–271; possible impact on policies of, 217–218; projects brought to scale using, 210, 227–229, 231, 235; Rockefeller Foundation's attempt to obtain charter under, 9; suggestions for relationships with legislators of, 224–227. *See also* Tax Reform Act of 1969; Taxes
Feedback: given when proposals declined, 47, 101–102, 105–106; from grantseekers, 40, 41
Fidelity Investments Charitable Gift Fund, 84, 275
Field notes, from site visits, 138–139, 186
Fine, A. H., 85, 92
Flattery, 40
Flexner, A., 8, 254
Flexner committee, 8–9
Ford, H., 269
Ford Foundation, 82, 227, 228, 263, 269
Formative evaluation, 90
Forum of Regional Associations of Grantmakers (RAGs), 264, 271
Fosdick, R. B., 10
Foundation Center, 34, 263
Foundation Directory (Foundation Center), 263
Foundation News and Commentary, 46, 48
Foundations: accommodation of program officers to, 31–32, 102, 164; bull market's effect on, 262–264; change orientation of, 25–27; defined, 1, 16, 39; diversity and, 264–265; freedom of, 22–23; grantmaking styles of, 27–28; history of, 1–16, 262; ideological position of, 219–221; increasing number of, 11–12, 263, 266; joint funding by, 197–199; limiting life span of, 13, 269–270; mode of operation of, 28–29; political activities of, 211–216, 219; public profile of, 29–31; referrals to other, 106–107; role of, 18–20, 278; Tax Reform Act of 1969 and, 12–16; types of, 16–17, 25–27. *See also names of specific foundations; specific types of foundations*
Foundations and Lobbying (Edie), 216
4-P continuum, 25–27; grantmaking style and, 27–28, 29; openness of grantmaker and, 54; priority setting and, 32; Q&C emphasis and, 113–114
Franklin, B., 3, 4, 230–231
Franklin Institutes, 3–4
Freeman, D., 15
Funding: collaborative, 198–199; cooperative, 198; for dissemination, 200, 201; for evaluation, 199–200; formulaic, 259–260; for social marketing, 200–201; for strategic communications, 200, 201. *See also* Budgets
Funding documents: abbreviations and acronyms in, 148; advantages and disadvantages of, 143–144; characteristics of successful, 145–146; contents of, 143; data in, 149, 151; definitions in, 148, 150; format for, 149–150; presenting, 153–166; rate of approval of, brought before boards, 154; tone test for, 150; writing, 144–152

G

Gates, F., 8, 10, 233
General Education Board, 8–9, 233, 270

George III (king of England), humorous Q&C from, 125–127

J. Paul Getty Foundation, 29

Gifts, 256–257

Irving S. Gilmore Foundation, 81

Girl Scouts, 274

Giving USA, 18, 19

Gladden, W., 9

Goddard, R., 234

Goff, F., 11

Goodwill Industries, 274

Gore, A., Sr., 12–13

"Gospel of Wealth, The" (Carnegie), 6

Government. *See* Federal government; Local government; State government

Grameen Bank, 274

Grant agreements: discussing provisions of, 175–177; statement of grant renewal policy in, 184

Grantees: relationship between foundations and, in initiative-based grantmaking, 235; reports from, 176, 186–190

Grantmaker Forum on Community and National Service, 229

Grantmakers. *See* Program officers

Grantmaking: bottom-line orientation of, 22; as calling versus profession, 23; cycle of, 192–194; differences between initiative-based and cluster, 234, 238–239; ethics of, 252–261; relational nature of, 53–55, 65; setting priorities in, 32–36; styles of, 27–28, 29. *See also* Initiative-based grantmaking

Grantmaking foundations, 28–29

Grants: learning, 36; leveraging impact of, 196–209, 227–229; planning, 72; renewing, 177, 183–185; terminating, 180–181

Grants management. *See* Management

Grantseekers: bill of rights for, 46–48; coaching, 56, 87–92, 119–121; communication with, 46–47, 55–56, 58; criticizing way in which proposals are declined, 96–97, 99, 103–107; inappropriate judgments of, 43–44; managing expectations of, 58–62, 110–111, 120–121, 131–132; money of, invested in project, 79; relationship between grantmakers and, 53–55, 65; responses of, to Q&Cs, 127–129; setting priorities with aid of, 32–33; telephone calls and meetings with, 56–62; unscrupulous, 62, 101–102

Grantwriters, contract, 74–75

Greenleaf, R. K., 51

Greenspan, A., 112

Gretzky, W., 95

Grossman, A., 271

Daniel and Florence Guggenheim Foundation, 234

H

"Hardening of the categories," 259–260

Havens, J. J., 265–266

Hawthorne effect, 91

Heidrich, K. W., 208

Hendrick, B. J., 7, 82

Henry VIII (king of England), 2

Heritage Foundation, 223

Howard Hughes Medical Research Institute, 29

Humor, when presenting funding document, 158–159

I

Ideas: in declined proposals, 98, 99–100; as focus of traditional philanthropy, 272; innovative, in good proposals, 77; relationship of proposals to, 72–74; sources of, 54

Ideological position, 219–221

Impact: of initiative-based grantmaking, 251; projects with potential for broader, 82; types of, on policies, 217–219. *See also* Leveraging impact

Impressionistic evaluation, 88

INDEPENDENT SECTOR, 10; on ethics in nonprofit sector, 260; government relations efforts of, 211, 271; lobbying handbook of, 217

Information worksheet, to accompany Q&C letter, 118

Initiative-based grantmaking, 26, 232–251; advantages of, 233–235; cluster grantmaking contrasted with, 234, 238–239; defined, 232; disadvantages of, 235–238; history of, 232–233; integrated action plan for, 239–245; management of, 238, 250–251; possible impact of, 251; request for proposals in, 246–248; starting process of, 238–239; strategic communications in, 248–249

Innovation, 19, 77

"Insider's Guide to Progressive Foundations, The" (Shuman), 46

Integrated action plan (IAP), 239–245

Integrity, 48

Intermediary organizations, to bring projects to scale, 207–208

Internal Revenue Service: audit by, 63; on political activities of nonprofits, 216–217; public charity guidelines of, 264–265. *See also* Taxes

Intersectoral activity, 274–277

J

James, W., 227, 277

Johnson, L. B., 229

Johnson Foundation, 212

Robert Wood Johnson Foundation, 82, 212, 263

Jones, S. E., 229, 230

Justinian (Roman emperor), 2

K

Kaiser Family Foundation, 82, 212

Kaplan, A. E., 18, 71

Karel, F., 249

W. K. Kellogg Foundation, 227; City Year grant from, 275; on cluster evaluation, 202; framework for public policy work, 221–223

Kerouac, J., 138

Kettering Foundation, 212

Kresge Foundation, 70

L

Layne, B., 185

Laziness, 44–46

Learn and Serve America, 228

Learning grants, 36

Lehman, R., 50

Lengsfelder, P., 84

Letters: declining proposals, 104–105, 129; to members of Congress, 226. *See also* Questions and concerns letters (Q&Cs)

Letts, C., 271

Leveraging funds, as focus of foundations, 19–20

Leveraging impact, 196–209; after closing project, 203–208; dissemination for, 193, 194, 204, 205; before funding project, 197–201; while project is active, 201–203; social marketing for, 204–205

Lilly Endowment, 263

Literature reviews, for priority setting, 34, 193

Lobbying: as component of projects, 215; direct, 213; guidebooks on, 216, 217; by nonprofits, 216–217; Tax Reform Act of 1969 restrictions on, 212–213

Local government, impact on public policies of, 218–219

Local Initiatives Support Corporation, 82

Logic model, of integrated action plan, 241, 243–245

M

Macdonald, D., 39

Magdalen Society, 4

Management, 167–182; anticipation as key in, 182; difficulties of, 167–169; discussing grant agreement provisions with grantees, 175–177; exit strategies, 181–182, 184–185, 208; of initiative-based grantmaking, 238, 250–251; notifying applicants of approval of project, 174; practical level of engagement in, 169–171; situations to be avoided in, 171–174; technical assistance (TA), 177–180; techniques for, 174–177; terminating grants, 180–181; withholding payments, 180

Mass media rule, 214

Mawby, R. G., 52, 101

Media: for dissemination, 204; foundations' public profile and, 29–31; mass media rule on advertising, 214; for social marketing, 200, 204–205

Meetings: documenting, 62; with intermediary representatives of grantseekers, 33; limiting number of, with applicants, 54, 57–58; with members of Congress, 225–226; project networking, 201–202; public versus private, during site visits, 135–136; rules for conducting, 58–62

Andrew W. Mellon Foundation, 263

Miller, L. F., 84

Millett, R. A., 92, 202

Mills, W., 14

Minnesota Public Radio, 84

Mondale, W., 14

Mott Fund, 227

Myerson, A. R., 272

N

National Center for Social Entrepreneurship, 84

National Society of Fund Raising Executives, 33

Networking: external, 203; internal, 201–203

Niche identification, 34, 193

Nizer, L., 157

Nonpartisan analysis and research, 214

Nonprofit Lobbying Guide, The (Smucker), 216, 217

Nonprofit Piggy Goes to Market (Simons, Lengsfelder, and Miller), 84

Nonprofits: foundations' contribution to income of, 19, 71; intersectoral activity by, 274–277; regulations on political activities of, 216–217

Nonverbal communication: in meetings, 60–61; in oral presentations, 160, 161–162; in site visits, 136–137

O

O'Malley, P., 114

O'Neill, T., 224

Operating foundations, 17, 28–29

Operating proposals, 70–71

Oral presentations, 153–166; audiovisual aids in, 155–156; declining proposals after, 164; do's and don'ts for, 157–160; enthusiasm as key in, 158; following up on, 163–164; humor in, 158–159; length of, 157, 159–160; nonverbal communication in, 160, 161–162; physical props in, 154–155; question-and-answer period following, 161–163; stage fright in, 153–154; using representatives of grantseeker in, 156–157

Organizational capacity: as element in reviewing proposals, 93–95; venture philanthropy's focus on, 271, 272

Organizational policy: defined, 210; impact on, 219

P

David and Lucile Packard Foundation, 41

Part of the Solution (Union of Experimenting Colleges and Universities), 84

Pascal, B., 67

Passive foundations, 25–26; grantmaking style of, 27, 28, 29; openness of grantmakers in, 54; priority setting by, 32

Patman, W., 12–13, 16

Patton, M. Q., 92

Payout rate: reduction of, 15, 170, 268; Tax Reform Act of 1969 provisions on, 14, 15, 22, 169–170; upward adjustment of, 15, 268–269

Peabody, G., 5

Peabody Education Fund, 5

Peremptory foundations, 27; grantmaking style of, 27, 28, 29; openness of grantmakers in, 54; priority setting by, 32; unsolicited proposals and, 66

Personal benefit, proposals for, 69

Philanthropy: Carnegie on best uses for, 6; ethics in, 252–261; as focus of foundations, 18–19; future of formal, 262–279; intersectoral activity in, 274–277; portion of total, from foundations, 18, 71; venture, 271–274

"Philanthropy in America," 263

Phone calls. *See* Telephone calls

Pifer, A., 38, 40, 52

Planning grants, 72

Plato's academy, 1, 2

Plimpton, G., 185

Points of Light Foundation, 227–228, 229

Policy. *See* Organizational policy; Public policy

Policy prototypes, 211

Politics. *See* Organizational policy; Public policy

Pratt Institute, 233

Prescriptive foundations, 26–27; grantmaking style of, 27, 28, 29; openness of grantmakers in, 54; priority setting by, 32; Q&C emphasis of, 113, 114

Price Waterhouse, 267

Priorities. *See* Setting priorities

Private foundations, 278; assets of, 263; future of, 262–289; history of, 5–16, 262; mandated spending by, 22, 169; prototypical, 5–10; Tax Reform Act of 1969 on, 16–17. *See also names of specific foundations*

Private sector, intersectoral activity by, 274–277

Proactive foundations, 26; grantmaking style of, 27, 28, 29; openness of grantmakers in, 54; priority setting by, 32; Q&C emphasis of, 113–114

Program officers: accommodation of, to employing foundations, 31–32, 102, 164; accountability of, 46, 252; behaviors and beliefs to be avoided by, 39–46, 252–261; communication from, to grantseekers, 55–56, 58; decision-making power of, 59, 68–69, 98, 112; desirable qualities for, 48–52; importance of, 38–39; initial review of proposals by, 112; openness by, about reasons for decline of proposals, 101–102, 105–106; preparation for, 21–22, 23; relationship between grantees and, in initiative-based grantmaking, 235; relationship between grantseekers and, 53–55, 65; relationships between board members and, 164–165; and relationships between colleagues, 64–65; renewal opportunities for, 260; sentry versus steward role of, 75–76, 167; terms for, 20–21

Programmatic proposals, 71–72

Project file, 63–64. *See also* Documentation

Project networking, 201–203

Projects: bringing, to scale, 206–208, 210, 227–229, 231, 235; closing, 183–195; investment of applicant's money in, 79; leveraging impact of, 196–209, 227–229; managing, 167–182. *See also* Evaluation

Proposals: approving, 59, 68–69, 75, 76, 102, 174; assessing organizational capacity from, 93–95; budgets in, 92–93; characteristics of good, 76–82; coaching grantseekers on preparing, 56, 87–92, 119–121; continuation plans in, 81–82, 83–85; declining, 49, 51–52, 60, 68–69, 75–76, 96–109; evaluation plans in, 81, 85–92; initial submissions of, 67–68; relationship of ideas to, 72–74; responding to, 110–129; reviewing, 46, 47, 66–95, 111–112; types of, 69–72; unsolicited, 66–67; written by contract grantwriters, 74–75

Public benefit, proposals for, 69, 70

Public charities, 17, 22, 264–265. *See also* Community foundations

Public policy: acceptable foundation activities regarding, 214–216, 219; defined, 210; developing messages on, 223–224; frame-work for work on, 221–223; funding prototypes of, 210–211; ideological position toward, 219–221; increase in foundation work on, 263–264; to leverage impact of grants, 227–229; making initiatives obsolescent, 236; prohibited foundation activities regarding, 213–214; projects brought to scale using, 210, 227–229, 231; public will and, 229–230; reasons for foundations' minimal involvement in, 211–213; relationships with makers of, 224–227; sources of information on, 216; threatening foundations, 211, 267–271; types of impacts on, 217–219

Public profile, 29–31

Public relations. *See* Strategic communications

Public support test, 16, 17

Public will, public policy and, 229–230

Q

Questions and concerns letters (Q&Cs), 112–129; as basis for coaching applicant, 119–121; declining proposal after sending, 128–129; emphasis in, and 4-P continuum, 113–114; format for, 114–117; grantseeker responses to, 127–129; information worksheet accompanying, 118; requesting addendum versus rewritten proposal, 115–116; sample, 121–127; selecting questions and concerns for, 118–119

R

Ratoff, G., 113

Rees, S., 223

Referrals to other foundations, 106–107

Relationships: between board members and program officers, 164–165; between foundations and grantees in initiative-based grantmaking, 235; between grantmakers and grantseekers, 53–55, 65; between program officers as colleagues, 64–65; with public policymakers, 224–227
Rendall, M., 265
Replication, 205–206
Reports: final evaluation, 188–190; final financial, 186–187; final narrative, 187–188; interim, 186; required, outlined in grant agreement, 176. *See also* Documentation
Request for proposals (RFP): in initiative-based grantmaking, 246–248; types of foundations using, 26, 27
Resources: on continuation, 84; on evaluation, 92; foundations as, for members of Congress, 226–227; on intermediary organizations, 208; on lobbying, 216, 217; on public policy, 216
Reviewing proposals, 66–95; assessing budget when, 92–93; assessing organizational capacity when, 93–95; characteristics of good proposals as guide in, 76–92; grantseekers' right to information about, 46, 47; guideposts for, 66–69; inappropriate judgments when, 43–44; in initial form, 67–68, 111–112; looking at ideas when, 72–74; sentry versus steward role in, 75–76; typology of proposals as aid in, 69–72; written by contract grantwriters, 74–75
Revolution of the Heart (Shore), 84
Ridings, D. S., 263
Rockefeller, J. D., Sr., 233, 270; as prototypical philanthropist, 8–10
Rockefeller, J. D., Jr., 10
Rockefeller, J. D., III, 10

Rockefeller Brothers Fund, 227
Rockefeller Foundation, 9–10, 30; establishment of, 9; General Education Board and, 8–9, 233, 270
Rosenwald Foundation, 270
Julius Rosenwald Fund, 11
Ryan, W. P., 271

S

Safe harbor, 215
Russell Sage Foundation, 10–11
Salamon, L. M., 19, 71, 275
Sarnoff, P., 10–11
Scaife Foundation, 220
Scatteration, 233–234
Schervish, P. G., 265–266
Seltzer, M., 83
Sentries, program officers as, 75–76
Setting priorities, 32–37, 193; consulting stakeholders in, 32–33, 34–36, 193; foundation style related to, 32; grantseekers as aid in, 32–33; learning grants for, 36; steps in, 34–36
Shakely, J., 43
Shore, B., 84
Shuman, M. H., 46
Siegal, M. A., 229, 230
Simons, R., 84
Site visits, 130–142; deciding which projects warrant, 130–131; declining proposals after, 139–141; field notes from, 138–139, 186; follow-up after, 139; grantseekers' rising expectations with, 131–132; people to conduct, 132, 141; public versus private conversations during, 135–136; setting agenda for, 134–135; signs of trouble observed in, 136–137; timing, 133–134; value of, 141–142, 186
John F. Slater Fund, 5
Smucker, B., 216, 217
Social marketing, 204–205; defined, 200; funding for, 200–201; outlined in integrated action plan, 242

Spirituality, 50–51, 144, 257–258

Stakeholders: consulted in setting priorities, 32–33, 34–36, 193; involved in evaluation, 85, 86–87; involvement of, evident in proposals, 78

Start-up, as focus of foundations, 20

State government, impact on public policies of, 218

Stewards, program officers as, 75, 76, 167

Strategic communications: defined, 200, 249; funding for, 200, 201; in initiative-based grantmaking, 242, 248–249; while project is alive, 203

Summative evaluation, 90

T

Tarbell, I., 9

Tax Reform Act of 1964, 13

Tax Reform Act of 1969, 13–16; community versus private foundation classifications in, 16–17; excise tax provisions of, 14, 15; payout rate mandated by, 14, 15, 22, 169–170; on political activities of foundations, 212–216

Taxes: community versus private foundation designation regarding, 16–17; estate, 267–268; excise, 14, 15, 211; penalty, if payout rate not met, 22, 169

Technical assistance (TA): to bring projects to scale, 207–208; given by foundations to units of government, 214–215; for managing projects, 177–180

Telephone calls: declining proposals by, 104, 129; to discuss grant agreement provisions, 175–177; documenting, 62; limiting number of, from applicants, 54, 57; notifying applicants of grant approval, 174; rules for, 58–62

Thayer, C. E., 85, 92

Thomas, F., 227

Thoreau, H. D., 237, 251, 252

Timberland Company, 275

Timelines: grant agreement's instructions on, 176–177; in integrated action plan, 241, 243; managing applicant's expectations regarding, 120–121

Tone test, for writing, 150

Trotter, D. W., 269

Troyer, T. A., 12, 13, 16

Truthfulness, 162–163, 255–256

Twain, M., 139, 163, 212, 255

U

Union Institute, 229

Union of Experimenting Colleges and Universities, 84

University of Chicago, 8, 233

Unsolicited proposals, 66–67

U.S. Treasury, 13

V

Venture philanthropy, 271–274

W

Wealth, intergenerational transfer of, 265–267

Weaver, W., 1, 3, 4

White, D., 46

White House Office of National Service, 228

White-Williams Foundation, 4

Wickersham, G., 9

Winthrop, J., 3

Writing: abbreviations and acronyms in, 148; for audience, 145–146; defining terms in, 148, 150; following format in, 145; rules for effective, 146; tone test for, 150

Y

Youth Service America, 227

Youth service movement, 227–229, 275

Youth Volunteer Corps of America, 227